DIE SCHÖNSTEN DAMAST-MESSER DER WELT

THE WORLD'S MOST BEAUTIFUL DAMASCUS KNIVES

Jim Cooper

Die schönsten Damastmesser der Welt

The world's most beautiful damascus knives

1. Auflage, 2023

Alle Rechte der Verbreitung sind vorbehalten.
Nachdruck, auch auszugsweise, nur mit schriftlicher Genehmigung des Verlags.

ISBN 978-3-948264-16-1

© copyright:
Wieland Verlag GmbH
Rosenheimer Str. 22
83043 Bad Aibling
Telefon 08061/38998-0
www.wieland-verlag.com

Fotos: Jim Cooper, SharpByCoop Photography
Bildtexte und Übersetzung: Ingrid Elser
Gestaltung, Satz: Caroline Wydeau
Schlussredaktion: Karola Wieland

Druck: Print Consult
Printed in EU

VORWORT | PREFACE

Das Messer ist eines der ältesten Werkzeuge der Menschheit. Unsere Entwicklungsgeschichte von den ersten Frühmenschen bis zu dem, was wir heute sind, ist ohne das Messer nicht vorstellbar. Es gehört wie die Nutzung des Feuers zu den Grundpfeilern unserer Existenz. Und es begleitet uns treu bis heute: So wie wir vor Hunderttausenden von Jahren mit einer Steinklinge unsere Jagdbeute zerteilt haben, so verwenden wir heute ein Taschenmesser, um das gerade gelieferte Amazon-Paket zu öffnen.

Das Messer hat sich im Laufe dieser Zeit von einem einfachen Faustkeil mit scharfer Bruchkante zu einer Vielzahl von hoch spezialisierten Werkzeugen entwickelt. Ihre Gemeinsamkeit ist, dass sie eine scharfe Schneide aufweisen, mit der man etwas zerteilen kann. Doch es ist viel mehr als nur ein Werkzeug: Das Messer ist ein Kulturgut, es kann ein Symbol einer nationalen Identität sein, ein Stück Handwerksgeschichte, ein ästhetischer Genuss, ein Sammelobjekt. In seiner höchsten Form verdient es den Namen Kunst. Ich scheue mich nicht, diesen Begriff zu verwenden.

Weltweit arbeiten begnadete Handwerker daran, das Messer als Objekt weiterzuentwickeln und zu vervollkommnen. Sie setzen ihre ganze Kreativität und ihr meisterhaftes Können ein, um einzigartige Objekte zu schaffen, die Begehrlichkeiten wecken und dem Ideal der Perfektion sehr nahe kommen. Dabei bildet die Vielfalt der Ergebnisse die Unterschiede in Geschmack, Prioritäten und ästhetischer Wahrnehmung ab.

Worin sich viele Messermacher wie Messersammler aber einig scheinen, ist ihre Vorliebe für Damaszenerstahl. Die Muster des Damasts bilden ein eigenes Universum, dessen Möglichkeiten unbegrenzt scheinen. Ursprünglich erschaffen, um die verschiedenen physikalischen Eigenschaften harter und weicher Stähle in einem Stück zu kombinieren, fasziniert heute an diesen Klingen ihre optische Erscheinung. Die Schmiede vereinen im Schmiedefeuer verschiedene Stahlsorten und erzeugen durch Falten, Verdrehen und Prägen die späteren Strukturen, die durch Ätzen und Schleifen sichtbar gemacht werden. In seiner höchsten Form, dem Mosaikdamast, werden vorgeformte Stahlstücke so zusammengefügt und verschmiedet, dass am Ende aufsehenerregende Muster und Bilder entstehen. Eine Damastklinge kann ein Kunstwerk innerhalb des Gesamtkunstwerks Messer sein.

Jim Cooper ist ein Chronist der Messer-Handwerkskunst. Der amerikanische Fotograf begleitet seit vielen Jahren die internationale Szene der handgefertigten Messer. Seine Signatur „Sharp by Coop" ist zu einem Markenzeichen geworden. Jim Cooper besucht die wichtigsten Custom-Knife-Ausstellungen und hält die schönsten Stücke in seinen ebenso kunstvoll arrangierten wie technisch perfekten Fotos fest. Er hat sich auf diese Weise ein einmaliges Archiv aufgebaut. Dieses Buch greift auf diese umfangreiche Sammlung zurück und präsentiert eine Auswahl von 100 handgefertigten Messern mit Damastklinge. Diese Auswahl folgt selbstverständlich dem subjektiven Empfinden und erhebt keinen Anspruch darauf, eine objektive Auszeichnung oder Rangfolge zu bilden. Sie soll jedoch die Bandbreite der heutigen Custom-Knife-Szene abbilden – auf allerhöchstem Niveau.

Hans Joachim Wieland
Herausgeber

The knife is one of the oldest tools of humankind. Our evolution from the earliest hominids to what we are today is unthinkable without the knife. It belongs to the basic pillars of our existence as much as the use of fire. And it still accompanies us as a trusted friend today: in the same way we used a stone blade to strip down a kill hundreds of thousands of years ago, we use a pocket knife nowadays to open the Amazon parcel we just received.

In this span of time, the knife has developed from a simple hand-axe with sharp fractured edge up to a multitude of highly-specialized tools. Their common feature is a sharp edge used to cut something. But the knife is more than a tool: it is a cultural heritage item, it can be a symbol of nationality, a piece of the history of craftsmanship, an aesthetic relish, a collectible. In its highest form it deserves the name „art". I don't shy away from using this expression.

Around the world, skilled craftspeople work to improve the knife even further and to bring it to perfection. They use all their creativity and their masterful skills to create unique objects which evoke desire and which are very close to the ideal of perfection. Here, the multitude of results represents the differences in taste, priorities and aesthetic perception.

The one point which unites many knifemakers as well as knife collectors is their preference for damascus steel. The patterns of damascus form a universe of their own with seemingly unlimited possibilities. Initially created to combine the different physical characteristics of hard and soft steel types in a single piece, nowadays these blades mainly fascinate due to their optical appearance. The bladesmiths unite different steel types in the fire of their forges and create the structures by folding, twisting and embossing, which subsequently become visible by etching and polishing. In its most developed form, the mosaic damascus, pre-shaped steel billets are put together and forged in such a way that exciting patterns are created in the end. A damascus blade can be a piece of art within the overall art of the entire knife.

Jim Cooper is a chronicler of knife craftsmanship. For many years this American photographer has been portraying the international scene of handmade knives. His signature "Sharp by Coop" has become a trademark. Jim Cooper attends the most important custom knife exhibitions and captures the most beautiful pieces in his photos. These compositions with artful arrangements and technical perfection approach the art of the original knives. In this way, he has created a unique archive. This book reflects that extensive archive and presents a selection of 100 handmade knives with damascus blades. Of course, this choice is due to subjective feelings and doesn't claim to be an objective honoring or ranking. But it is meant to show the bandwidth of today's scene of custom knives – at top level.

Hans Joachim Wieland
publisher

INHALT | CONTENT

8	Russ Andrews		108	Stuart Kerr
10	Bruce Barnett		110	Kevin Klein
12	Jordon Berthelot		112	Vladimir Kolenko
14	Ron Best		114	Jamie Lundell
16	Tashi Bharucha		116	Samuel Lurquin
18	Bruce Bingenheimer		118	Collin Maguire
20	Andrew Blomfield		120	R. J. Martin
22	Tobias Bockholt		122	Mareko Maumasi
24	William Brigham		124	Andrew B. Meers
26	David Broadwell		126	Mardi Meshejian
28	Edward Burke		128	Adam Millé
30	Shayne Carter		130	David Mirabile
32	Kevin Casey		132	Trevor Morgan Jr.
34	Jon Christensen		134	Theo Nazz
36	Greg Cimms		136	Will Newham
38	Samuel Cobb		138	Olamic Cutlery
40	John M. Cohea		140	Matt Parkinson
42	Bubba Crouch		142	Logan Pearce
44	Mauricio Daletzky		144	Ben Pittman
46	Alan Davis		146	Bill Poor
48	Peter Del Raso		148	Jean-Pierre Potvin
50	Dikristo		150	Joshua Prince
52	Rian Doudle		152	Mike Quesenberry
54	Rick Dunkerley		154	Lin Rhea
56	Dwayne Dushane		156	Bertie Rietveld
58	Jason Ellard		158	Javan Roberts
60	Charlie Ellis		160	Charles Roddenberry
62	Kay Embretsen		162	Kyle Royer
64	Chris Farrell		164	Brian Sellers
66	Steve Filicietti		166	Chris Sharp
68	Jerry Fisk		168	Steven Skiff
70	Stephan Fowler		170	Andrew K. Smith
72	Dennis Friedly		172	Stuart Smith
74	Scott Gallagher		174	Sobral Brothers
76	Tommy Gann		176	Tim K. Steingass
78	Aidan Garrity		178	Will Stelter
80	Charles Gedraitis		180	Johnny Stout
82	Randy Haas		182	Peter Swarz-Burt
84	Marshall Hall		184	André & Marietjie Thorburn
86	Don Hanson III		186	Brian Tighe
88	Jerarmie Heywood		188	Corin Urquhart
90	Tobin Hill		190	Noah Vachon
92	Tony Hughes		192	Kelly Vermeer-Vella
94	Brandon Hyner		194	Javier Vogt
96	James Ingram		196	Michael Walker
98	Paul Jarvis		198	Aaron Wilburn
100	Benjamin Kamon		200	Henning Wilkinson
102	Alexandre H. Kaspary		202	Josh Wisor
104	Derick Kemper		204	Owen Wood
106	Chad Kennedy		206	John Worthington

INHALT | CONTENT

INHALT | CONTENT

INHALT | CONTENT

RUSS ANDREWS

Russ Andrews aus Sugar Creek in Montana fertigt am liebsten Bowiemesser. Für die 10 Zoll lange Klinge dieses Sub-Hilt-Bowies schmiedete er einen speziellen Duplex-Leiter-Damast mit Schneidkern. Auch Handschutz, Sub-Hilt und die Griffkappe sind aus Damast gefertigt. Der Griff besteht aus Sambar-Hirschhorn, die Scheide nähte Paul Long.

Russ Andrews from Sugar Creek, Montana, loves to make Bowie knives. He forged the 10"-blade of this sub-hilt Bowie with a duplex ladder damascus on top of plain steel. The guard, sub-hilt and pommel are made of damascus, too. The handle is made of sambar stag; the sheath was sewn by Paul Long.

BRUCE BARNETT

Bruce Barnett aus Australien baut die verschiedensten Messer, darunter auch klassische amerikanische Taschenmesser. Dieses Sowbelly wurde auf der Sydney Knife Show 2022 als „Best Folder" ausgezeichnet. Die Klingen bestehen aus selbstgeschmiedetem Federdamast, die Backen und Liner aus rostbeständigem Stahl. Für die Griffschalen verwendete Bruce ausgesucht helles Perlmutt.

Bruce Barnett from Australia makes a wide variety of different knives with classic American folders among them. This sowbelly was awarded „Best Folder" at the Sydney Knife Show 2022. The blades are made of the maker's own feather damascus; bolsters and liners are made of stainless steel. As material for the handle scales, Bruce selected especially bright mother-of-pearl.

JORDON BERTHELOT

Jordon Berthelot aus New Braunfels in Texas will sich auf Integralmesser spezialisieren. Sein erstes Halbintegral hat er komplett von Hand gefeilt. Den Damast mit Schneidkern aus O1-Werkzeugstahl schmiedete Justin Reynolds. Der Griff ist aus Ahorn-Maserknolle gefertigt.

Jordon Berthelot from New Braunfels, Texas wants to specialize in integral knives. He filed his first half-integral completely by hand. The damascus with a core of O1 tool steel was forged by Justin Reynolds. The handle is made of maple burl.

JORDON BERTHELOT

RON BEST

Ron Best aus Stokes in North Carolina ist Mitglied der amerikanischen Messermachergilde und berühmt für seine herausragenden Back-Lock-Dolche. Dieser hier wurde aus Leiter-Damast mit geriffelten Goldintarsien gemacht, die sich auf dem Griff fortsetzen. Der Griff besticht auch durch farbenfrohes Timascus.

Ron Best from Stokes, North Carolina is a member of the American Knifemaker's Guild and is famous for his outstanding lockback daggers. This one was made of ladder damascus with fluted gold inlays which continue on the handle. The handle is also highlighted by colorful timascus.

TASHI BHARUCHA

Die Formensprache des französischen Messermachers Tashi Bharucha ist sehr markant – man erkennt sie auf den ersten Blick. Für diesen Folder verwendete er Damast aus der Werkstatt des ebenfalls sehr bekannten belgischen Messerschmieds Sam Lurquin. Die Liner und der Clip sind aus anodisiertem Titan gefertigt, der Backspacer aus Zirkonium.

The design language of French knifemaker Tashi Bharucha is very pronounced and can be recognized at first glance. For this folder, he used damascus from the workshop of Belgian bladesmith Sam Lurquin. The liners and clip are made of anodized titanium; the backspacer is made of zirconium.

BRUCE BINGENHEIMER

Der leider verstorbene amerikanische Messerschmied Bruce Bingenheimer schaffte es, klassische Materialien mit zeitlosem Design zu kombinieren. Für sein *BingaLor* schmiedete er Mosaikdamast mit einzigartigem Muster. Backen und Clip aus Stahl wurden hitzecoloriert. Die Griffschalen sind aus ausgesuchtem Hirschhorn gefertigt.

The late American bladesmith Bruce Bingenheimer managed to combine classic materials with a timeless design. For his *BingaLor*, he forged mosaic damascus with a unique pattern. The steel bolsters and steel clip were heat-colored. The handle scales are made from especially selected stag.

ANDREW BLOMFIELD

Der Pesh Kabz ist eine Jahrhunderte alte persische Messerform mit sehr komplexem Klingenschliff und versickter Spitze. Dieser moderne Nachbau stammt vom australischen Messermacher Andrew Blomfield. Für die Klinge schmiedete er sieben Bahnen tordierten („türkischen") Damast.
Der Griff ist aus besonders hellem Mammut-Elfenbein gefertigt.

The Pesh Kabz is an ancient Persian knife shape with complex blade grind and lock-beaded blade tip. This modern version was made by Australian knifemaker Andrew Blomfield. The blade was forged from seven bars of twisted („Turkish") damascus. The handle was made from especially light-colored mammoth ivory.

TOBIAS BOCKHOLT

Trotz seines deutschen Namens ist der Messerschmied Tobias Bockholt waschechter Australier und lebt auf der schönen Insel Tasmanien. Seine Spezialität sind Kochmesser. Für dieses Modell schmiedete er Damast aus 1095- und 15N20-Stahl. Für den Griff verwendte er gefärbte und stabilisierte Ahornwurzel.

Despite his German name, knifemaker Tobias Bockholt is a true Australian and lives on the pretty Tasmanian island. His specialty is kitchen knives. For this model, he forged damascus from 1095 and 15N20 steels. For the handle he used dyed and stabilized maple roots.

TOBIAS BOCKHOLT

WILLIAM BRIGHAM

Das Damastmuster erinnert an einen Engelsflügel – deshalb nennt Messerschmied William Brigham es auch „Seraphim Pattern". Die Form der Klingen passt er weitestgehend dem Verlauf des Musters an. Den rostbeständigen Damast für diese Halbintegralmesser schmiedete er aus AEB-L- und 304-Stahl. Der Griff besteht aus gefärbter Ahorn-Maserknolle.

This damascus pattern reminds one of angel wings – thus William Brigham calls it „Seraphim pattern". He lets the shape of his blades mostly follow the flow of the pattern. Brigham forged the stainless damascus for this half-integral from AEB-L and 304 steels. The handle was made from dyed maple burl.

DAVID BROADWELL

David Broadwell ist sehr bekannt für seine organisch aussehenden Messerdesigns und taktischen Kugelschreiber. Dieses *Art Deco Egyptian Revival* hat er bereits viele Jahre gedanklich mit sich herumgetragen. Der Damast für diesen Dolch wurde von Dave Lisch hergestellt. Die Griffschalen aus rostfreiem Stahl und der Rahmen wurden von Ray Cover graviert, der sie auch mit Feingold, Platin und Kupfer verzierte. Er schuf auch den ägyptischen Kopf aus Rotgold, Gelbgold und Zirkonium. David Broadwell sagt: „Dieses Messer ist eine der aufwändigsten Arbeiten, die wir je zusammen erledigt haben."

David Broadwell is most well-known for his organic-looking knife designs and tactical pens. This *Art Deco Egyptian Revival* is something he had on his mind for many years. The damascus for the dagger was made by Dave Lisch. The stainless steel handle scales and frame were engraved by Ray Cover who also inlaid them with fine gold, platinum and copper. He also created the Egyptian head in rose gold, yellow gold and zirconium. David Broadwell states: „The knife represents some of the most complex work we have done together."

EDWARD BURKE

Der weniger bekannte amerikanische Messermacher Ed Burke aus Bethlehem, Connecticut, kreierte dieses einmalige Klappmesser mit Leiter-Damast von Matt Parkinson. Die Griffbacken, die den Öffnungsmechanismus des Springmessers verdecken, wurden aus Torsionsdamast gefertigt, ebenfalls von Matt Parkinson. Die besonders hübschen Feilarbeiten auf Platinen und Griffrücken wurden aus farbenfrohem Titan erschaffen. Die Griffschalen sind aus Knochen gefertigt.

The rather unknown American knifemaker Ed Burke from Bethlehem, Connecticut, created this unforgettable folder with ladder damascus by Matt Parkinson. The bolsters, which conceal the switchblade mechanism, were made from twisted damascus, also by Matt Parkinson. The especially pretty filework on liners and backspacer was created of colorful titanium; the handle scales were made from bone.

SHAYNE CARTER

Dieser *Fighter* von Meisterschmied Shayne Carter aus Payton, Utah, wurde als „Best Bowie" bei der Blade Show West 2022 ausgezeichnet. Shayne schmiedete den Federdamast für die 8 Zoll lange Klinge selbst. Auch Handschutz und Zwinge sind aus seinem eigenen Damast gemacht. Die Griffschalen bestehen aus erlesenem Hirschhorn.

This *Fighter* by Master Smith Shayne Carter from Payton, Utah, was awarded „Best Bowie" at the Blade Show West 2022. Shayne forged the feather damascus for the intriguing 8"-blade himself. Guard and ferrule are made of his own damascus as well; the handle scales are of exquisite stag.

SHAYNE CARTER

KEVIN CASEY

Kevin Casey ist ein bekannter ABS (American Bladesmith Society) Meisterschmied aus Lander, Wyoming. Sein *Equus*-Bowie hat eine 6,5 Zoll lange Klinge aus Federdamast, den Casey selbst aus Kohlenstoffstahl geschmiedet hat. Der Griff aus Grenadill-Holz mit dem namensgebenden Pferd wurde in Zusammenarbeit mit dem russischen Künstler Konstantin Pushkarev gestaltet. Der Pferdekopf besteht aus „Blacklip"-Perlmutt, seine Kontur und die Mähne wurden aus Silberdraht erschaffen. Im Messerknauf ist ein Opal eingelegt.

Kevin Casey is a well-known maker from Lander, Wyoming. His *Equus*-bowie has a 6.5"-blade of feather damascus forged from carbon steel by Casey himself. The blackwood handle, sporting the name-giving horse, was created as a collaboration with the Russian artist Konstantin Pushkarev. The horse head is made from blacklip mother-of-pearl; its outline and the mane were created with silver wire. The knife's pommel features an inlaid opal.

JON CHRISTENSEN

Jon Christensen, der ABS-Meisterschmied aus Stevensville, Montana, nannte diesen feststehenden Dolch *Garden Walk* – ein passender Name für den geschnitzten Griff, der Schmetterlinge, einen Vogel und eine herrliche Gartenumgebung auf fossilem Walross-Elfenbein zeigt. Die 10 Zoll lange Klinge wurde vom Messermacher selbst aus „Rose Garden"-Damast geschmiedet. Die Zwinge besteht aus Schmiedeeisen mit Bronze-Akzenten.

Jon Christensen, the ABS Master Smith from Stevensville, Montana, named this fixed dagger *Garden Walk* – a fitting name for the carved handle which depicts butterflies, a bird and gorgeous garden scenery on fossil walrus ivory. The 10"-blade was forged from „Rose Garden" mosaic damascus by the maker himself. The ferrule is made from wrought iron with bronze accents.

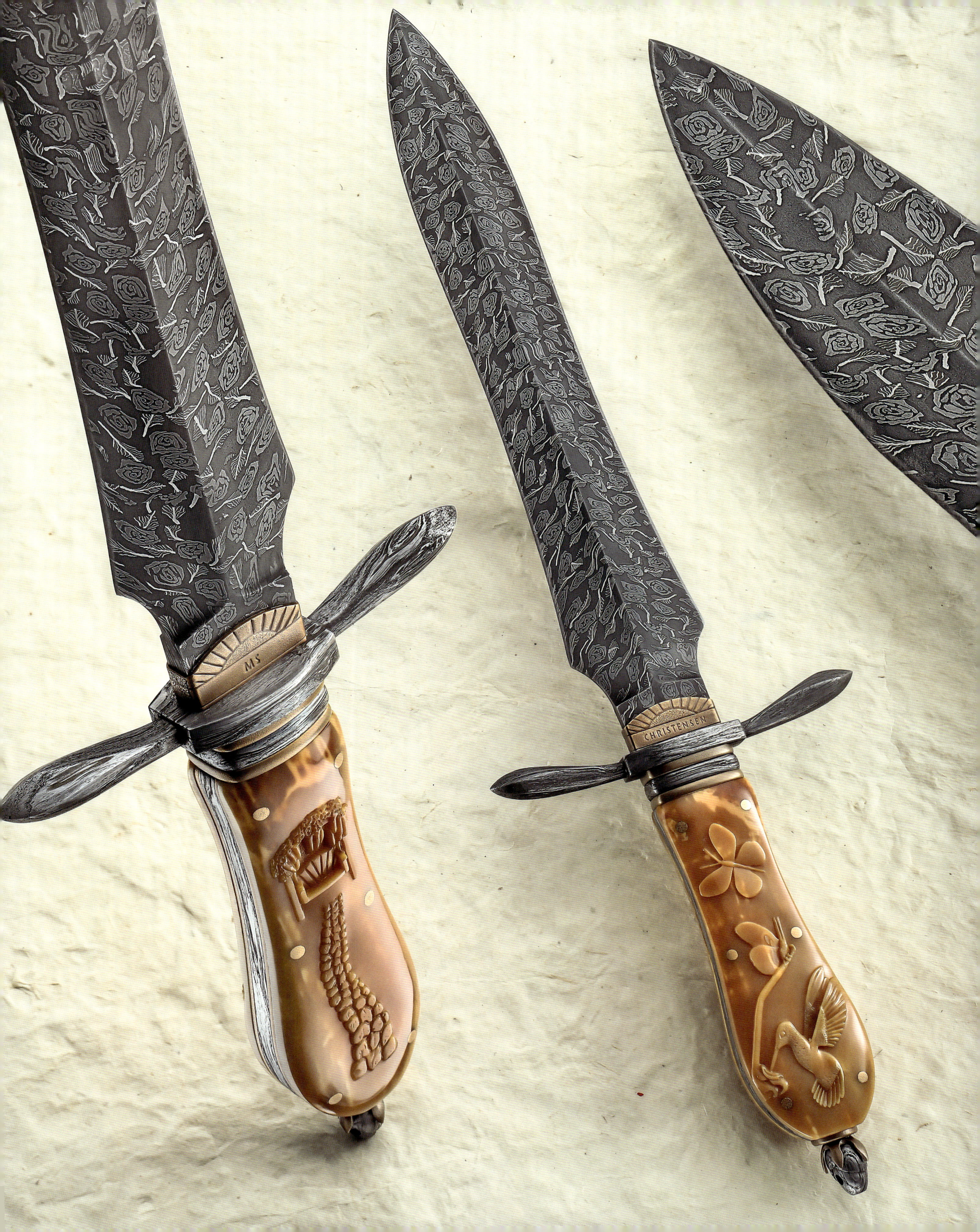
MS
CHRISTENSEN

GREG CIMMS

Der ABS-Journeyman-Schmied Greg Cimms hatte schon eine Menge verschiedener Berufe, bevor er schließlich zum Messermacher wurde. Er arbeitete unter anderem in der Gastronomie, wo er sowohl seine Liebe zum Kochen entdeckte als auch zu den Messern, die im Kochberuf benötigt werden. Dieses Küchenmesser im japanischen Stil ist das Resultat von Gregs Leidenschaft für beides. Der Mosaikdamast der Klinge zeigt verzerrte Schädel – ein Markenzeichen von Greg Cimms.

ABS Journeyman Smith Greg Cimms had a lot of jobs before he finally settled on being a knifemaker. One of the jobs was in the restaurant industry, where he fell in love with cooking as well as the knives needed in the profession of being a chef. This Japanese style kitchen knife is the outcome of Greg's passion for both. The mosaic damascus of the blade depicts distorted skulls – one of the trademarks of Greg Cimms.

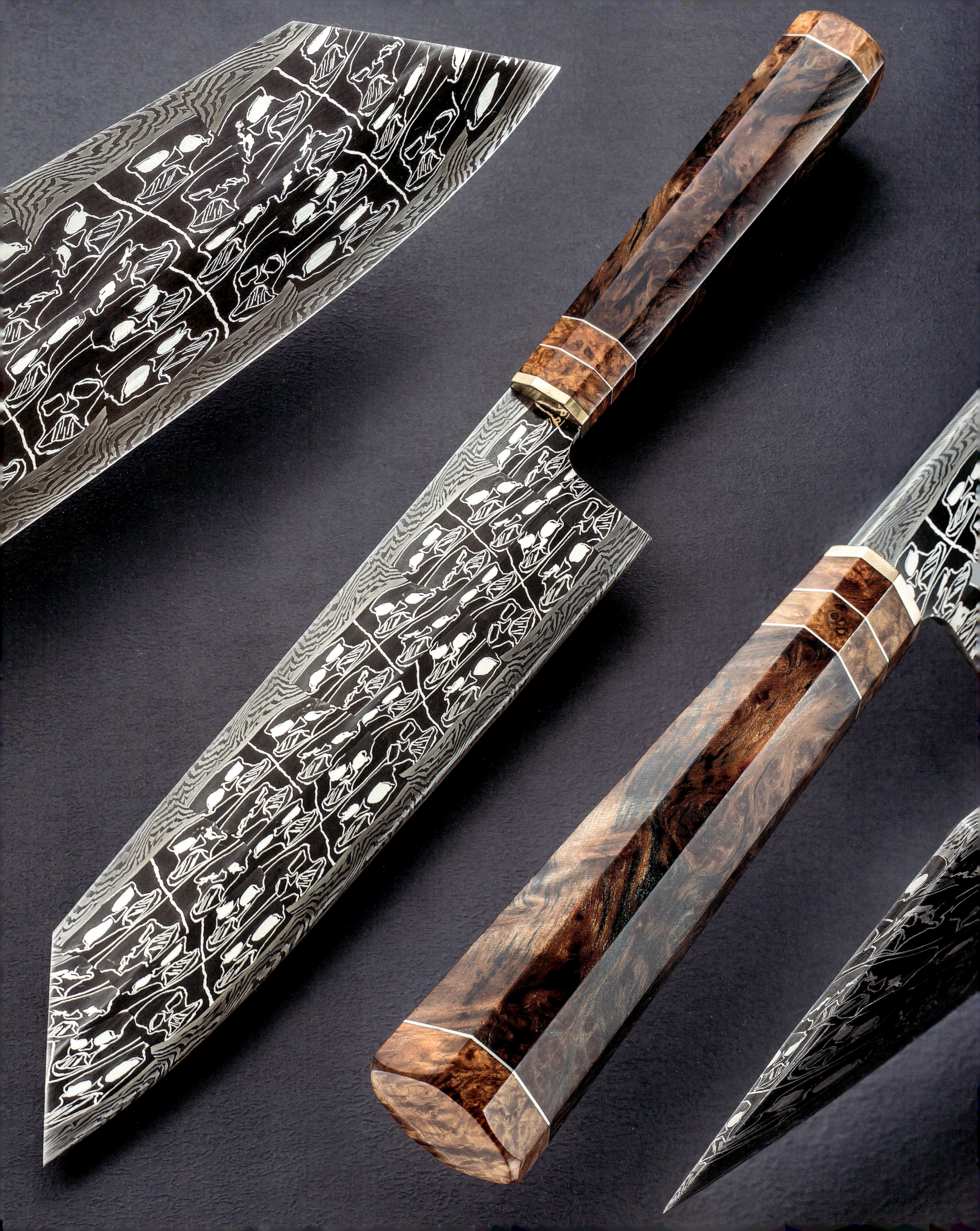

SAMUEL COBB

Samuel Cobb aus Bland, Missouri, ist der Schöpfer dieses attraktiven Bowies. Der Leiterdamast für die Klinge wurde von Robert Scott auf einen Kern aus 80CrV2-Stahl geschmiedet. Handschutz, Zwinge und Knauf bestehen aus rostfreiem 416-Stahl. Der Griff wurde aus Kohlefaser mit einem Flechtmuster geformt.

Samuel Cobb from Bland, Missouri, is the maker of this attractive Bowie. The ladder pattern damascus for the blade was forged by Robert Scott over 80CrV2 steel. Guard, ferrule and pommel are made of stainless 416 steel; the handle is shaped from carbon fiber in a basket-weave pattern.

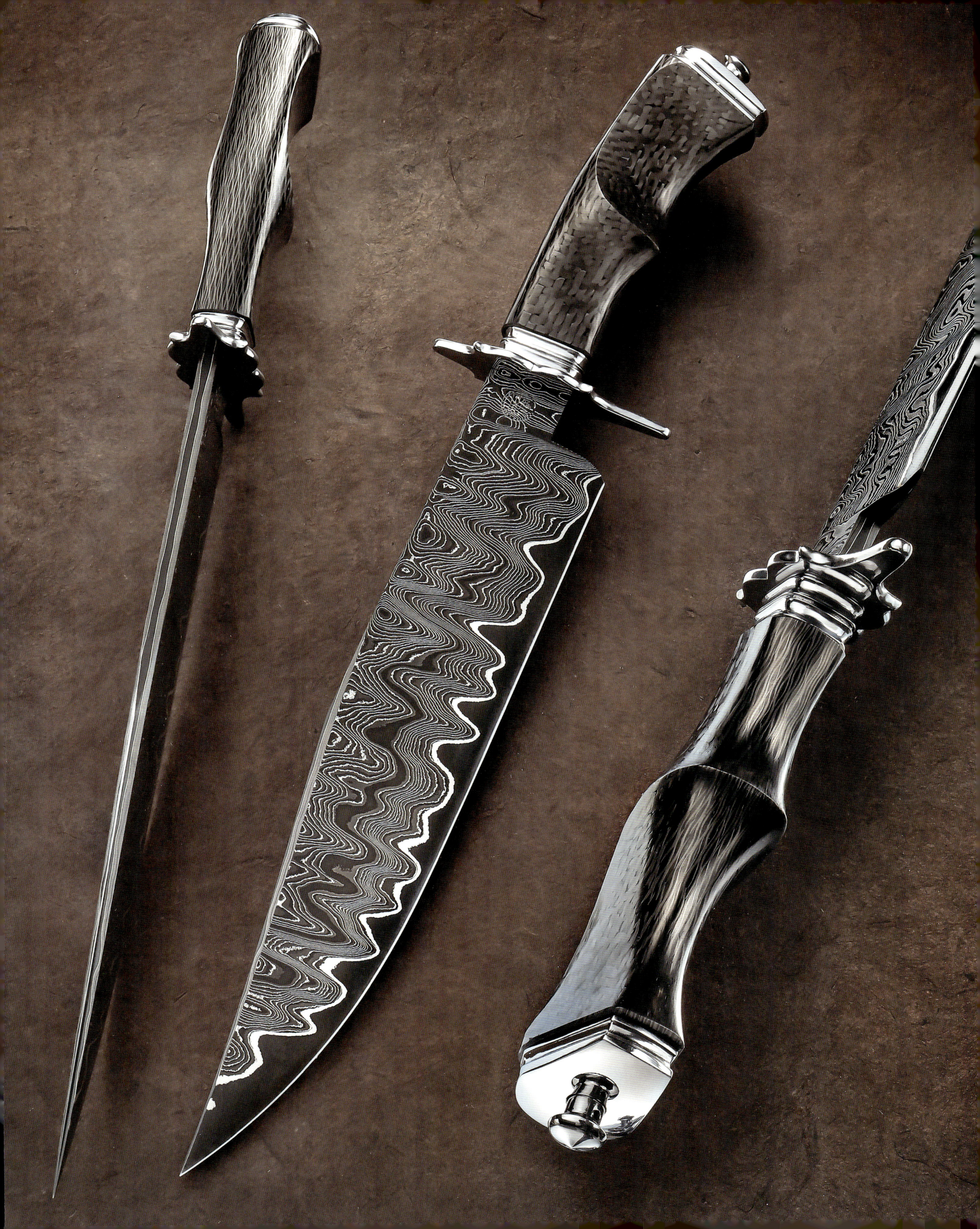

JOHN M. COHEA

John M. Cohea aus Nettleton, Mississippi, ist bekannt für seine Messer und Tomahawks im Stil der amerikanischen Pionierzeit. Für die Klinge seines *Bear Jaw Bowie* benutzte er Damast von Chad Nichols mit einem Zufallsmuster. Der Unterkiefer eines Schwarzbären dient als Griff. Der blattförmige Handschutz und die Griffzwinge wurden aus Kupfer hergestellt. Cohea fertigte auch die Scheide aus Rohhaut an.

John M. Cohea of Nettleton, Mississippi, is well-known for his frontier-style knives and hawks. For the blade of his *Bear Jaw Bowie* he used Chad Nichols damascus with a random pattern. A black bear's lower jaw forms the handle. The leaf-shaped guard as well as the bolster are made from copper. Cohea also made the sheath of rawhide.

JOHN M. COHEA

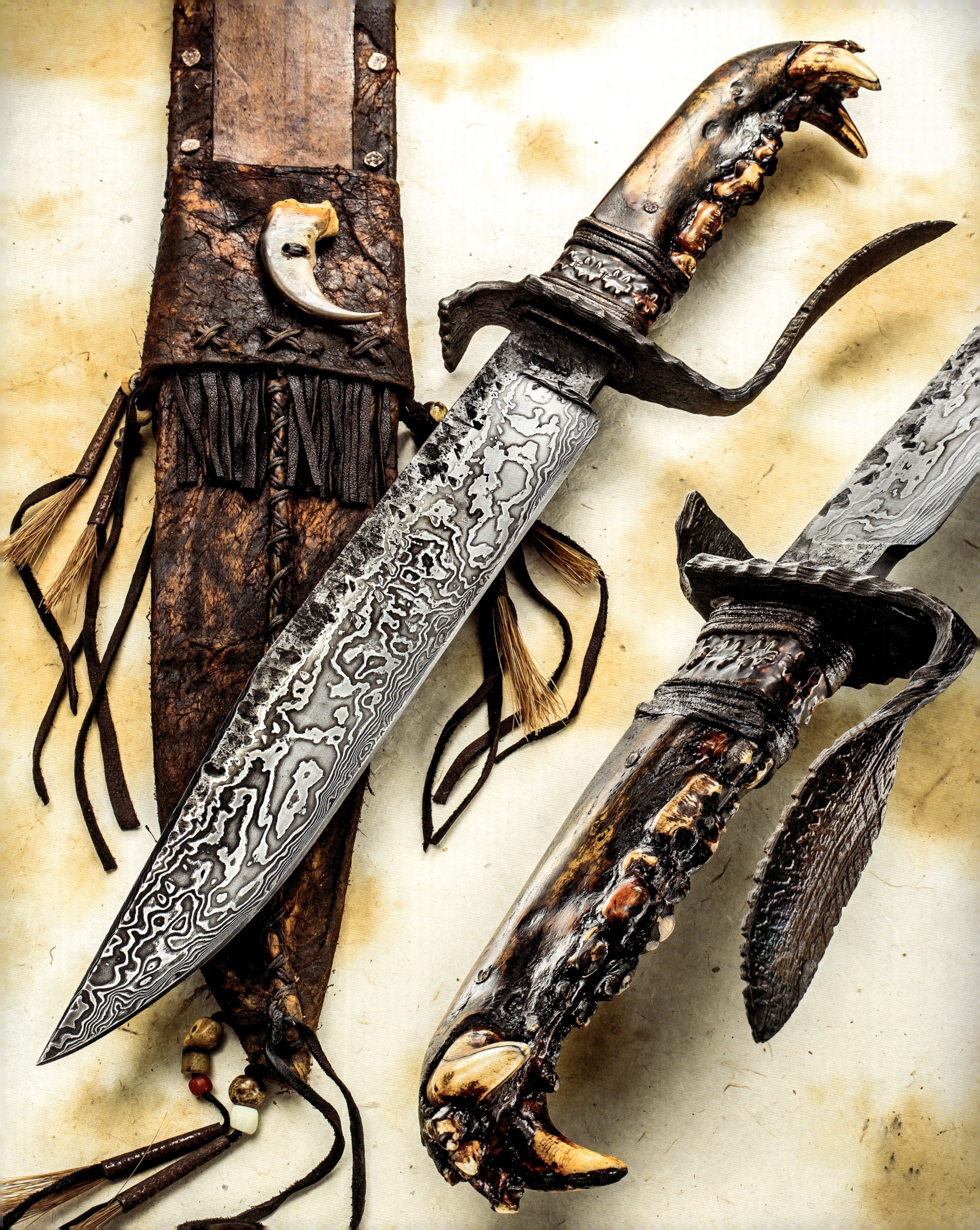

BUBBA CROUCH

Dieses schöne Slipjoint-Trapper wurde von Bubba Crouch aus Pleasonton, Texas, hergestellt. Die hohlgeschliffene Einzelklinge dieses Klappmessers besteht aus Federdamast von Bill Burke. Der „Wespennest"-Damast für die Griffbacken wurde von Chris Mark geschmiedet. Die Griffschalen aus geflämmtem Hirschhorn und das Filework mit Rankenmuster auf der Rückenfeder tragen zur Schönheit des Messers bei und machen es zu einem Kunstobjekt.

This pretty slipjoint Trapper was made by Bubba Crouch from Pleasonton, Texas. The single, hollow-ground blade for this folder is made of feather damascus by Bill Burke. The „wasp nest" damascus for the bolsters was forged by Chris Mark. The handle scales from torched stag and the filework with rose vine pattern on the backspring add to the beauty of this knife and turn it into a piece of art.

BUBBA CROUCH

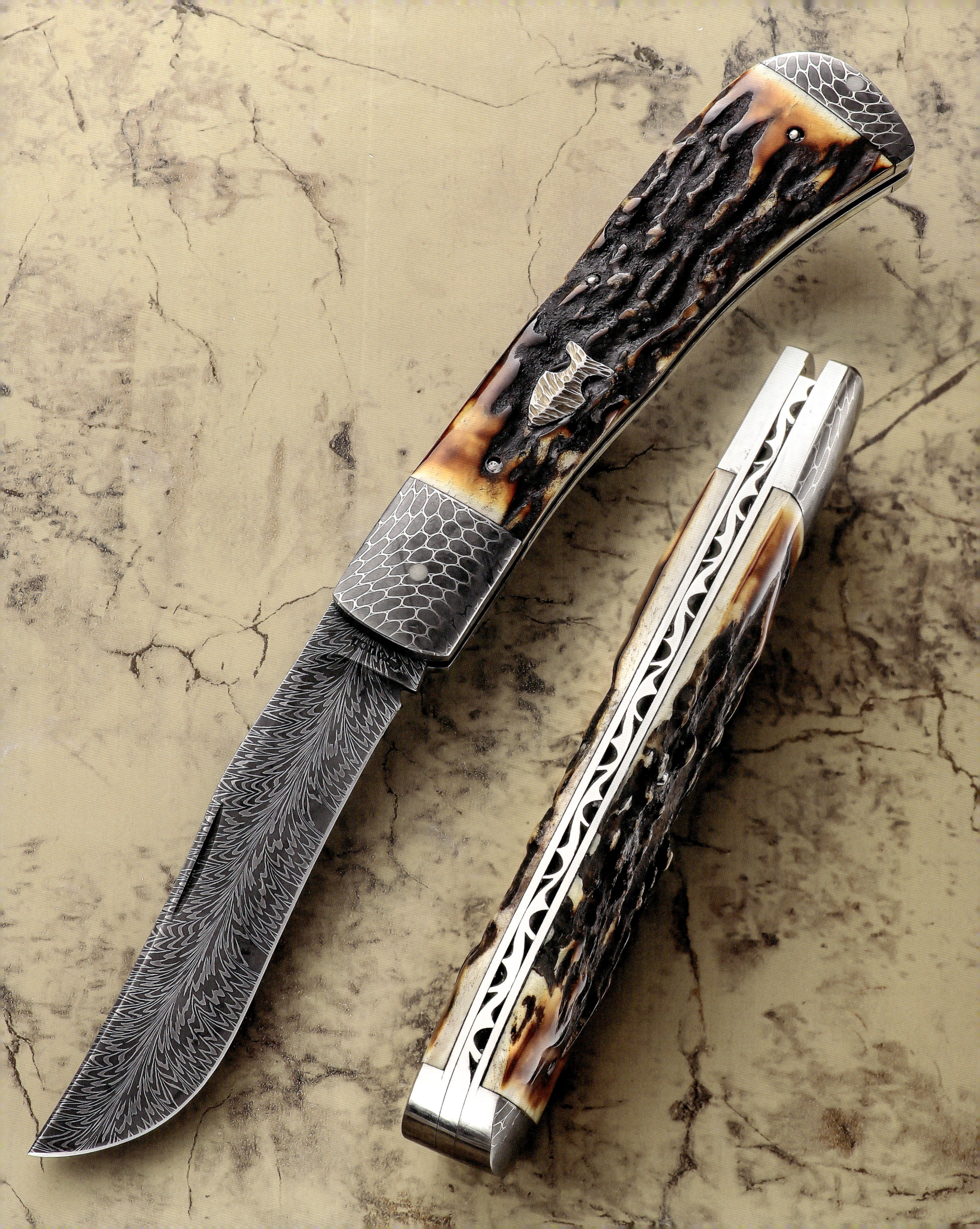

MAURICIO DALETZKY

Ein weiteres Kunstobjekt ist dieses wunderbare *Presentation Criollo Knife* von Mauricio Daletzky aus Argentinien: die 9 Zoll lange Klinge mit dem Strom des „Feuerfluss"-Damasts, die 24-karätigen Goldeinlagen auf Klingenrücken und Scheide, die Beschläge und der Knauf aus gebläutem Stahl und die Griffschalen aus Kohlefaser mit Holzmaserung – sie alle zusammen bilden ein einzigartiges Meisterstück.

Another piece of art is this wonderful *Presentation Criollo Knife* by Mauricio Daletzky from Argentina: the 9"-damascus-blade with the flow of its „River of Fire"-pattern, the 24k gold inlays on the blade back and sheath, the fittings and pommel of blued steel and the handle scales of carbon fiber with a wood grain structure – they all combine into a unique masterpiece.

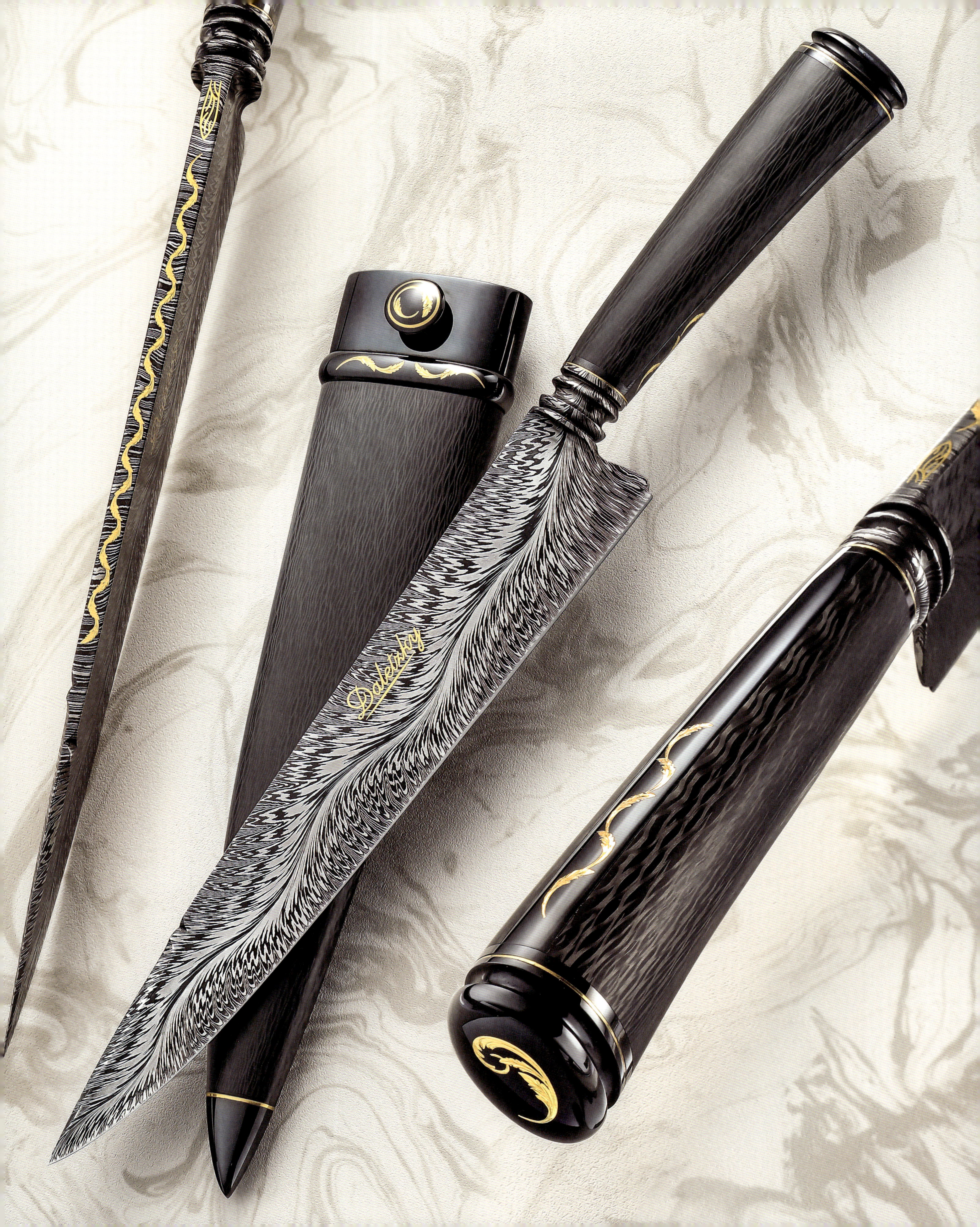
Doletzky

ALAN DAVIS

Dieses Gentleman-Klappmesser von Alan Davis aus Boerne, Texas, sticht sofort ins Auge: Die Klinge wurde aus Bill Burkes „River of Fire" (Feuerfluss)-Damast geformt, die Griffbacken bestehen aus Bertie Rietvelds „Nebula"-Damast. Die Griffschalen aus der Rinde eines Mammut-Stoßzahns und die Platinen aus gebläutem und mit Feilmuster versehenem Titan verstärken den Gesamteindruck dieser Schönheit.

This Gent's folder by Alan Davis from Boerne, Texas, immediately catches one's eye: the blade is shaped of Bill Burke's „River of Fire" damascus, the bolsters are made from Bertie Rietveld's „Nebula"damascus. Handle scales of mammoth bark and liners from blued and fileworked titanium enhance the overall look of this beauty.

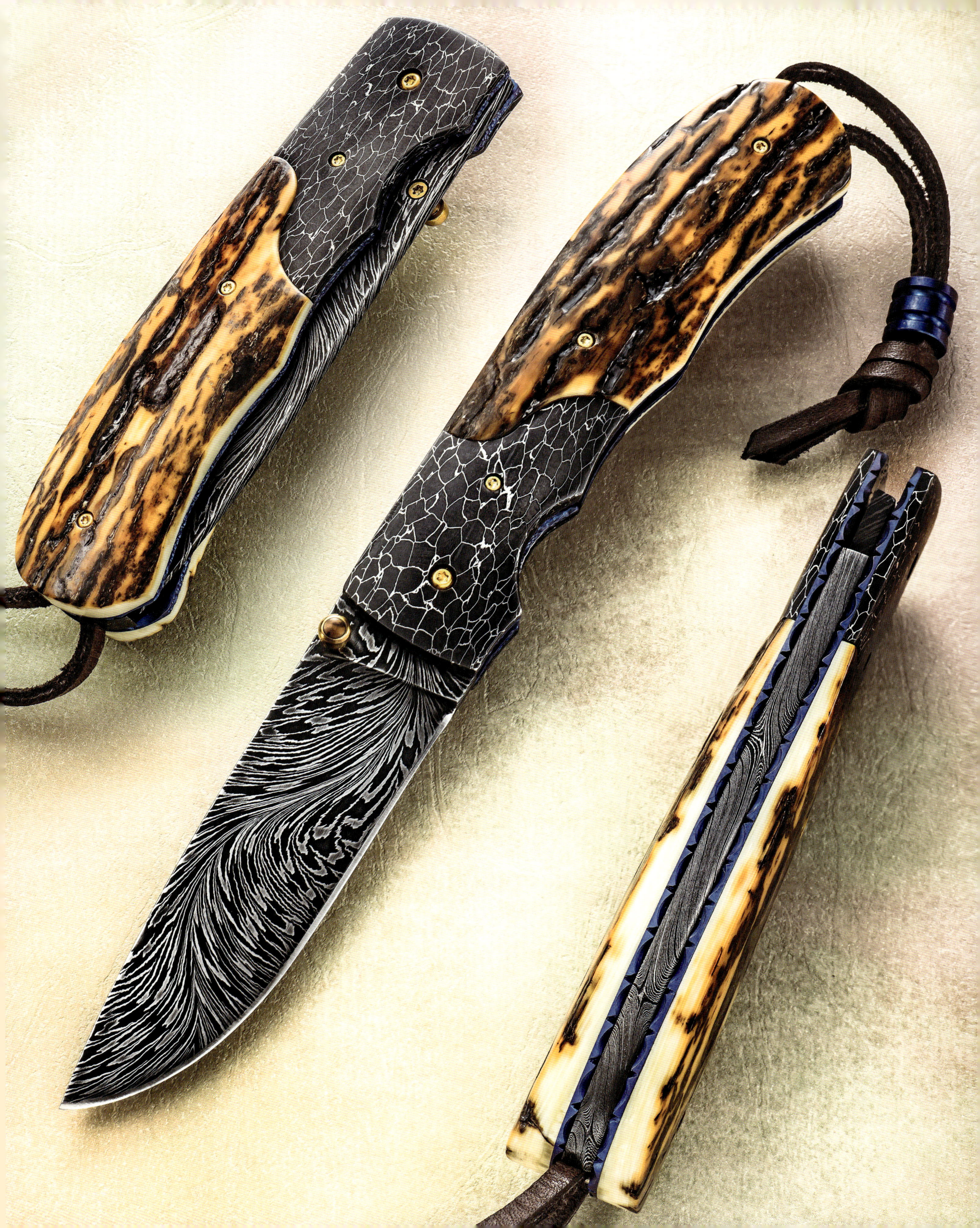

PETER DEL RASO

Peter Del Raso ist ein Mitglied der australischen Messermachergilde. Seine meisterhaften Fähigkeiten werden bei diesem „Persian Fighter" offensichtlich. Die San-Mai-Klinge hat einen Kern aus VG-10, flankiert von Lagen aus Takefu DP15. Die Griffbacken bestehen aus rostfreiem 416-Stahl, graviert von Marcello Pedini, der auch die goldenen Greifköpfe kreierte. Die Griffschalen sind aus Giraffenknochen mit in Messing gefassten Granaten gefertigt. Die zugehörige Scheide wurde ebenfalls von Del Raso handgefertigt.

Peter Del Raso is a member of the Australian Knifemakers Guild. His masterful skills become obvious with this Persian fighter. The San Mai blade has a core of VG-10 sandwiched between layers of Takefu DP15. The bolsters are of 416 stainless steel engraved by Marcello Pedini who also created the golden griffin heads. The handle scales are made of giraffe bone with garnets set in brass. The accompanying sheath was also handcrafted by Del Raso.

PETER DEL RASO

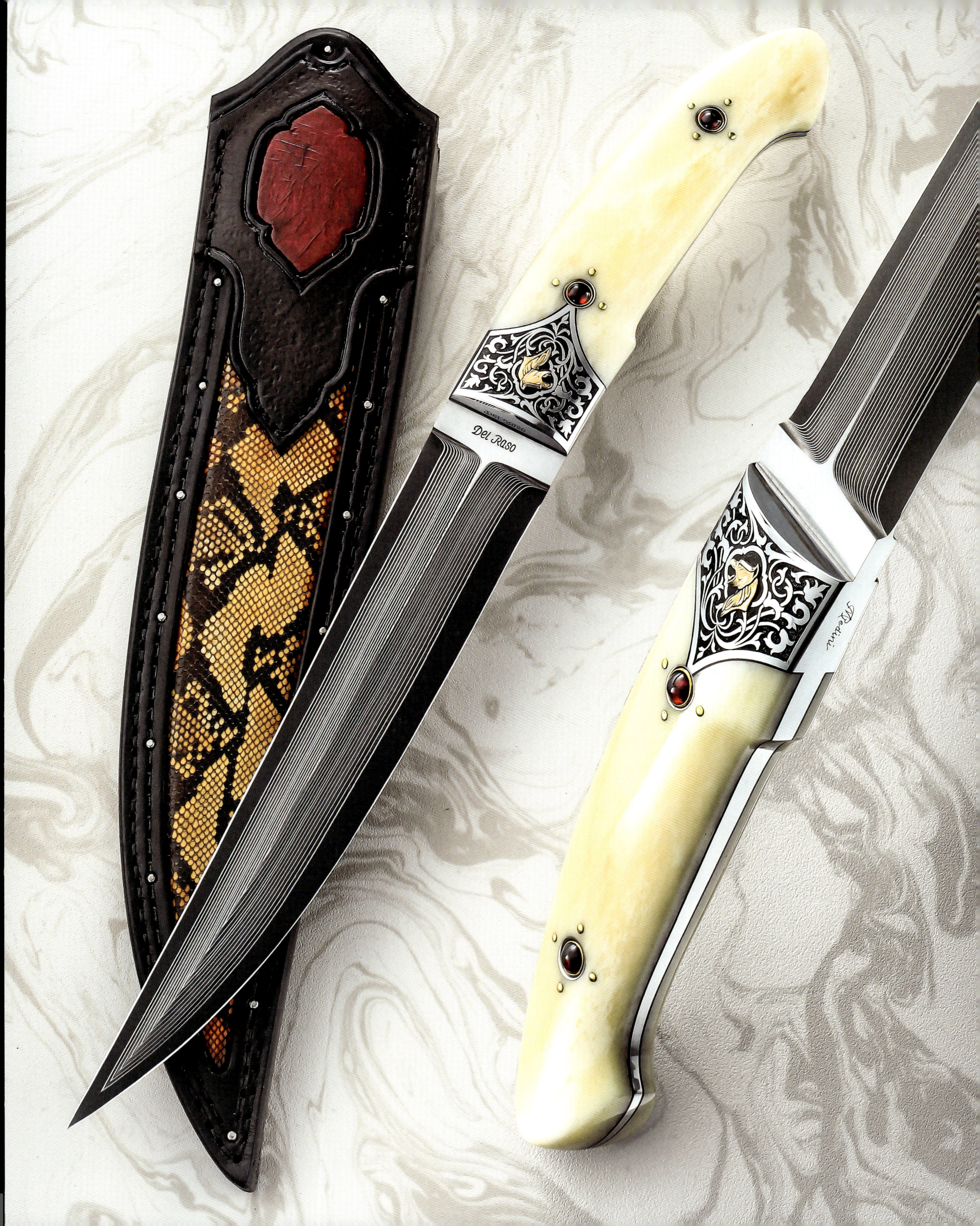
Del Raso

DIKRISTO

Dikristo ist der Künstlername des griechischen Messermachers Stelios Drakopoulos. Er liebt es Küchenmesser zu fertigen und benennt diese mit Worten aus der griechischen Mythologie. Das *Chaos* auf diesem Foto hat eine Klingenlänge von 230 mm und stellt Mokume aus Kupfer, Messing und rostfreiem Stahl zur Schau, das einen Kern von Kohlenstoffstahl ummantelt. Griffschalen und Scheide sind aus Oliven-Maserknolle geformt, das Logo des Messermachers dagegen wurde aus Kupfer und Kunstharz gefertigt.

Dikristo is the artist name of the greek knife maker Stelios Drakopoulos. He loves to make kitchen knives and names them with words from Greek mythology. The *Chaos* on this photo has a blade length of 230 mm and sports mokume of copper, brass and stainless steel cladded over a core of carbon steel. The handle scales and sheath are shaped of olive burl with the maker's logo outlined in copper and resin.

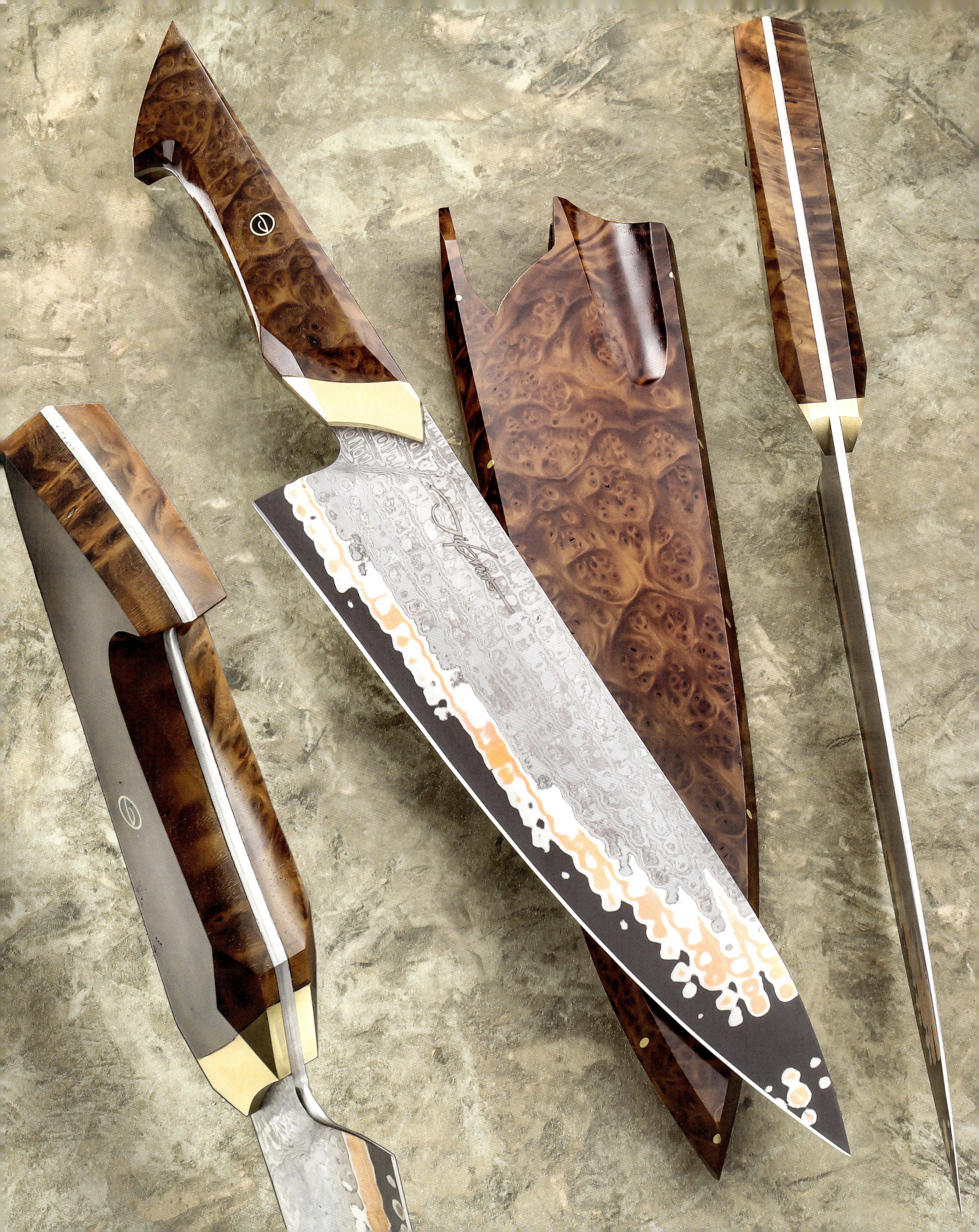

RIAN DOUDLE

Rian Doudle aus Redwood Park in Südaustralien schmiedete den Mosaikdamast für sein Halbintegral-Messer selbst. Dafür nahm er 1084- und 15N20-Stahl, die einen schönen Kontrast ergeben. Der Griff aus Arizona Ironwood fühlt sich sehr komfortabel an. Die roten Distanzstücke und das geflochtene Lederband sind zusätzliche Highlights.

Rian Doudle from Redwood Park, South Australia, forged the mosaic pattern damascus for this half-integral knife himself. For this he used 1084 and 15N20 steels which provide a nice contrast. The handle of Arizona Ironwood feels very comfy in your hand. The red spacers and braided leather lanyard set additional highlights.

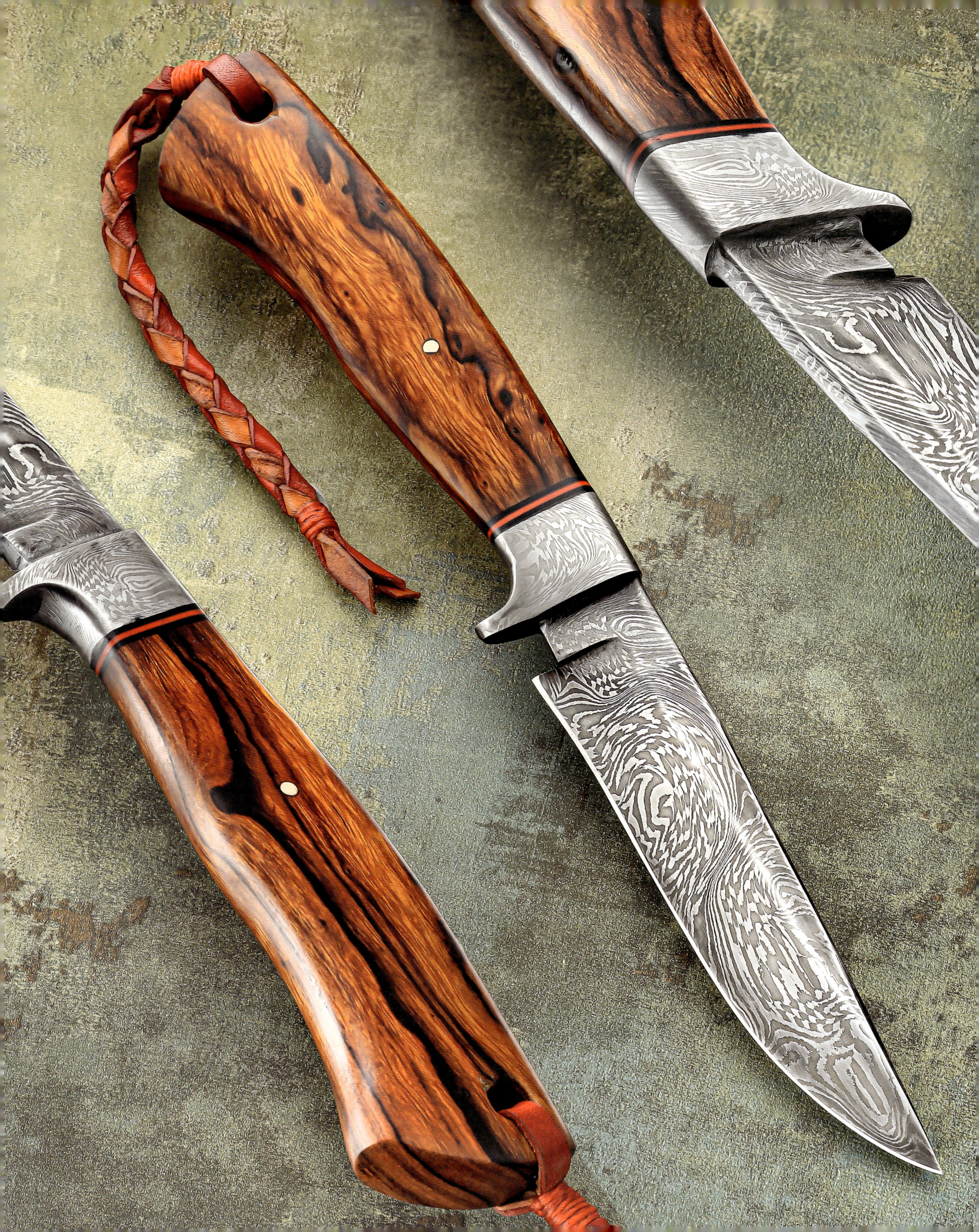

RICK DUNKERLEY

Rick Dunkerley muss nicht erst vorgestellt werden. Der amerikanische Meisterschmied ist Alleinautor dieses außergewöhnlichen Folders. Für Klinge und Griffbacken wurde derselbe Damast benutzt. Die Schnitzarbeit aus fossilem Walross-Elfenbein passt perfekt zum Verlauf dessen Musters. Auch das komplexe Filework auf dem Griffrücken und sogar die gefeilten Schrauben sind Hingucker und tragen dazu bei, ein einfaches Werkzeug in ein meisterhaftes Kunstwerk zu verwandeln.

Rick Dunkerley doesn't need to be introduced. The American ABS Master Bladesmith is sole author of this extraordinary folder. The same damascus was used for blade and bolsters . The carving on the handle scales of fossil walrus ivory fits perfectly to the flow of this pattern. The intricate filework of the backspacer and even the filed screws are eyecatchers as well and contribute in turning a simple tool into masterful art.

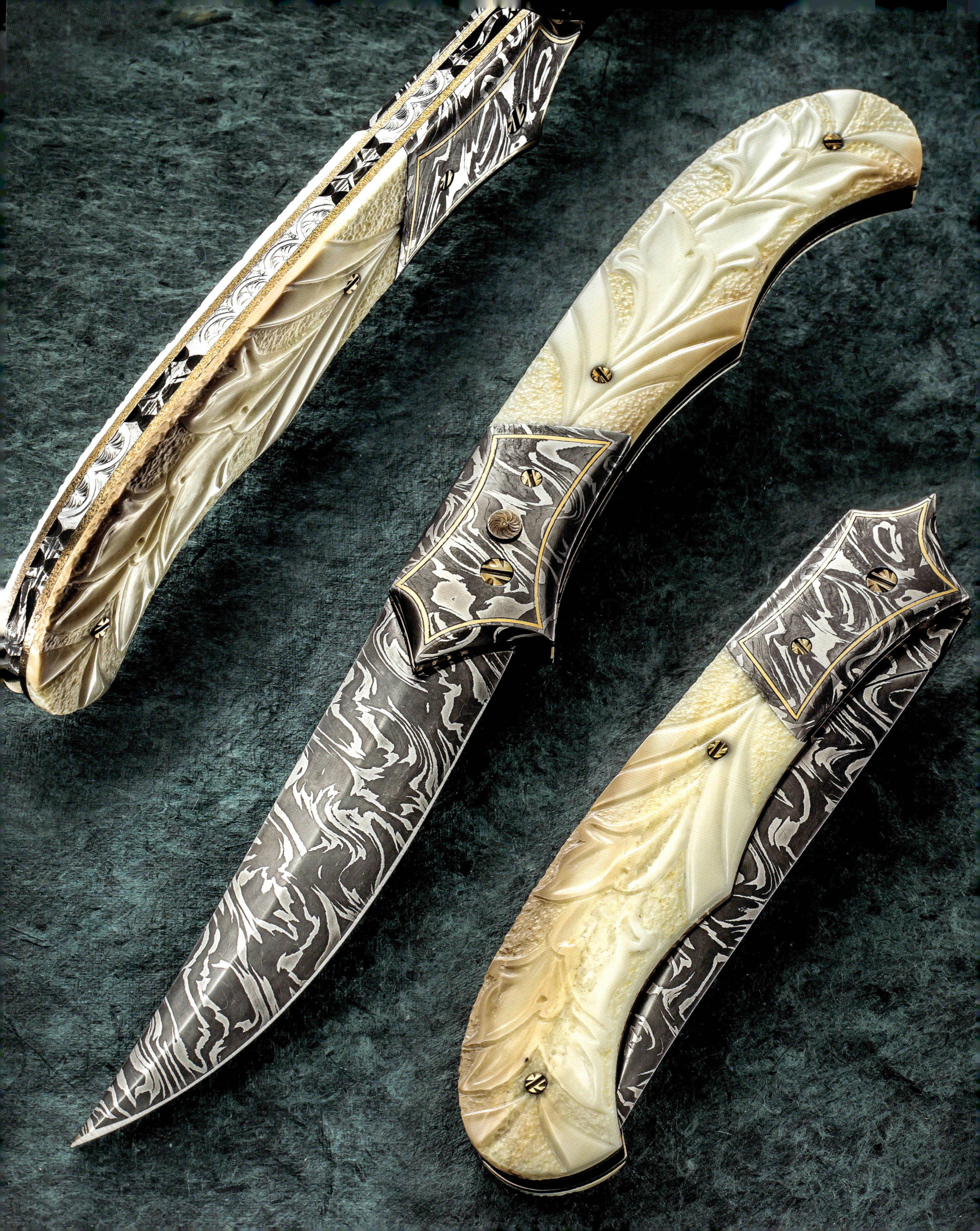

DWAYNE DUSHANE

Das aufwändige Damastmuster dieser Klinge und der Griffbacken wurde vom Messermacher Dwayne Dushane selbst geschmiedet. In seiner Werkstatt in Andrews, Texas, formte er auch die Griffschalen aus Mastodon-Elfenbein für sein *Eclipse*-Klappmesser und schuf auch die elegante Feilarbeit für die gebläuten Titanplatinen.
Ein Augenschmaus!

The intricate damascus pattern of this blade and bolsters was forged by the knifemaker Dwayne Dushane himself. In his workshop in Andrews, Texas, he also shaped the handle scales of mastodon ivory for his *Eclipse* folder and created the elegant filework for the blued titanium liners. A treat for the eyes!

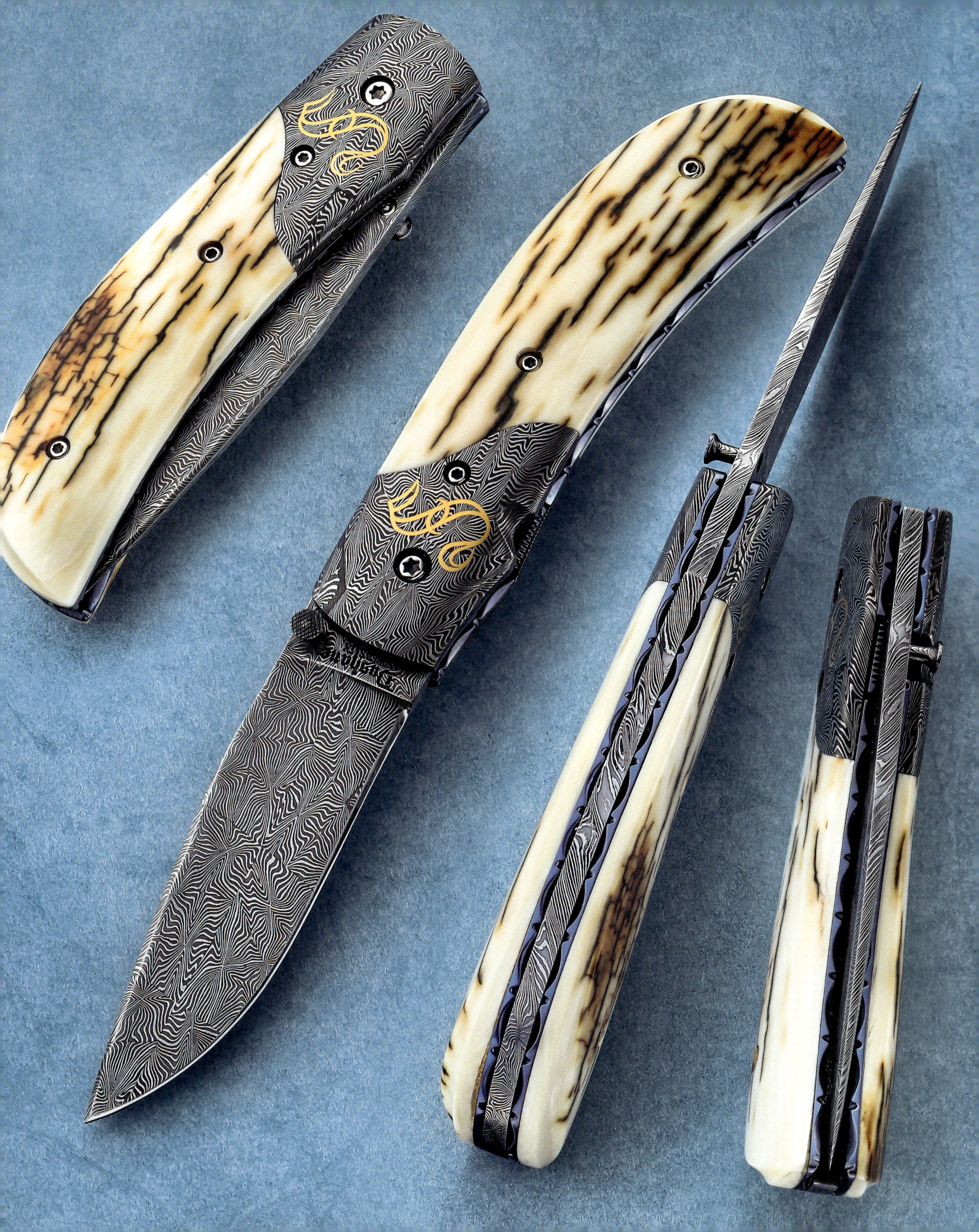

JASON ELLARD

Jason Ellard ist ein junger und vielversprechender Messermacher aus Australien. Trotz seiner Jugend hat er bereits die Kunst gemeistert, schönen Damast herzustellen – ohne die Verwendung eines Maschinenhammers. Um das komplizierte Muster für sein integrales Mosaik-Kochmesser herzustellen, verwendete er die Stahlsorten 1084 und 15N20. Die Klinge wird durch eine elegante Edelstahlzwinge vom Griff aus Tasmanian Blackwood abgegrenzt.

Jason Ellard is a young and promising Australian knifemaker. Despite his youth, he has already mastered the art of creating beautiful damascus – without using a power hammer. For this integral mosaic chef, he used 1084 and 15N20 steels to create the complicated pattern. It is set apart from the handle of stabilized Tasmanian blackwood by a spacer of stainless steel.

JASON ELLARD

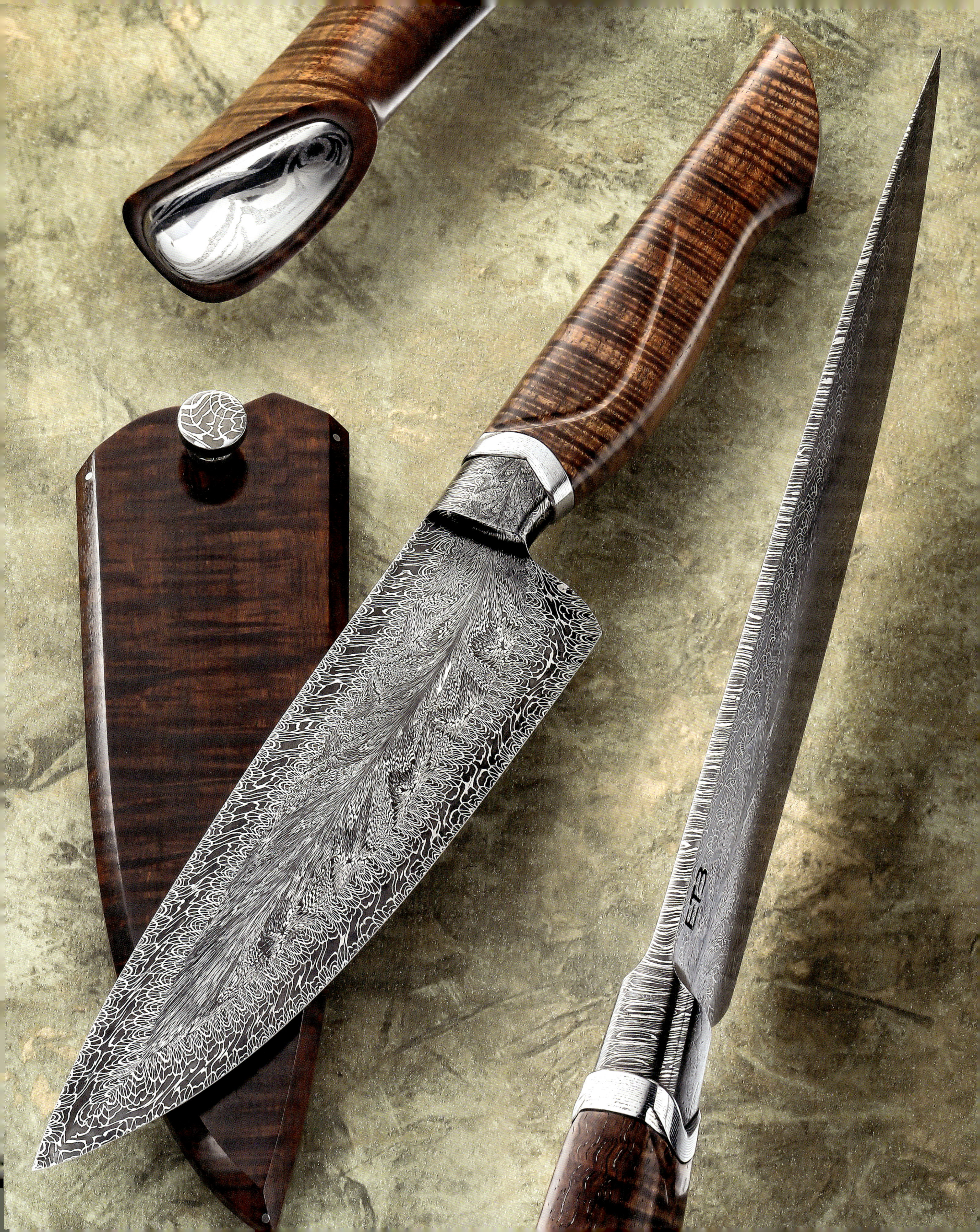
ETB

CHARLIE ELLIS

Das *Royal Integral Chef* von Charlie Ellis aus Leicester, North Carolina, besitzt eine sehr schöne Leiter-Damastklinge, die aus den Stählen 1084 und 15N20 geschmiedet wurde. Der Griff besteht aus stabilisierter Maserbirke mit einem auffallenden violetten Farbton. Die Zwinge aus „dunkler Materie" (Kohlefaser) bildet eine Verbindung zwischen der Maserung des Holzes und dem Muster des Damasts.

This *Royal Integral Chef* by Charlie Ellis from Leicester, North Carolina, shows a beautiful ladder damascus blade forged from 1084 and 15N20 steels. The handle is shaped from stabilized curly maple exhibiting an eyecatching violet hue. The ferrule from „dark matter" carbon fiber forms a connection between the grain of the wood and the pattern of the damascus.

CHARLIE ELLIS

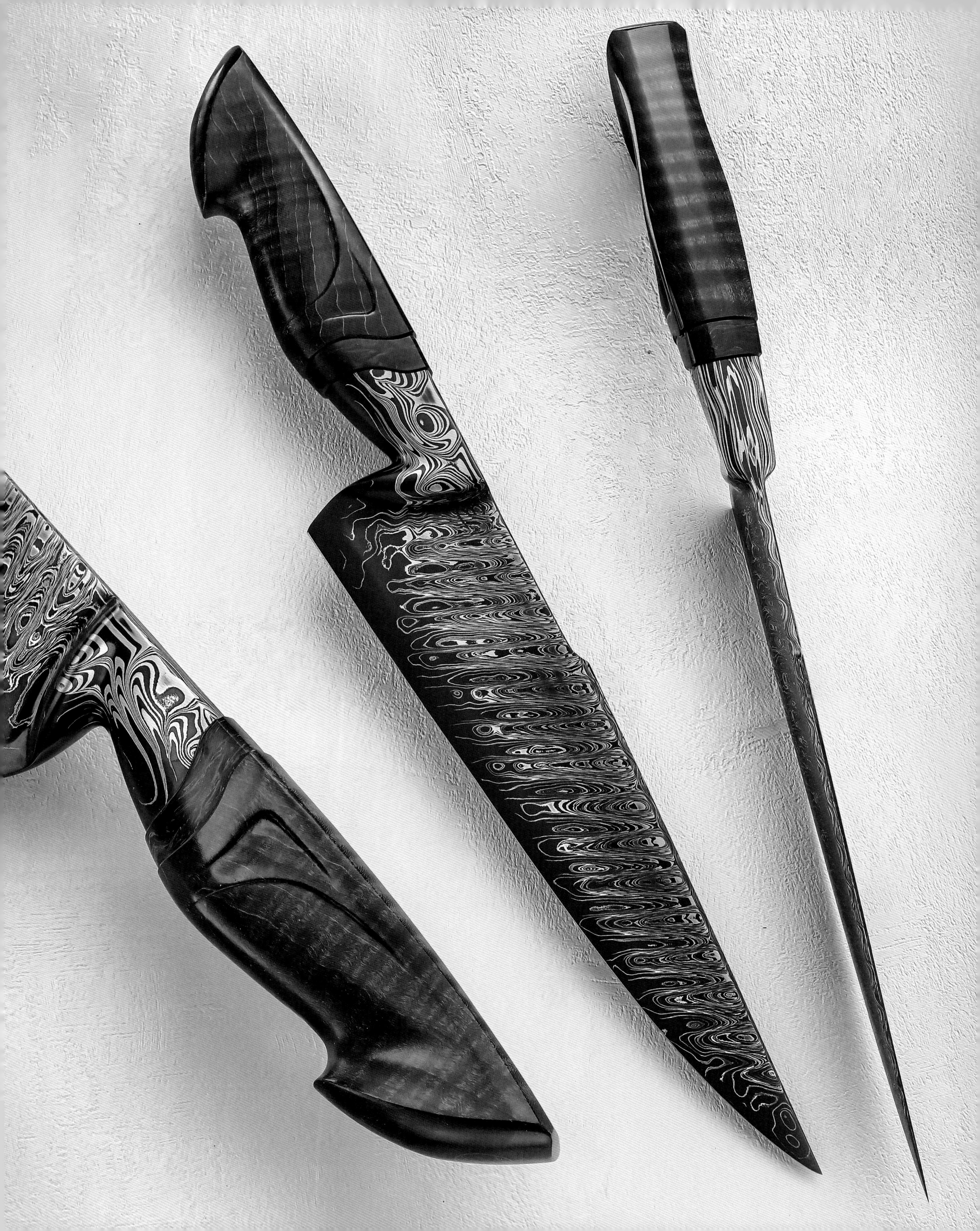

KAY EMBRETSEN

Ein Messer im typisch skandinavischen Stil ist dieses schöne feststehende Exemplar von Kay Embretsen aus Edsbyn in Schweden. Kay macht alles selbst: Er schmiedete sowohl den hübschen Leiter-Damast für die San-Mai-Klinge als auch den Damast für das Zwischenstück am Griff. Er bearbeitete die Maserbirke für den ansprechenden und komfortablen Griff und bläute den Stahl für die Zwinge. Er fertigte auch die zugehörige Lederscheide.

A typical Scandi-type knife is this beautiful fixed blade by Kay Embretsen of Edsbyn, Sweden. Kay makes everything himself: He forged the lovely ladder damascus for the San Mai blade as well as the damascus for the bolster. He shaped the curly birch for the pretty and comfy handle and blued the steel for the ferrule. He also made the accompanying leather sheath.

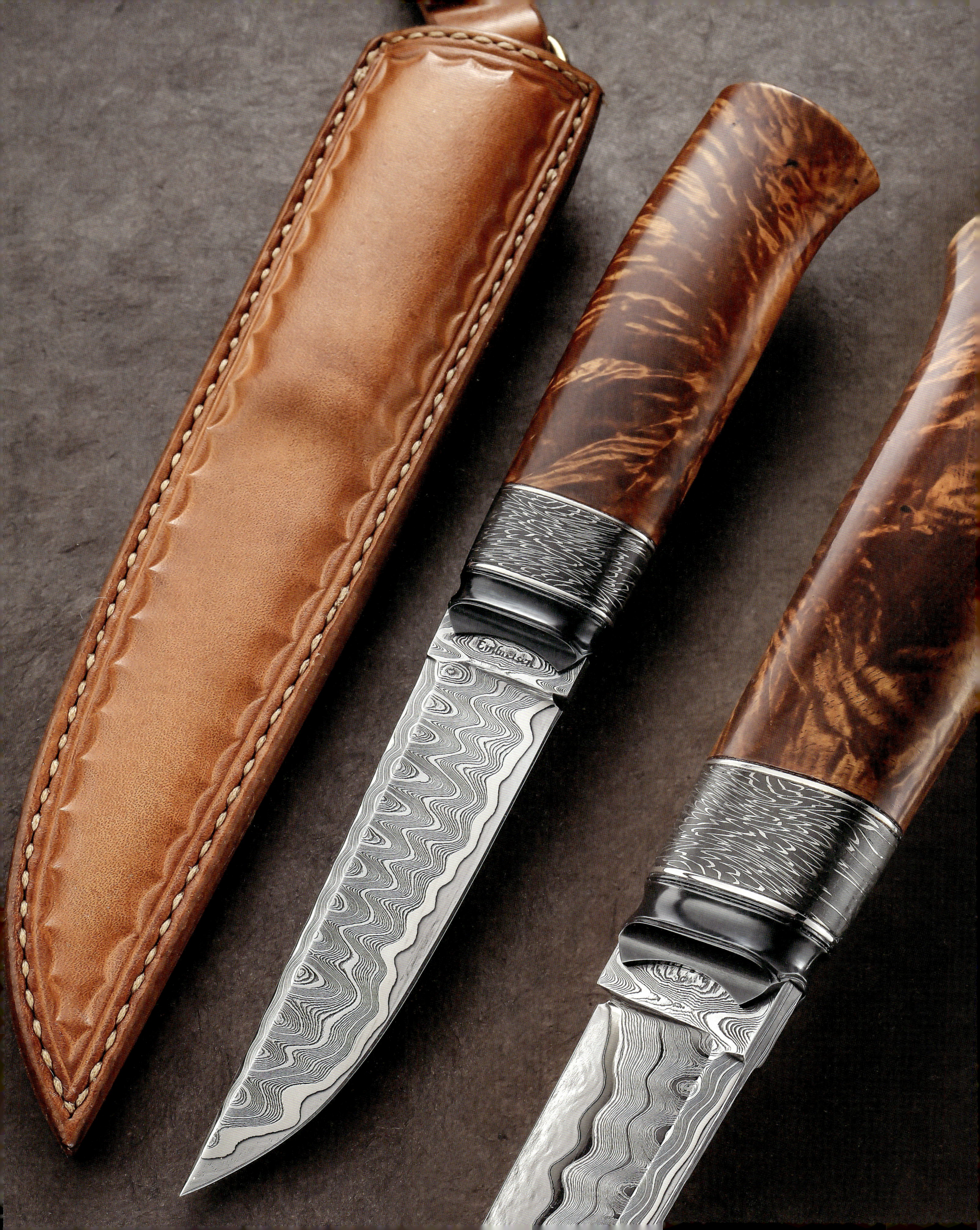

CHRIS FARRELL

Das amerikanische Magazin „Blade" druckte die Überschrift „My, oh, my, Copper-Mai!", nachdem die Journalisten dieses herausragende Messer gesehen hatten. In der Tat nutzte Chris Farrell aus Elgin, Texas, Damast und Kupfer vom Hersteller Baker Forge, um die Klinge seines „Húrin" in San-Mai-Technik herzustellen. Der Griff besteht aus stabilisierter und gefärbter Kastanien-Maserknolle, die aufwändig geformt und mit Mosaikpins verziert ist.

The American Blade Magazine used the headline „My, oh, my, Copper-Mai!" upon seeing this outstanding knife. Indeed, Chris Farrell from Elgin, Texas used San Mai of damascus and copper from Baker Forge to shape the blade of his „Húrin". The handle is made of stabilized and dyed buckeye burl shaped in an intricate way and embellished with mosaic pins.

CHRIS FARRELL

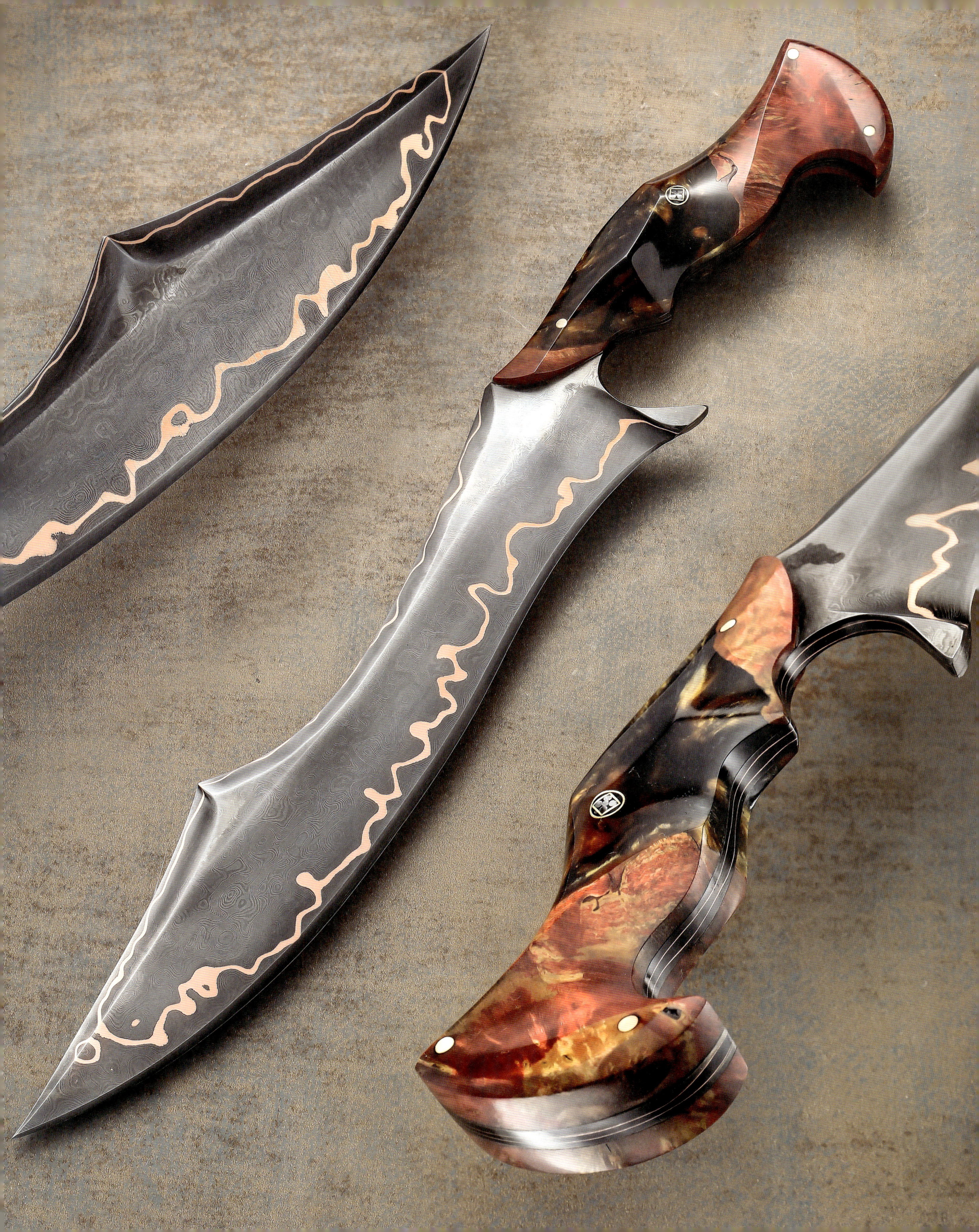

STEVE FILICIETTI

Steve Filicietti ist Mitglied der „Queensland Metal Artisans Collective" und spezialisiert darauf, seinen eigenen Damast herzustellen. Die Klinge dieses großen Bowies besteht aus einem aufwändig geschmiedeten Mosaikdamast. Parierstange und Zwischenstück wurden hitzecoloriert, um die verschiedenen Farben hervorzurufen. Der Griff besteht aus stabilisiertem geringeltem Gidgee – einem sehr dichten Holz. Spacer und eingesetztes Schild aus rostfreiem Stahl vervollständigen dieses Kunstwerk.

Steve Filicietti is a member of the Queensland Metal Artisans Collective and specializes in making his own damascus steel. This big Bowie shows an intricate pattern of mosaic damascus on its blade. The guard and bolsters were heat-treated to reveal different colors. The handle is made of stabilized ringed gidgee – a very dense wood type. Spacers and shield of stainless steel complete this piece of art.

STEVE FILICIETTI

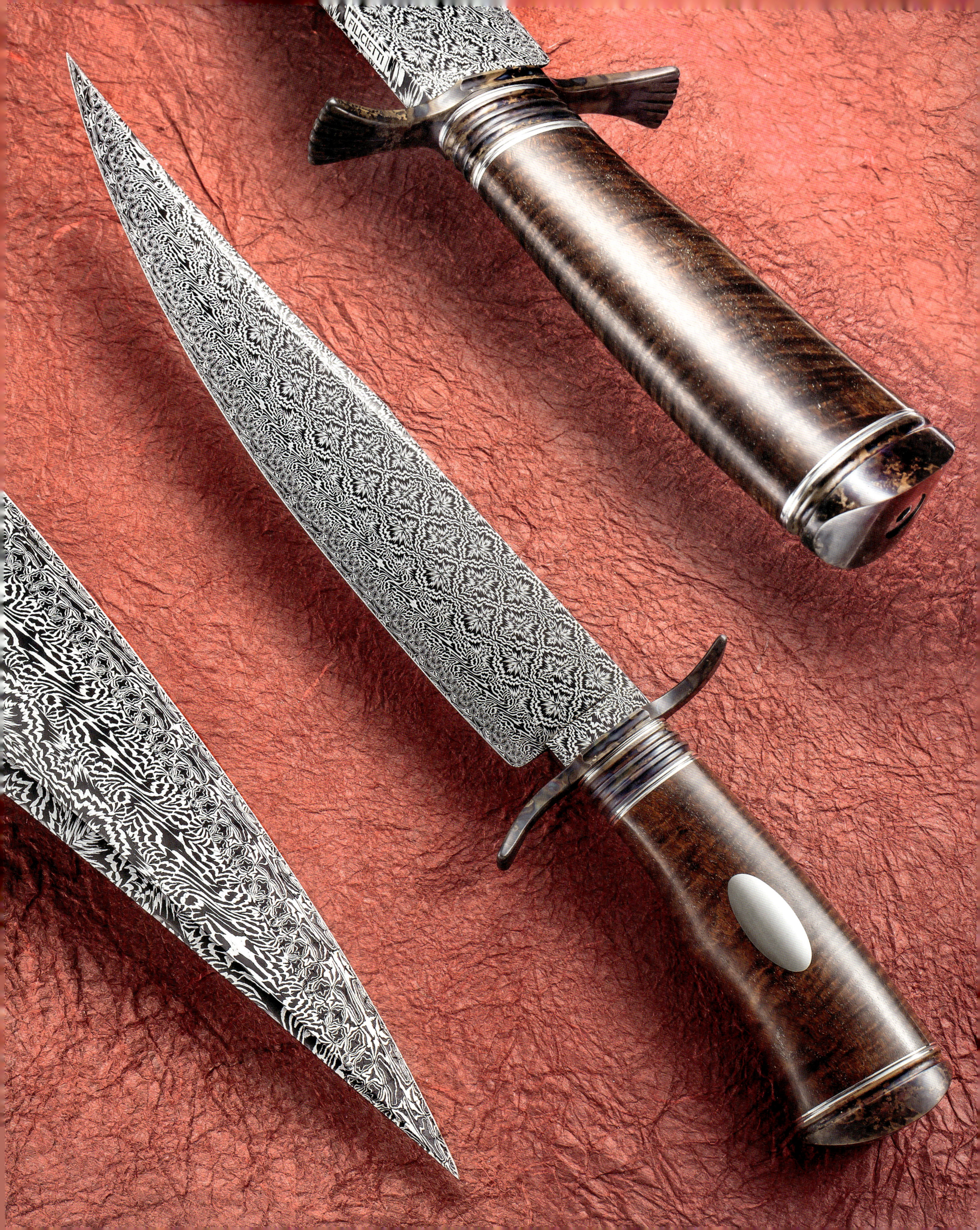

JERRY FISK

Meisterschmied Jerry Fisk ist schon seit geraumer Zeit in der Branche. Er ist in der „Hall of Fame" der American Bladesmith Society und wurde sogar zum „National Living Treasure" ernannt. Das Foto zeigt zwei seiner kleinen feststehenden Gebrauchsmesser, das *Sendero* mit Hirschhorn-Griff und das *Gamemaster* mit einem Griff aus attraktiver Maserknolle. Der Damast für beide Messer wurde natürlich vom Meister persönlich geschmiedet.

Master Smith Jerry Fisk has been around for some time. He is in the American Bladesmith Society's „Hall of Fame" and even was named „National Living Treasure". The photo shows two of his small utility fixed blades, the *Sendero* with stag handle and the *Gamemaster* with a handle of attractive burl. The damascus for both was, of course, forged by the master himself.

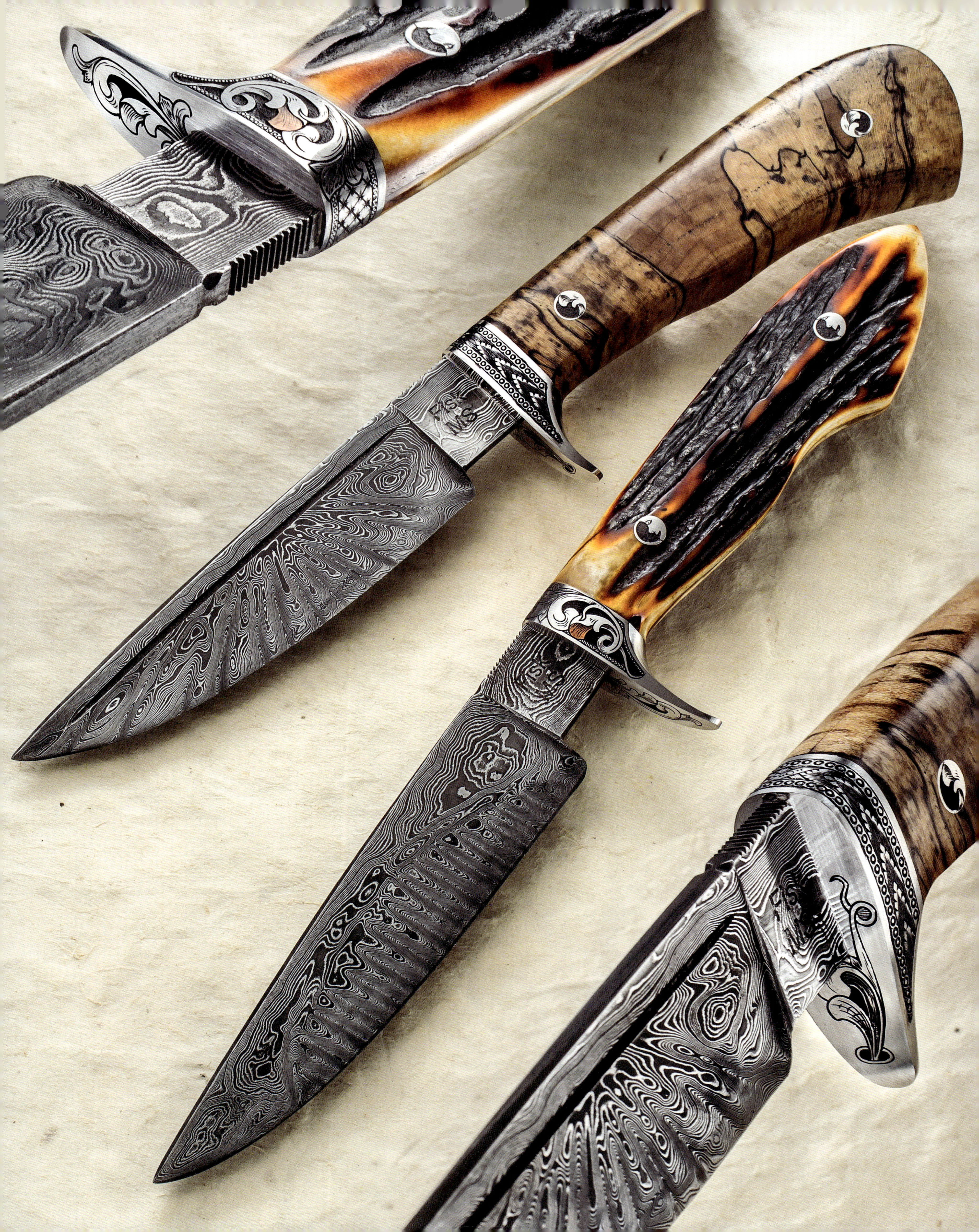

STEPHAN FOWLER

Stephan Fowler ist ein Journeyman Smith aus Dallas, Georgia, und war eine Zeitlang auch Präsident der Messermachergilde von Georgia. Die 8½-Zoll-Klinge seines *Koa Bowie* besteht aus Stephans eigenem Zebra-Damast. Auch die Parierstange ist aus Stephans eigenem Material gefertigt. Der Griff wurde aus Koa passend zum Muster geformt. Eine gefärbte Lederscheide vervollständigt sein Bowie-Messer.

Stephan Fowler is a Journeyman Smith of Dallas, Georgia, and was also President of the Georgia Knife Makers Guild for some time. The 8½"-blade of his *Koa Bowie* is made of Stephan's own zebra damascus. The guard, too, is of Stephan's own material. The handle is shaped from corresponding curly Koa. A sheath of dyed leather completes his Bowie knife.

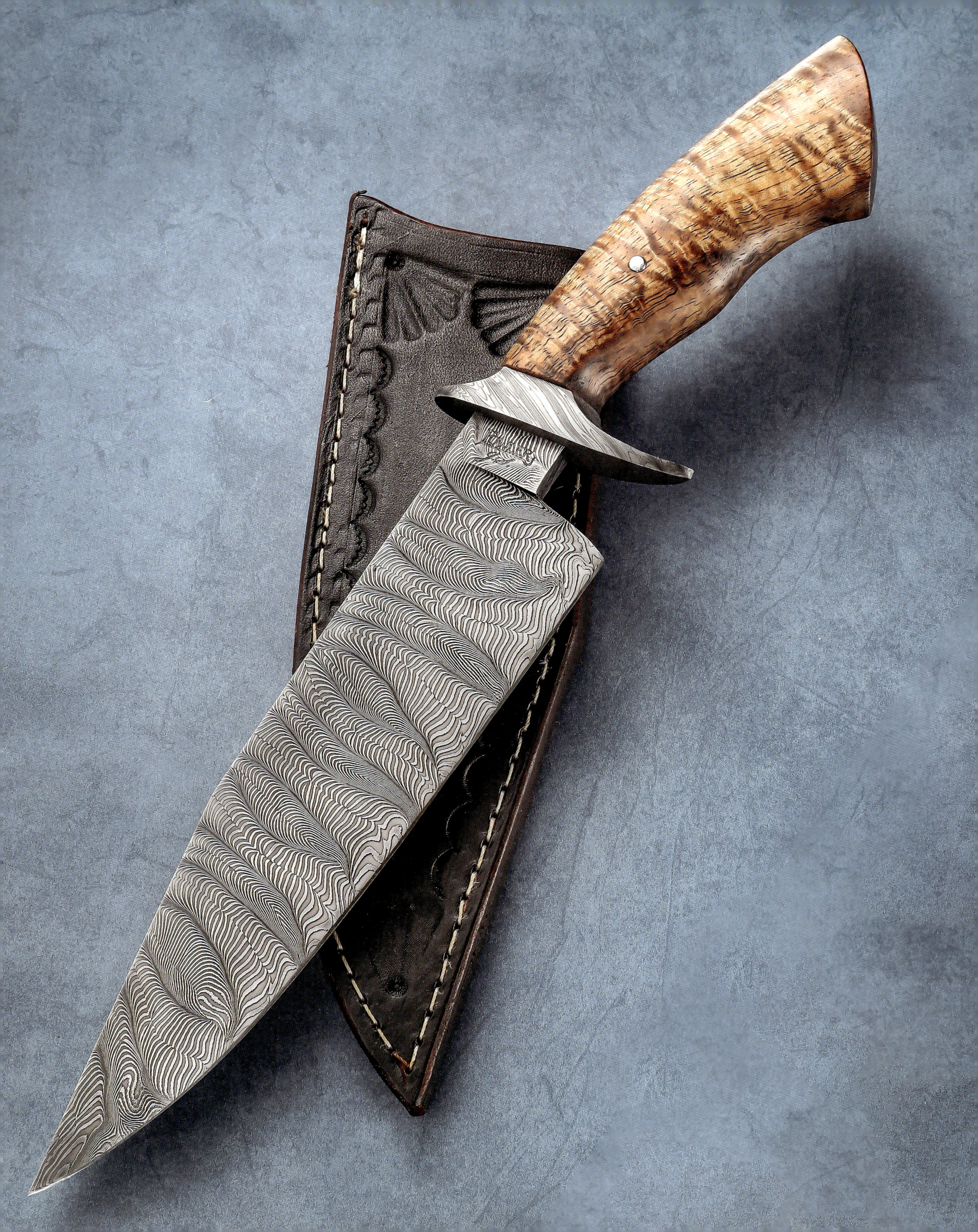

DENNIS FRIEDLY

Ebenfalls kein Unbekannter ist Dennis Friedly aus Cody, Wyoming. Er fertigte die hohlgeschliffene Klinge aus rostfreiem Damast von Mike Norris von Hand und formte und polierte auch den Griff aus Picasso-Marmor. Die mit Salzen gebläute Parierstange, die Zwinge und der Knauf wurden von Gil Rudolph mit floralen Motiven und Schmetterlingen dekoriert.

Dennis Friedly from Cody, Wyoming is also not an unknown. He hollow-ground the blade of Mike Norris stainless damascus by hand and also shaped and polished the handle of Picasso marble. The nitre-blued guard, bolster and pommel were decorated with floral motifs and butterflies by Gil Rudolph.

DENNIS FRIEDLY

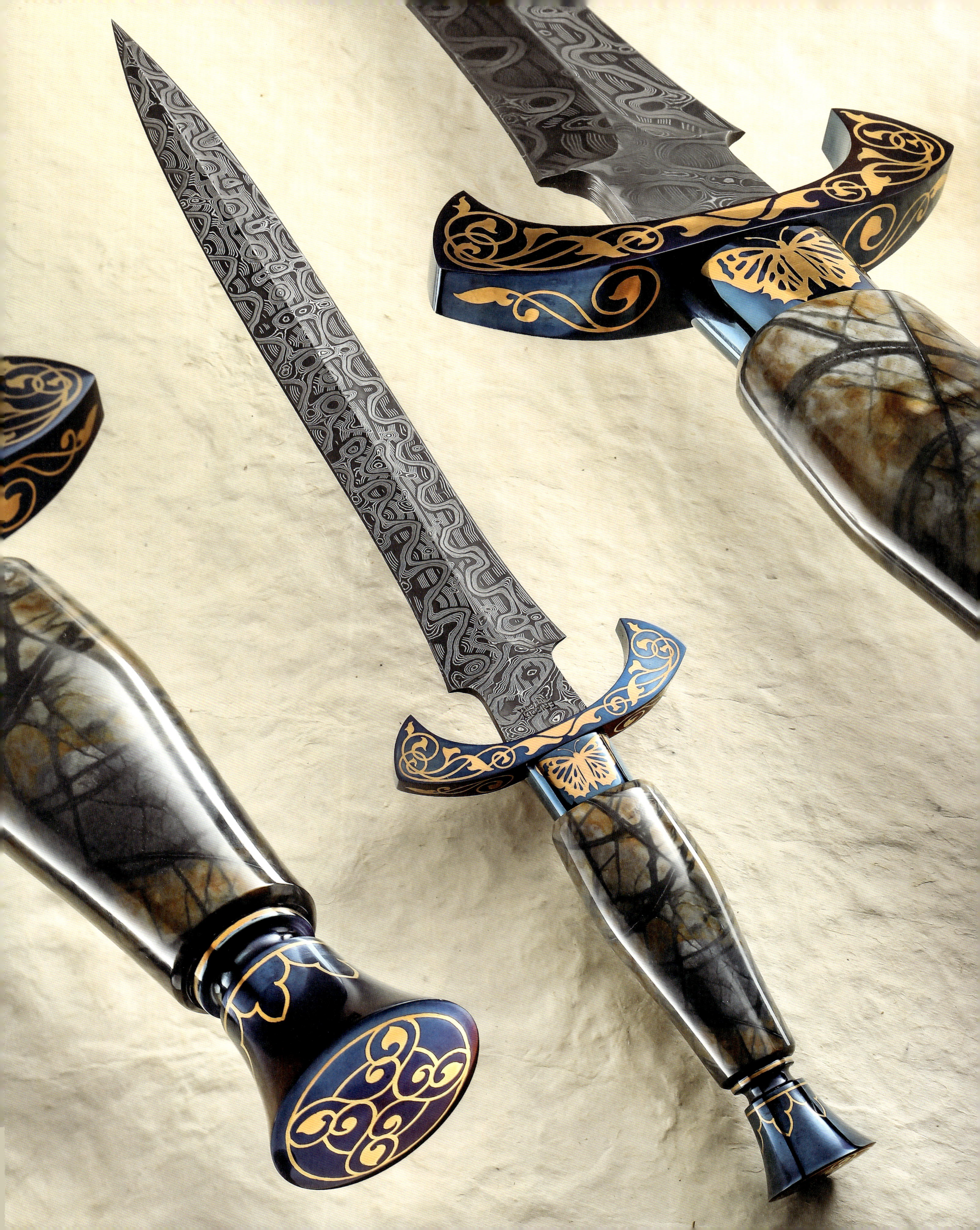

SCOTT GALLAGHER

ABS-Meisterschmied Scott Gallagher aus Defuniak Springs, Florida, erschuf den Mosaik-Damast sowohl für diese Klinge als auch für den Handschutz und die Beschläge. Die Rundung der Klinge setzt sich in dem Griff aus fossilem Walross-Elfenbein fort. Ein schlankes Distanzstück mit Filework sorgt für ein zusätzliches Highlight auf diesem Meisterstück. Die punzierte Lederscheide spendet eine weitere ästhetische Note.

ABS Master Bladesmith Scott Gallagher from Defuniak Springs, Florida, created the mosaic damascus for this blade as well as the guard and fittings. The curve of the blade continues up to the handle of fossil walrus ivory. A slim fileworked titanium spacer provides an additional highlight for this masterpiece. The embossed leather sheath contributes a further aesthetic note.

SCOTT GALLAGHER

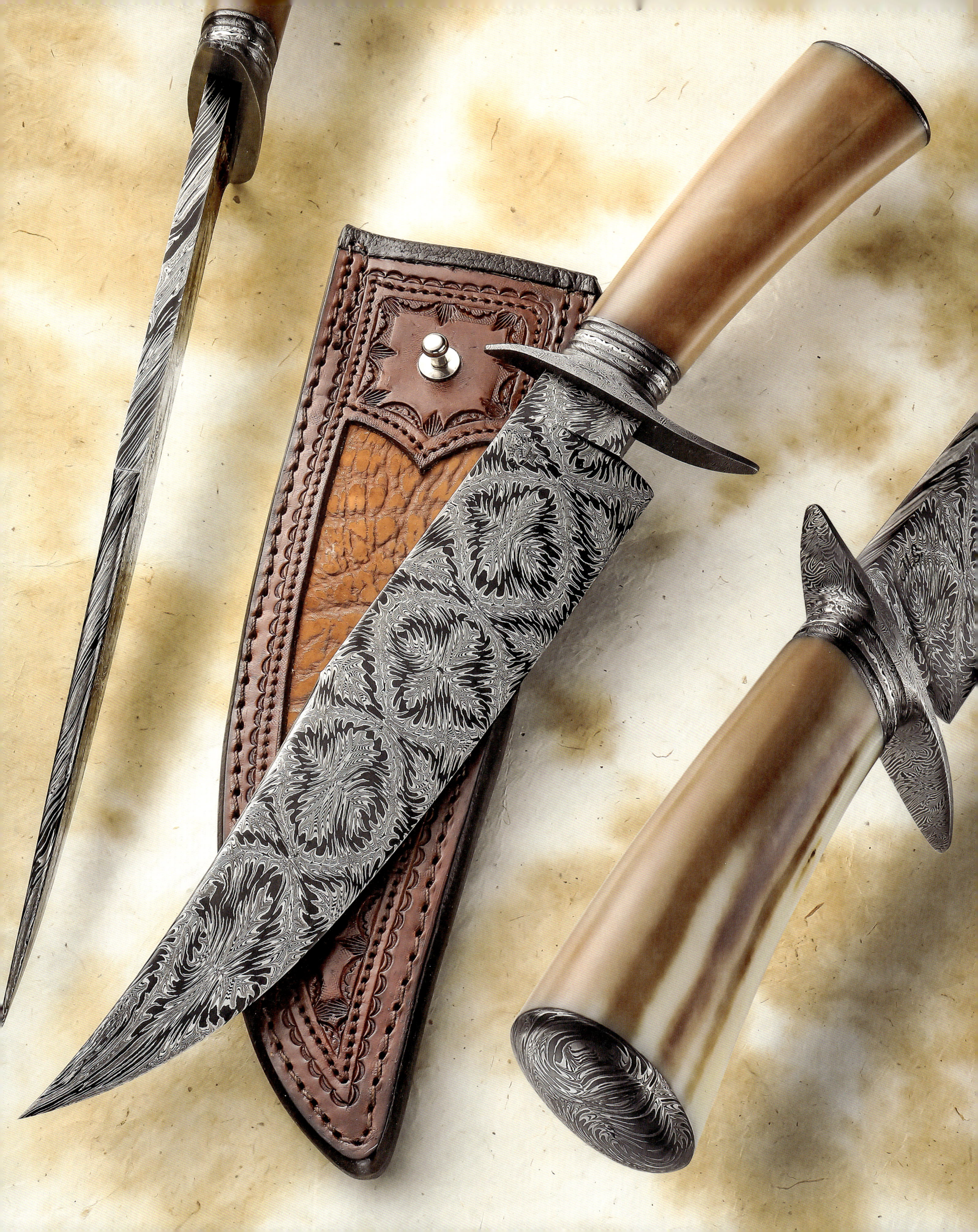

TOMMY GANN

Dieses Messer von Tommy Gann wurde als „Best Bowie" auf der Blade Show Texas 2022 ausgezeichnet. Der ABS-Master-Bladesmith aus Canton, Texas, verwendete selbst hergestellten Mosaikdamast für die 10-Zoll-Klinge und wählte Torsionsdamast für Handschutz und Zwinge. Der sargförmige Griff dieses schönen Bowies ist aus Walross-Stoßzahn gefertigt und von der Flachangel durch Platinen aus Neusilber abgegrenzt.

This knife of Tommy Gann was awarded „Best Bowie" at the Blade Show Texas 2022. The ABS Master Bladesmith from Canton, Texas, used mosaic damascus of his own making for the 10"-blade and chose his twisted damascus for the guard and ferrule. The coffin-type handle of this beautiful Bowie was created of walrus tusk, separated from the tang by liners of nickel silver.

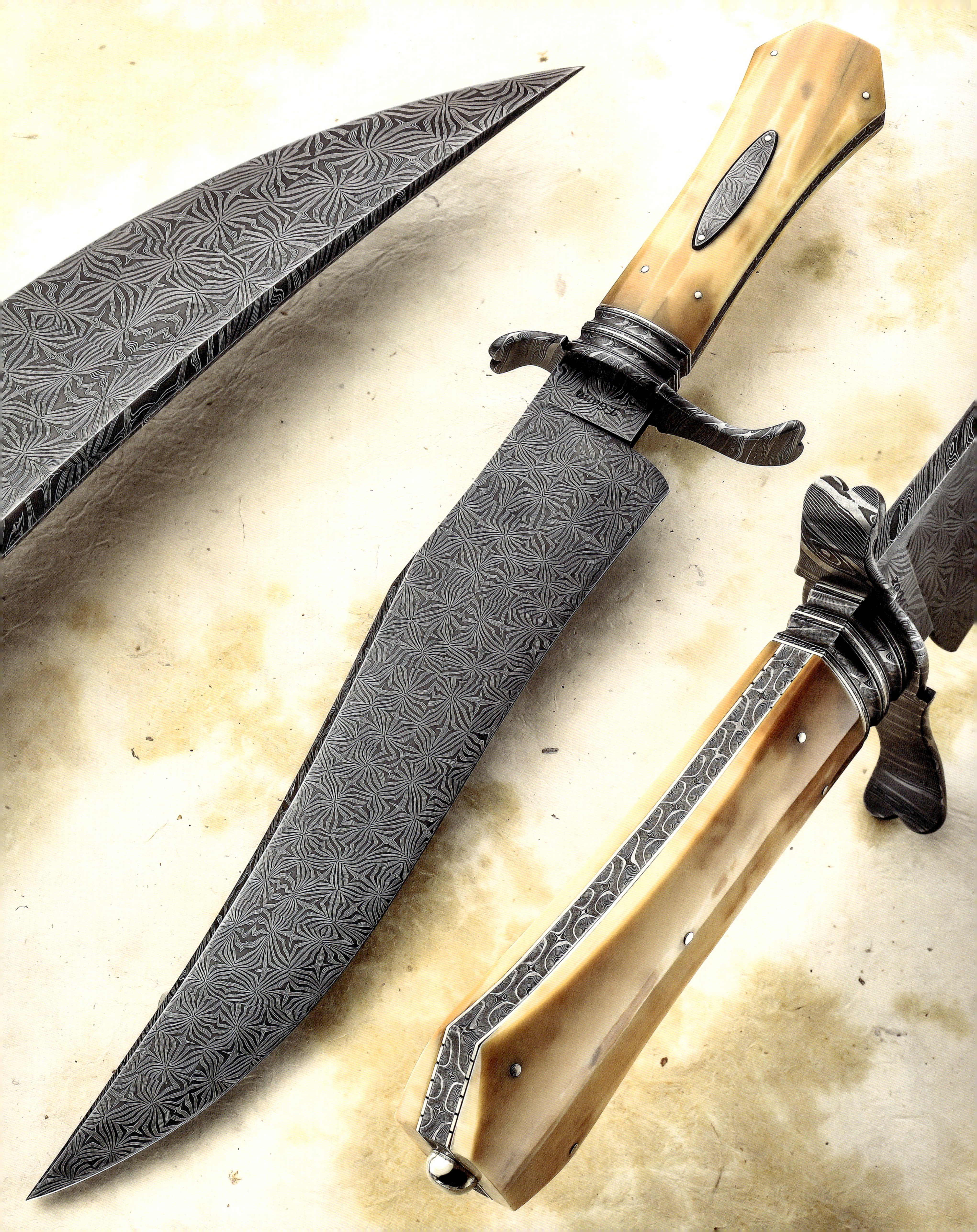

AIDAN GARRITY

Aidan Garrity aus Madison, Connecticut, ist der Macher dieses französisch-persischen Küchenmessers. Sein Design ist eine Fusion aus persischem Kampfmesser und französischem Kochmesser. Garrity schmiedete den Damast für die Klinge und den integrierten Kropf aus den Stahlsorten 15N20, 1095 und 52100. Der Griff sieht aus wie Elefanten-Elfenbein, ist aber komplett aus Elforyn gefertigt.

Aidan Garrity of Madison, Connecticut, is the maker of this French/Persian kitchen knife. Its design is a fusion between Persian fighter and French chef's knife. Garrity forged the damascus for blade and integral bolster from 15N20, 1095 and 52100 steel types. The handle looks like elephant ivory, but was entirely made of Elforyn.

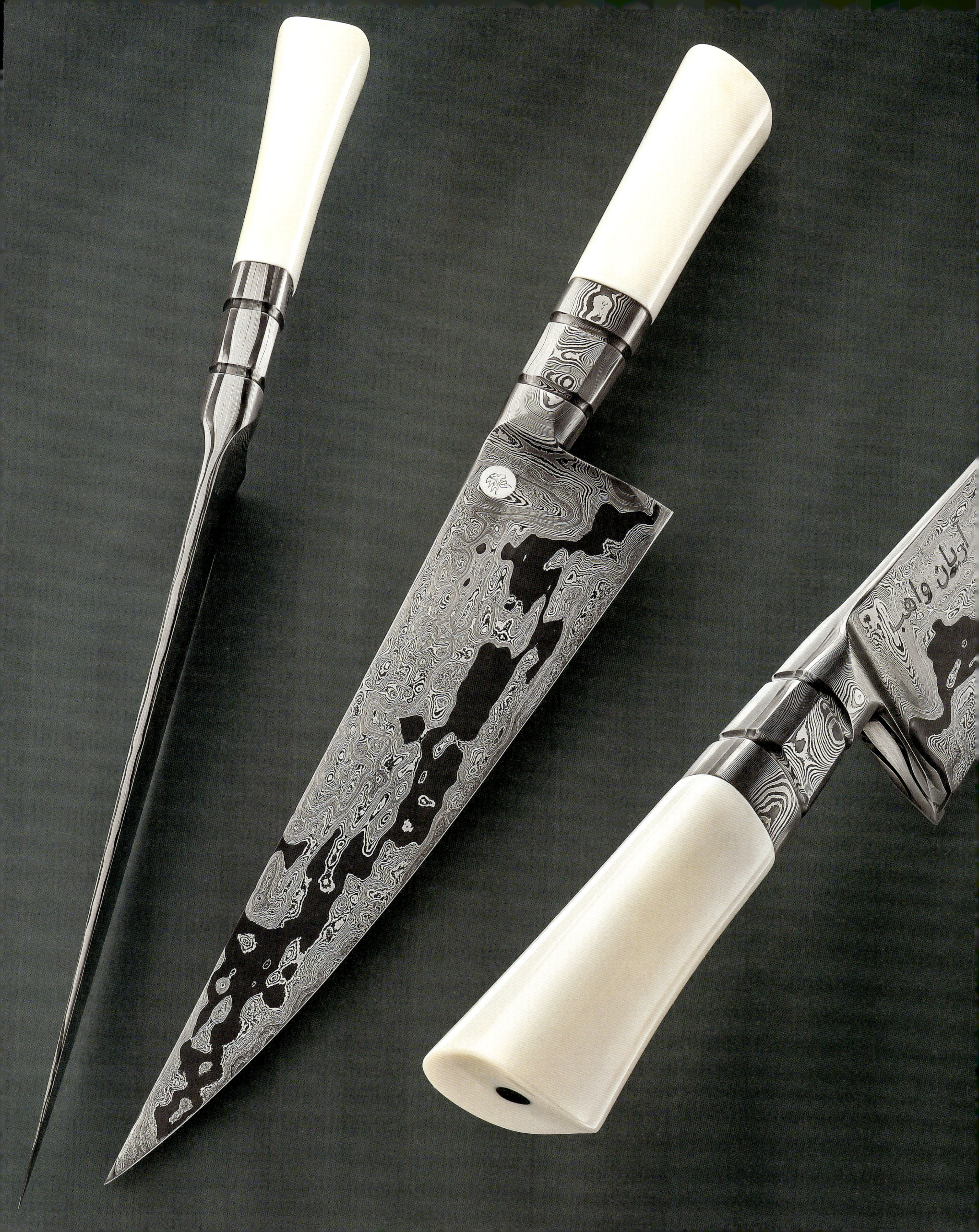

CHARLES GEDRAITIS

Ein Taschenmesser mit Füßen und dem Namen *Clever Girl*? Das erinnert einen doch an Jurassic Park, oder nicht? Allerdings sind die Füße nur Teil des handgefertigten Ständers für dieses wunderschöne Springmesser mit einer Damastklinge im persischen Stil. Der autodidaktische Messermacher Charles (Chuck) Gedraitis aus Holden, Massachusetts, formte die hinteren Griffbacken als Kopf eines Raubsauriers, die Klinge dagegen fungiert als Schwanz des Reptils. Der Körper des vorsintflutlichen Tieres wird mit Hilfe der Griffschalen aus Mammut-Elfenbein verdeutlicht, während die Füße aus Damast von Jerry Rados geformt wurden. Die Platinen bestehen aus blau anodisiertem Titan.

A folder with feet named *Clever Girl*? Doesn't that remind one of Jurassic Park? Actually, the feet are only part of the handmade stand for this beautiful switchblade knife with Persian-style damascus blade. Self-taught knifemaker Charles (Chuck) Gedraitis from Holden, Massachusetts, shaped the rear bolster as the head of a raptor; the blade in turn constitutes the reptile's tail. The ancient dinosaur's body is made visible by means of the handle scales of mammoth ivory, while the rest of the critter and the feet are shaped of Jerry Rados damascus. The liners are made of blue anodized titanium.

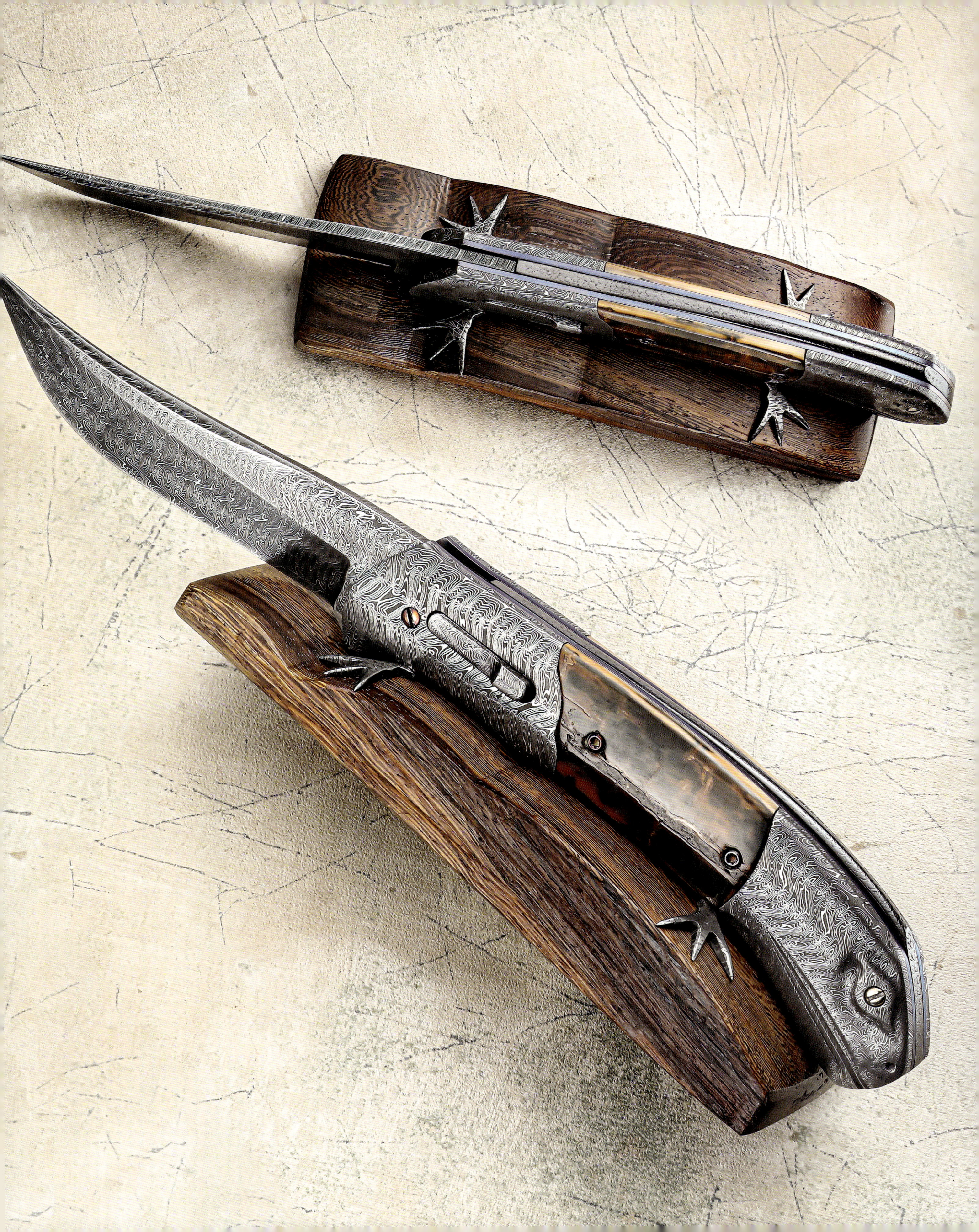

RANDY HAAS

Randy Haas, Eigentümer von HHH Custom Knives in Marlette, Michigan, hat sich auf individuelle Küchenmesser spezialisiert. Dieses prächtige Stück ist mit einer Klinge aus seinem eigenen Vogelaugen-Damast versehen. Der Klingenrücken ist mit einem hübschen gefeilten Rankenmuster verziert. Die Zwinge besteht aus Randys Mosaik-Damast und ist mit einem charmanten cremefarbenen Griff aus fossilem Walross-Stoßzahn verbunden.

Randy Haas, owner of HHH Custom Knives in Marlette, Michigan, specializes in custom kitchen knives. This gorgeous piece was made with a blade of his own bird's eye damascus. The blade's back is nicely fileworked with a vine pattern. The ferrule is made of Randy's mosaic damascus and is attached to the charming cream-colored handle of fossil walrus tusk.

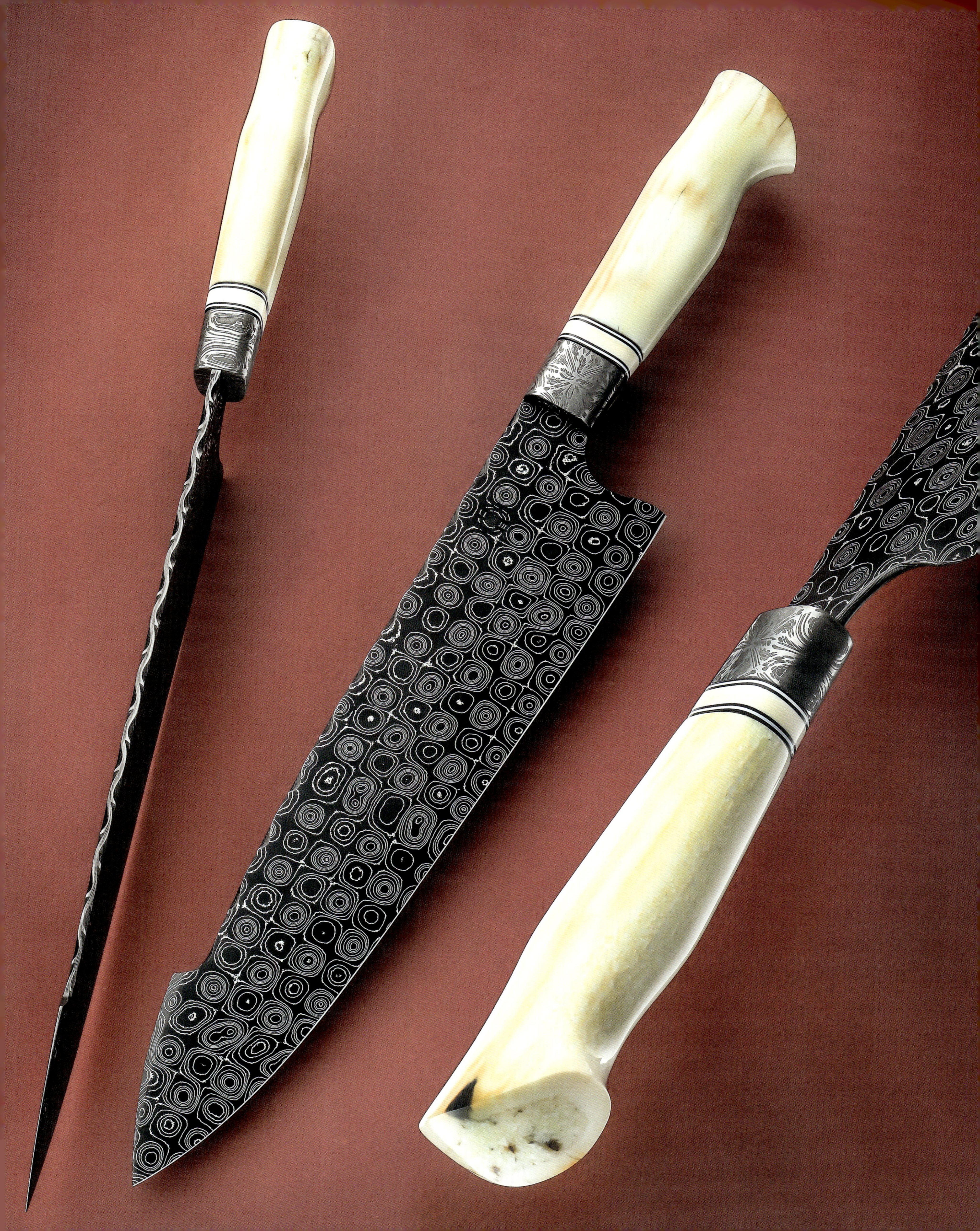

MARSHALL HALL

Marshall Hall ist ein eher unbekannter Messermacher aus Casselberry, Florida. Nichtsdestotrotz ist er dazu fähig, sehr attraktive Messer wie zum Beispiel dieses feststehende Exemplar zu machen. Der Damast für die Klinge wurde von Doug Ponzio geschmiedet. Marshall verschönerte sie mit einem gefeilten Zopf entlang und um die gesamte Flachangel herum. Die Griffschalen bestehen aus Mammut-Backenzahn.

Marshall Hall is a rather unknown knifemaker from Casselberry, Florida. Nevertheless, he is able to create very attractive knives like this fixed blade. The damascus for the blade was forged by Doug Ponzio, and Marshall embellished it with a fileworked braid along and around the entire tang. The handle is made of mammoth tooth.

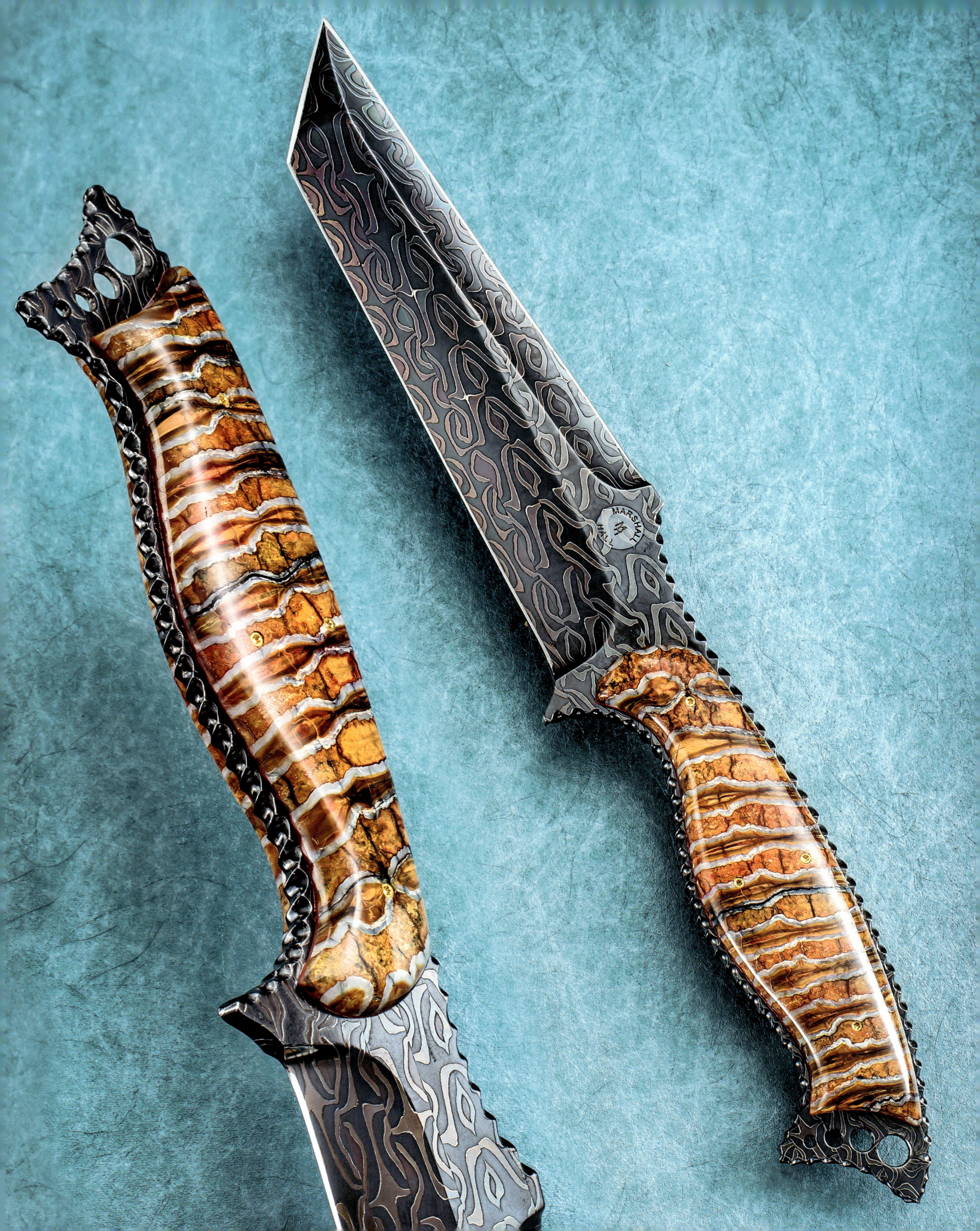
MARSHALL
HALL

DON HANSON III

Don Hanson III, Eigentümer der Schmiede Sunfish Forge in Success, Missouri, ist ein ABS-Meisterschmied und wahrer Künstler. Hier abgebildet ist sein *Blue Devil* mit einer Gesamtlänge von 13 Zoll. Die 8 Zoll lange Klinge dieses wunderschönen Bowies wurde vom Meister genauso selbst geschmiedet wie der Damast für den Handschutz des Halbintegrals. Die Griffschalen bestehen aus blauem Mammut-Elfenbein.

Don Hanson III, owner of Sunfish Forge in Success, Missouri, is an ABS Master Smith and true artist. Depicted here is his *Blue Devil* with an overall length of 13". The 8"-blade of this beautiful Bowie was forged by the master himself as was the damascus for the guard of this half-integral. The handle scales are of blue mammoth ivory.

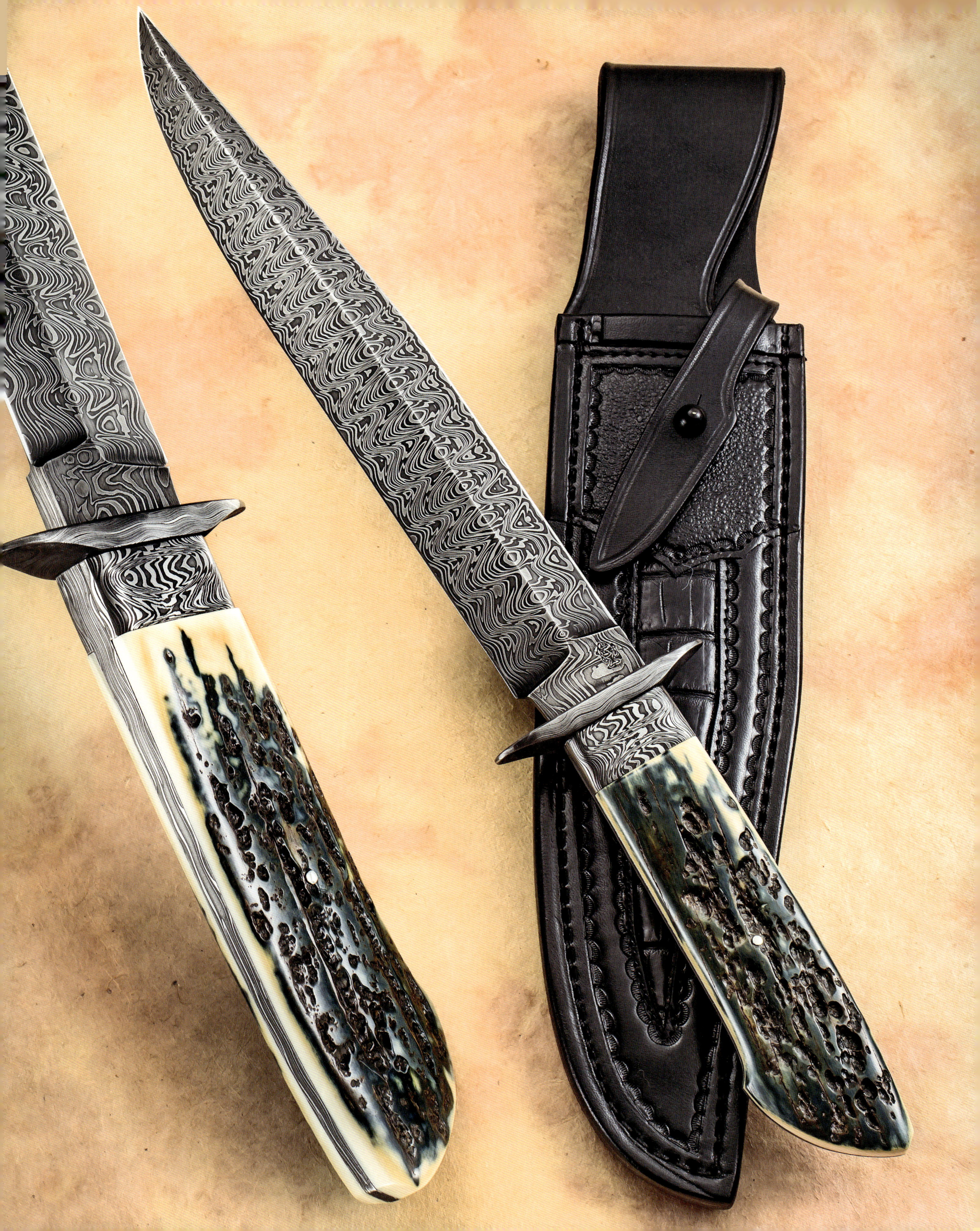

JERARMIE HEYWOOD

Der australische Messermacher Jerarmie (Jezz) Heywood aus Newcastle, New South Wales, kreierte dieses rustikal aussehende Küchenmesser. Der Kern der Klinge wurde aus Tiegelstahl geschmiedet. Zusätzliche Lagen aus grobem Damast wurden dazu in einer Weise hinzugefügt, dass ein Teil der Schmiedehaut noch auf der Klinge sichtbar ist. Das Griffmaterial wird als „individueller Verbundstoff" beschrieben.

Australian knifemaker Jerarmie (Jezz) Heywood from Newcastle, New South Wales, created this rustic-looking kitchen knife. The blade's core was forged from crucible steel, to which layers of coarse damascus were added in a way that some of the forging scales are still visible on the blade. The handle material is described as „custom composite".

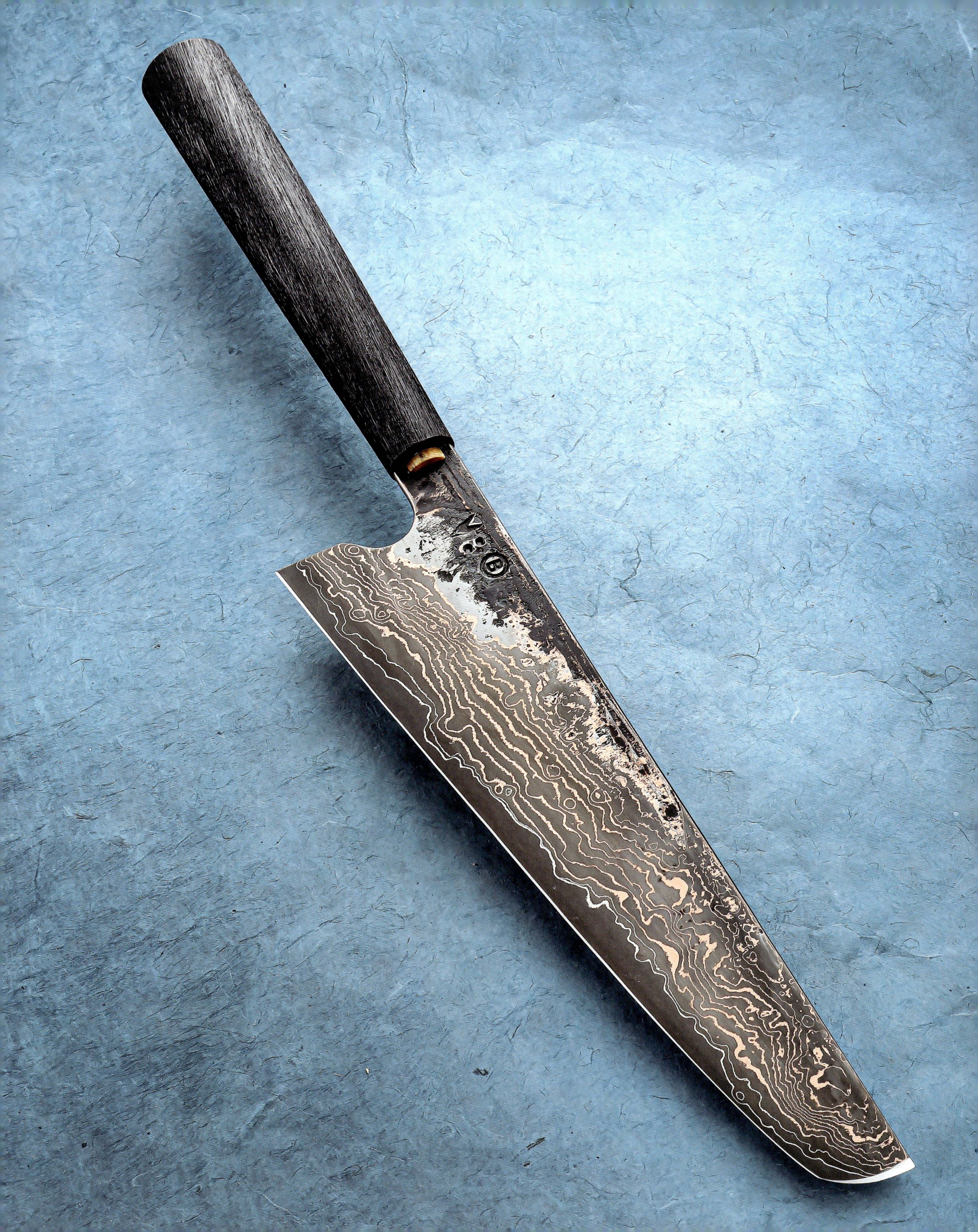

TOBIN HILL

Tobin Hill ist nicht nur ein Stadtteil von San Antonio, sondern teilt sich den Namen mit einem Messermacher aus Pleasonton, Texas. Er erschuf dieses klassische „Texas Toothpick" mit hohlgeschliffenen Klingen aus „Tri Star"- Damast von Joe Burke, gerillten Backen aus rostfreiem 416-Stahl, die durch Filework verbunden sind, und Griffschalen aus erlesenem Hirschhorn. Die Platinen sind aus rostträgem 410-Stahl gefertigt.

Tobin Hill is not only a district of San Antonio, but shares its name with a knifemaker in Pleasonton, Texas. He created this classical Texas Toothpick with hollow-ground blades of Tri Star Damascus by Joe Burke, fluted bolsters of stainless 416 steel connected by filework and handle scales made of exquisite stag. The liners are made of stainless 410 steel.

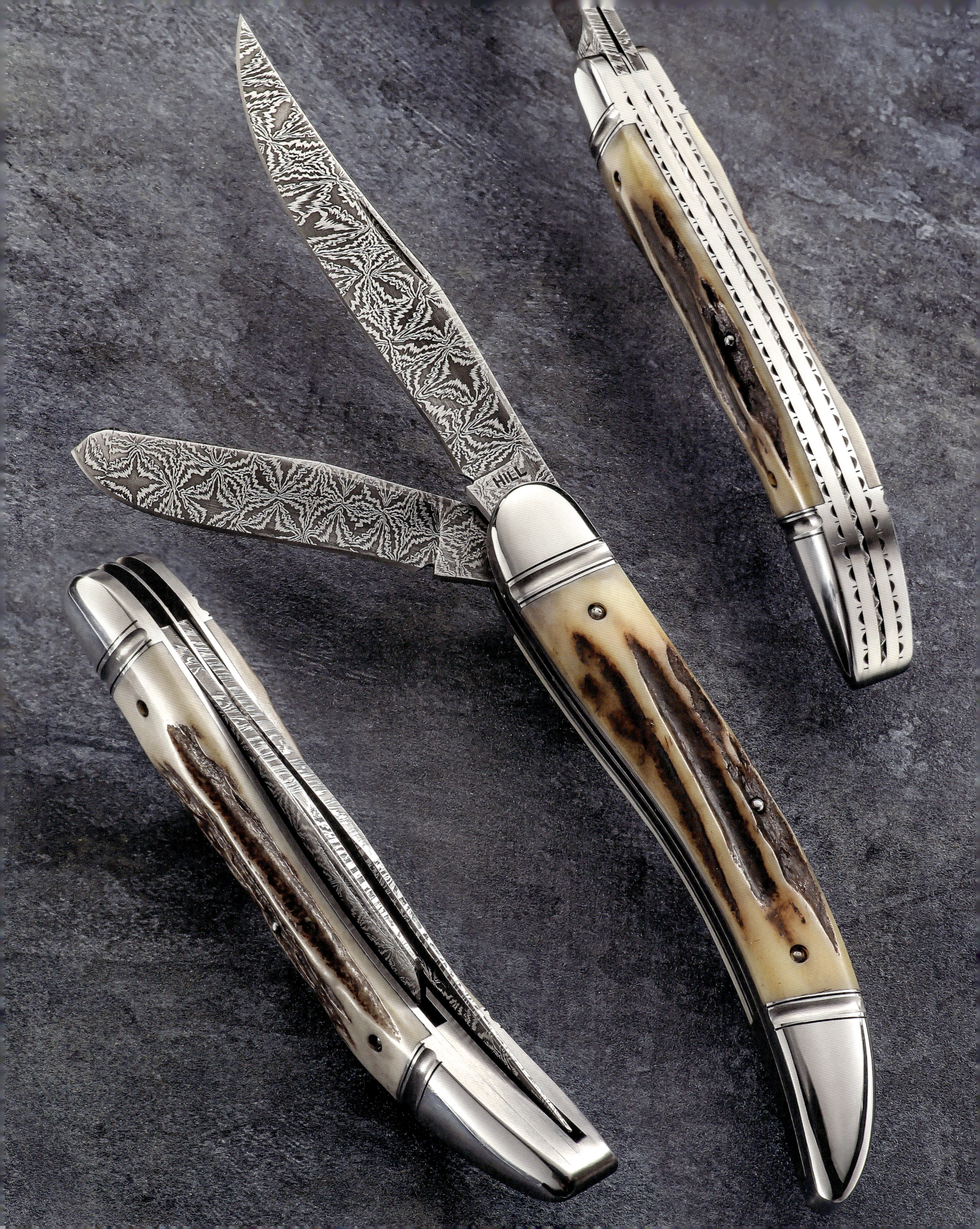
HILL

TONY HUGHES

ABS Journeyman Smith Tony Hughes aus Littleton, Colorado, ist Schöpfer dieses wunderschönen Gentleman-Automatikmessers. Das Explosionsmuster des Mosaikdamasts auf den Griffbacken fällt sofort ins Auge. Der Klingendamast, der auch von Tony geschmiedet wurde, zeigt ein ähnlich explosives Mosaik. Das Material für die Griffschalen stammt von der Innenseite eines Mastodon-Stoßzahns. Die mit Feilarbeit versehenen Platinen bestehen aus hitzekoloriertem 15N20 Stahl. Ein herausragendes Stück Handwerkskunst!

ABS Journeyman Smith Tony Hughes of Littleton, Colorado, is the maker of this beautiful Gent's automatic folder. The explosion pattern of the mosaic damascus is an immediate eyecatcher on the bolsters. The damascus on the blade, which was also forged by Tony, displays a similar explosive mosaic. The handle scales were made of the interior of mastodon tusk. The fileworked liners are of heat-blued 15N20 steel. All in all, an outstanding piece of art!

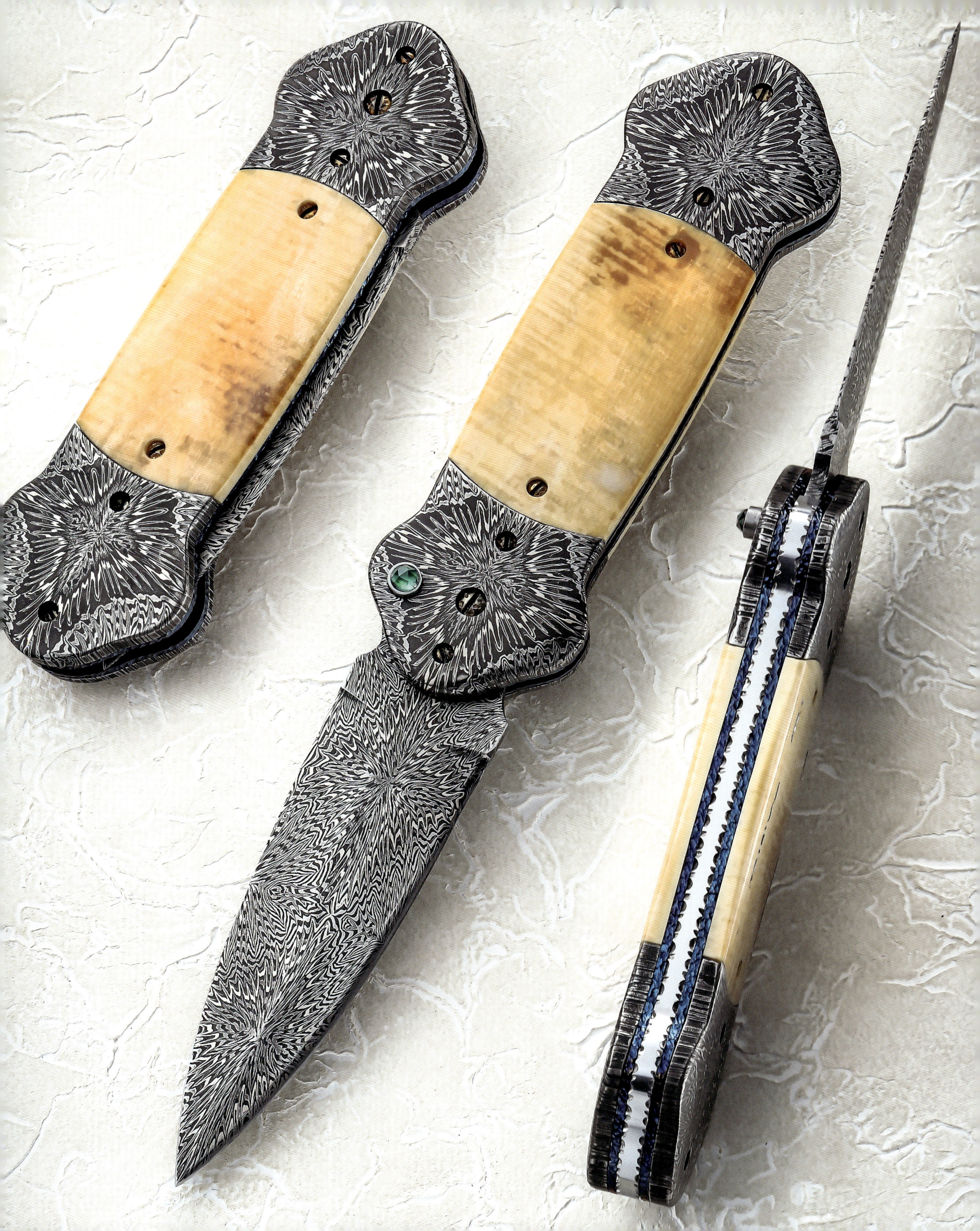

BRANDON HYNER

Dieses *Damascus Gentleman's Hunter* wurde von Brandon Hyner aus New London, Connecticut, erschaffen in Erinnerung an sein allererstes Damastmesser aus seiner Anfangszeit als Messerschmied. Wie bei seinem früheren Jagdmesser, so wurde auch diese Klinge aus nur wenigen Lagen seines Torsionsdamasts hergestellt. Die Griffbacken wurden aus Kohlefaser geformt und sind von den Griffschalen aus Wüsteneisenholz durch dünne Messing-Distanzstücke getrennt.

This *Damascus Gentleman's Hunter* was created by Brandon Hyner from New London, Connecticut, in memory of the very first damascus knife he made when starting out as a bladesmith. As with his earlier hunter, this one's blade was made from only a few layers of his twisted damascus. The bolsters are shaped of carbon fiber, separated from the desert ironwood handle scales by thin spacers of brass.

BRANDON HYNER

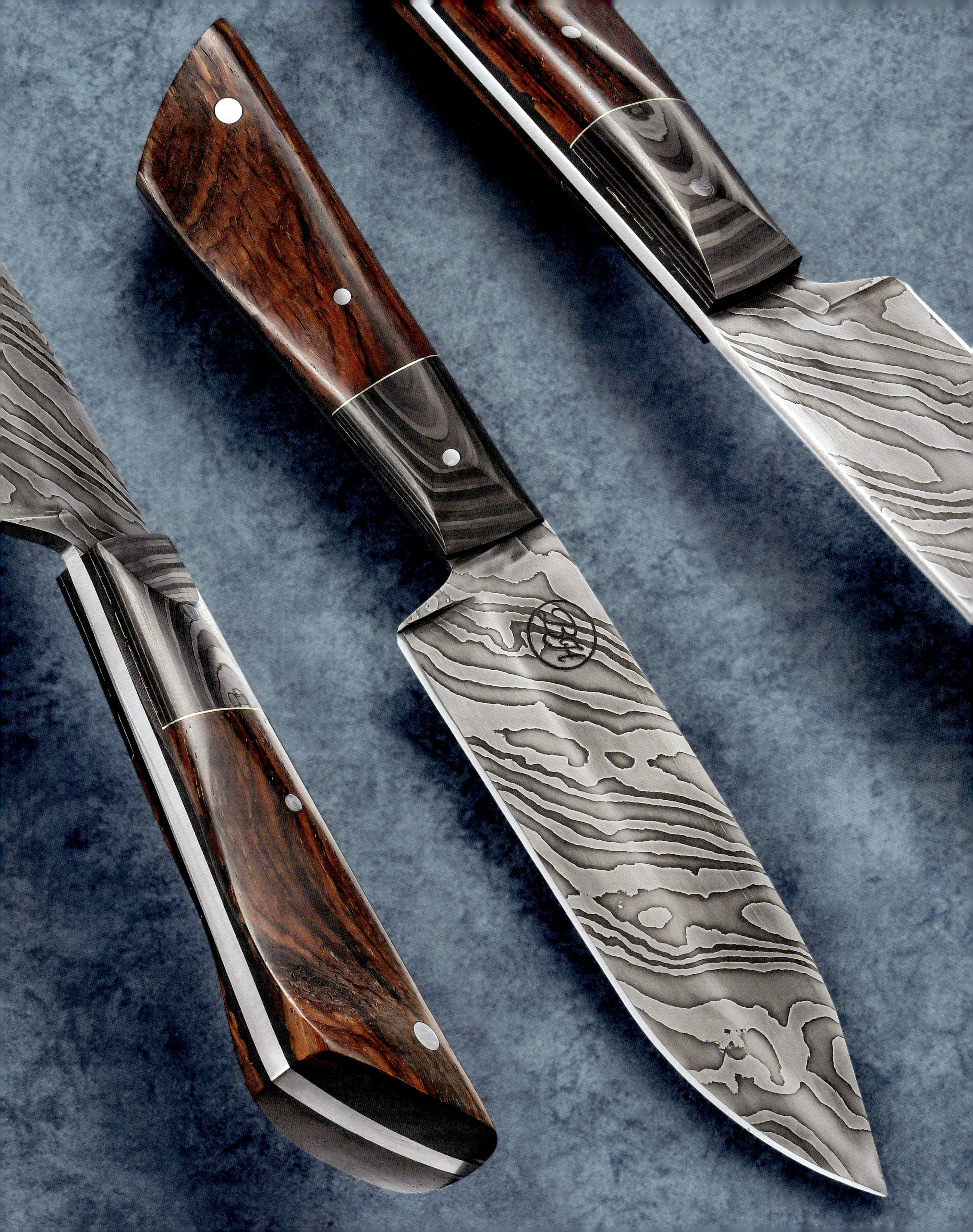

JAMES INGRAM

James Ingram aus Yuma in Arizona ist Schöpfer einer Vielzahl unterschiedlicher Messertypen. Auf dem Bild ist ein sehr ansprechender Flipper mit einer 3½ Zoll langen Klinge aus Federdamast zu sehen, der von Mike Tyre aus den Stahlsorten 1080 und 15N20 geschmiedet wurde. Die Griffschalen bestehen aus Mammut-Elfenbein mit einem hübschen braunen Farbton, der einen netten Kontrast zu Griffbacken und Clip aus rostfreiem 416er-Stahl bildet. Die Titanplatinen und das Rückenstück sind mit Feilarbeiten verziert. Das Filework am Rücken harmoniert besonders schön mit dem Federdamast der Klinge.

James Ingram from Yuma, Arizona, makes a wide variety of different knife types. Depicted here is a very pretty flipper with a 3½"-blade of feather damascus made by Mike Tyre of 1080 and 15N20 steel. The handle scales are made of mammoth ivory with a beautiful brown hue which gives a nice contrast to the bolsters and clip of stainless 416. The titanium liners as well as the backspacer are fileworked. The backspacer's filework corresponds especially nicely to the feather pattern of the blade's damascus.

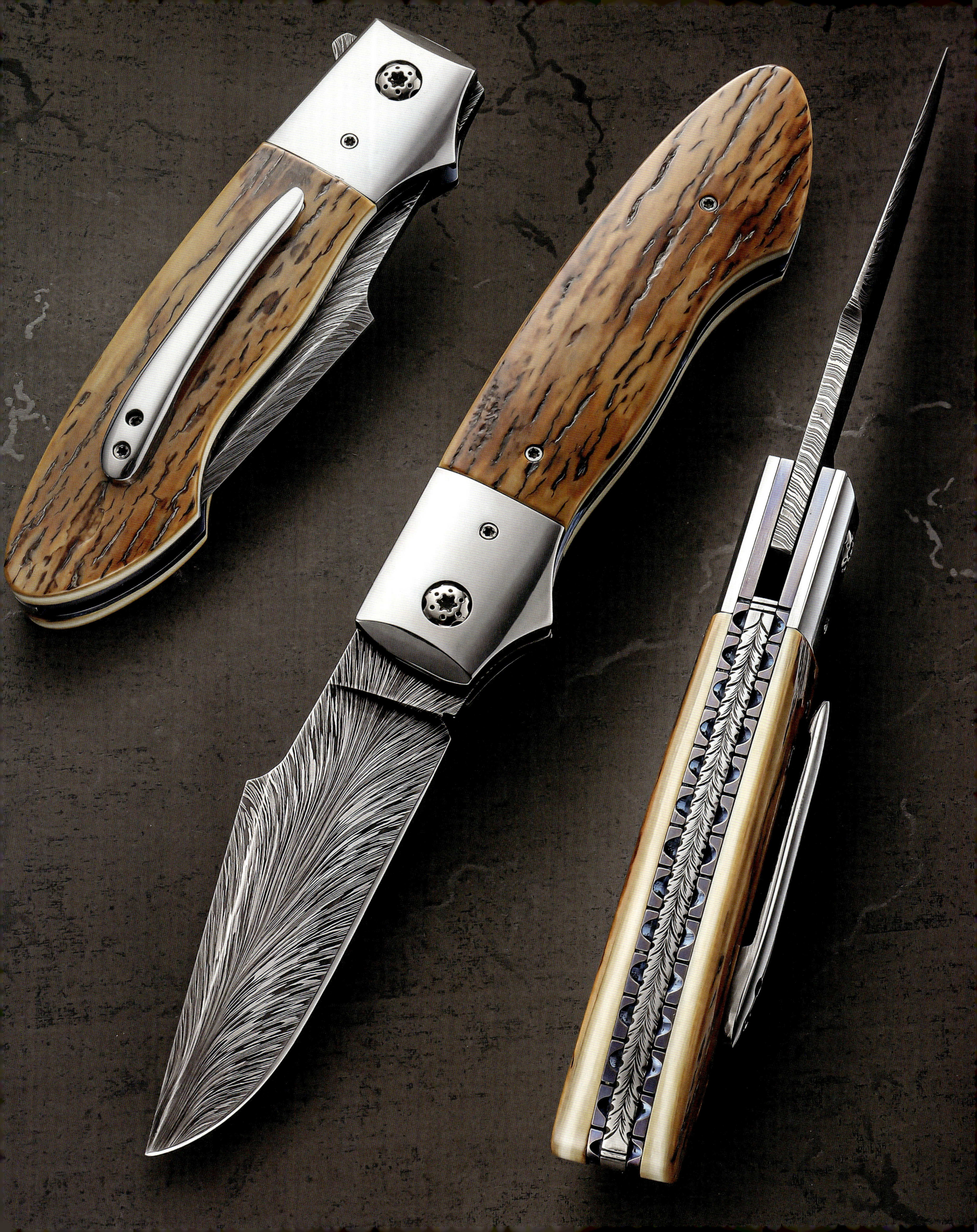

PAUL JARVIS

Paul Jarvis aus Cambridge, Massachusetts, produziert nicht viele Messer pro Jahr, aber wenn er eines macht, dann ist das Resultat herausragend. Dieser Dolch mit einer Gesamtlänge von 20 Zoll wurde über einen Zeitraum von drei Monaten gebaut. Die Damastklinge wird von Zwinge und Handschutz aus graviertem Sterling-Silber, Nickel und Bronze eingerahmt. Der Griff aus stabilisiertem Mammut-Backenzahn passt zur Farbe der Granate, die in Parierstange und Knauf eingesetzt wurden.

Paul Jarvis from Cambridge, Massachusetts, doesn't make many knives per year, but when he does make one, the result is outstanding. This dagger with an overall length of 20" was built over the timespan of three months. The damascus blade is framed by ferrule and guard of carved sterling silver, nickel and bronze. The handle of stabilized mammoth tooth is matched in color by the inset garnets of quillon and pommel.

PAUL JARVIS

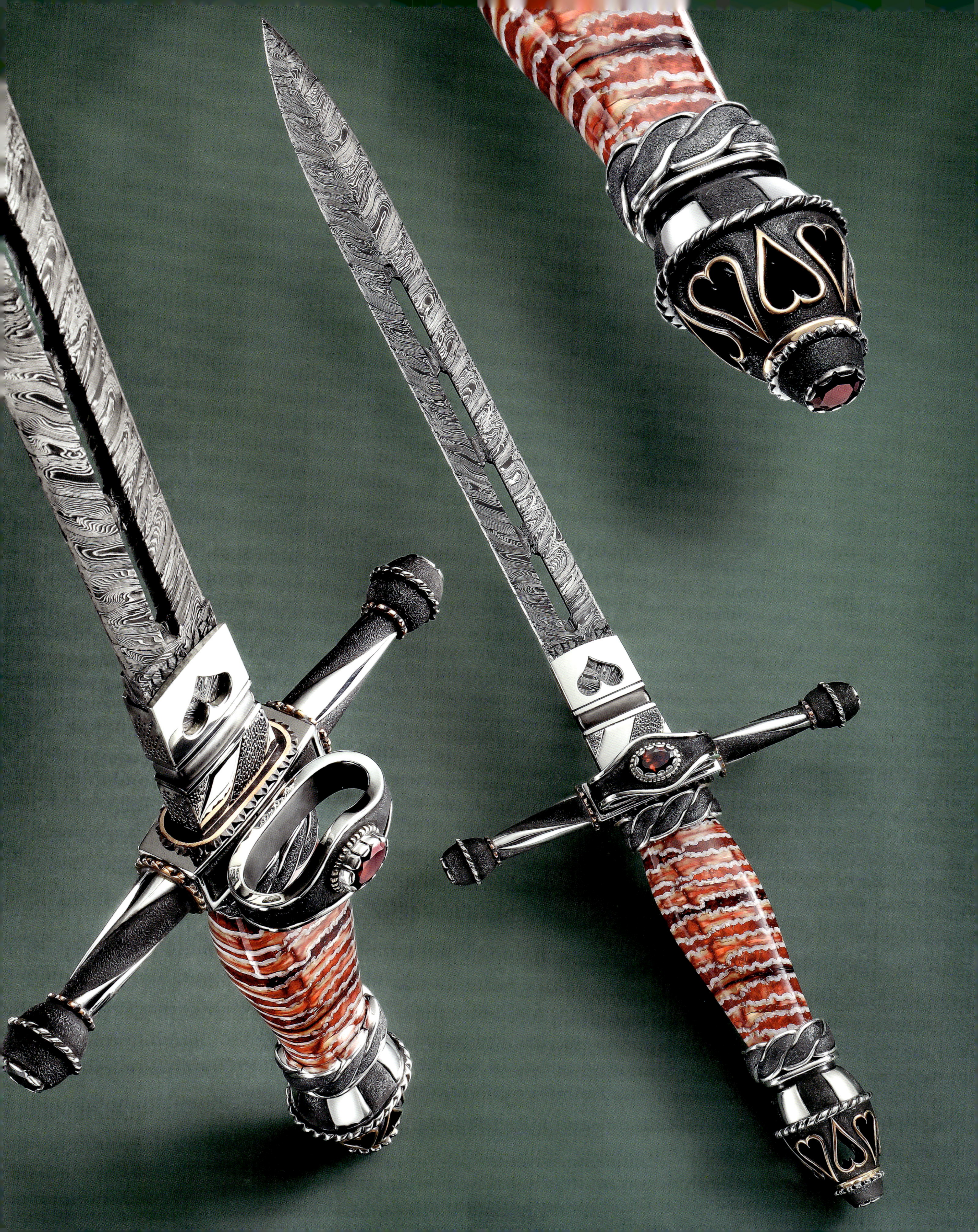

BENJAMIN KAMON

Benjamin Kamon aus Korneuburg in Österreich schmiedet erlesene Küchenwerkzeuge. Für dieses *GV No. 2* kooperierte er mit den Gründern von „GoldVein", Tobias Hangler, David Wolkerstorfer und Abe Shaw. Die „Gold-Ader" aus 24-karätigem Gold wirkt wie ein Hamon (Härtelinie) auf der Klinge aus kohlenstoffreichem Stahl und kohlenstoffarmem Baustahl. Der Griff aus exquisiter australischer Mooreiche wird durch goldplattierte Schrauben fixiert, die in Kontrast zum geschwärzten Zirkon von Zwinge und Griffabschluss stehen.

Benjamin Kamon is a maker of fine kitchen tools from Korneuburg in Austria. For this *GV No. 2*, he teamed up with „GoldVein" founders Tobias Hangler, David Wolkerstorfer, and Abe Shaw. The gold vein of 24k gold looks like a hamon on the blade of high-carbon and mild steels. The handle of exquisite Australian bog oak is held in place by gold-plated screws contrastingly set into the blacked zirconium ferrule and handle butt.

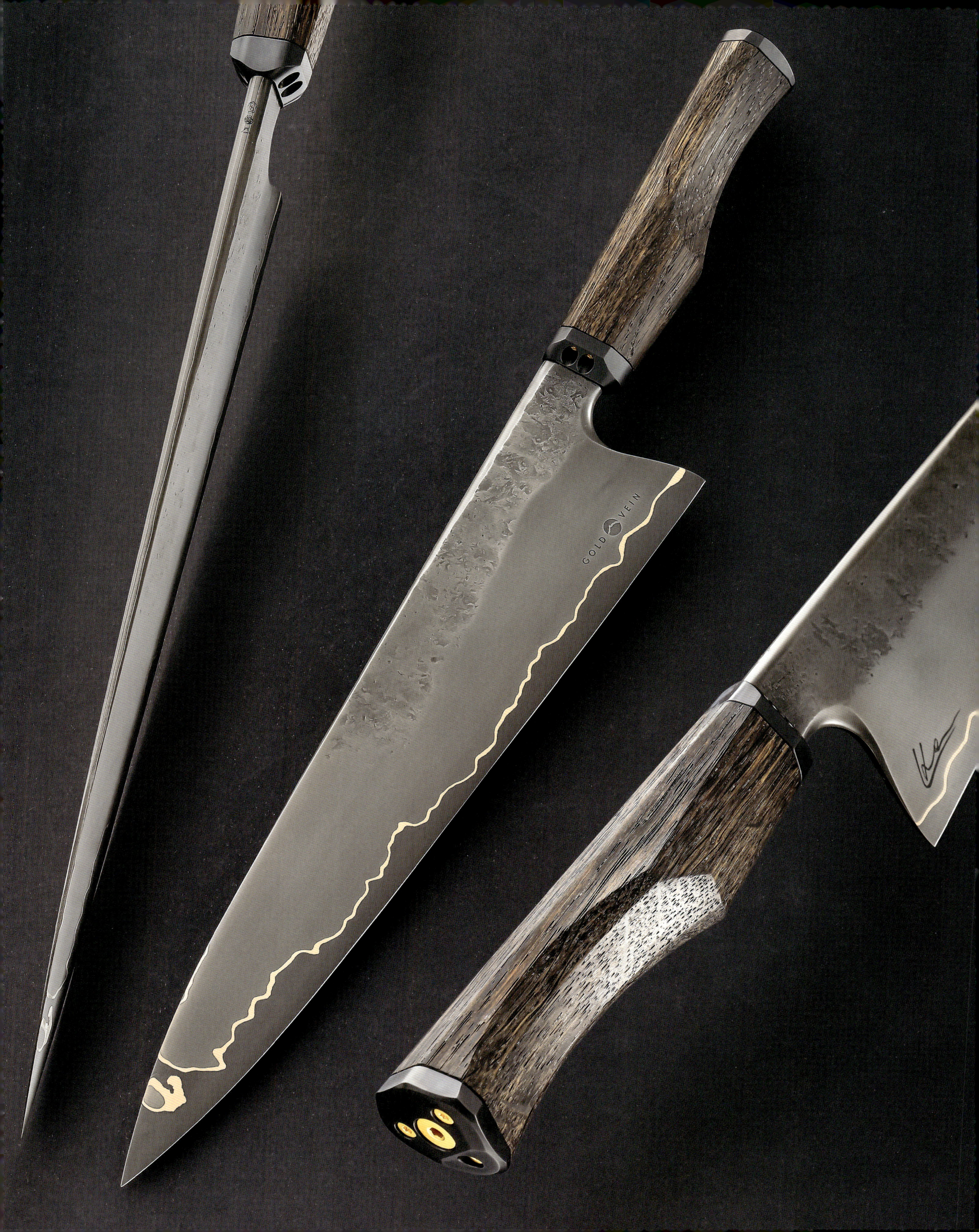
GOLD VEIN

ALEXANDRE H. KASPARY

Alexandre Kaspary, ein brasilianischer Messermacher und ABS-Mitglied, ist der Schöpfer dieses eleganten Bowies. Die Klinge wurde aus „türkischem" Damast hergestellt, der aus 1084 und 15N20 geschmiedet ist. Der Griff besteht aus Grenadill-Holz und hat ein eingelegtes Elfenbein-Schildchen. Die zugehörige Lederscheide besticht durch seinen passenden dunklen Farbton.

The Brazilian knifemaker and ABS member Alexandre Kaspary is the creator of this pretty Bowie. The blade was forged from Turkish damascus made of 1084 and 15N20 steels. The handle is shaped from African blackwood and has an inlaid ivory shield. The accompanying leather sheath complements it with a matching dark color.

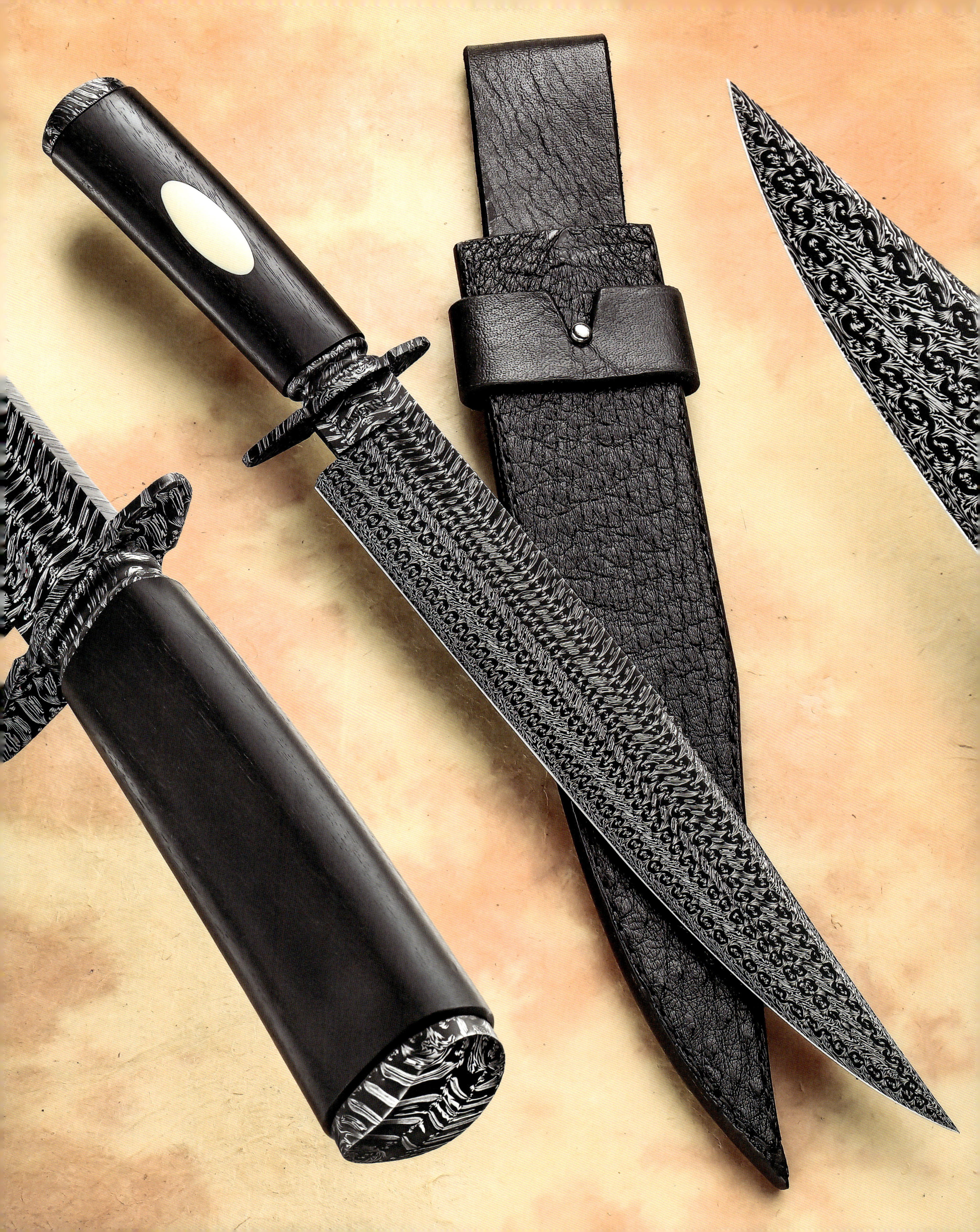

DERICK KEMPER

Dieser schottische Dirk wurde von Derick Kemper aus York, Pennsylvania, als eine Ehrung der Jakobiten-Rebellion von 1745 erschaffen. Derick schmiedete den Klingendamast aus W2-Werkzeugstahl und nutzte 15N20 für einen ansprechenden Kontrast im kurvigen Muster. Als Griffmaterial nahm er gealtertes Eschenahorn-Holz, das von zwei Distanzstücken aus Sterlingsilber eingerahmt wird. In die Zwinge des Messers sind zwei Kleinlibellen und die Initialen des Messermachers graviert – das Logo seiner „Damselfly Forge". Die Gravur wurde von D. Brent ausgeführt. Er gravierte auch das lateinische Motto auf dem Knauf, das übersetzt werden kann als „Wer das meiste Anrecht darauf hat zu regieren".

This Scottish Dirk was crafted by Derick Kemper, based in York, Pennsylvania, as a tribute to the Jacobite Rebellion of 1745. Derick forged the damascus for the blade from W2 tool steel and used 15N20 to provide a nice contrast in the curly pattern. As handle material he used aged boxelder framed by spacers of sterling silver. The knife's ferrule is engraved with two damselflies and the maker's initials – the logo of his Damselfly Forge. The engraving was done by D. Brent. He also engraved the Latin motto on the pommel, translated as "Who hath best right to reign".

QUE OPTIME REGNARE IUS HABET

CHAD KENNEDY

ABS-Journeyman-Schmied Chad Kennedy aus Wichita Falls, Texas, kreierte dieses hübsche Damast-Kampfmesser im Stil von Bill Moran. Er schmiedete den wunderschönen Federdamast für die Klinge aus den Stählen 1084 und 15N20 und schuf auch den Torsionsdamast für Handschutz und Zwinge. Griff und Scheide aus geringeltem Ahornholz sind mit Silberdraht eingelegt.

ABS Journeyman Smith Chad Kennedy from Wichita Falls, Texas, created this lovely damascus fighter in Bill Moran style. He forged the beautiful feather damascus for the blade from 1084 and 15N20 steels and also made the twisted damascus for guard and ferrule. Handle and sheath of curly maple are inlaid with silver wire.

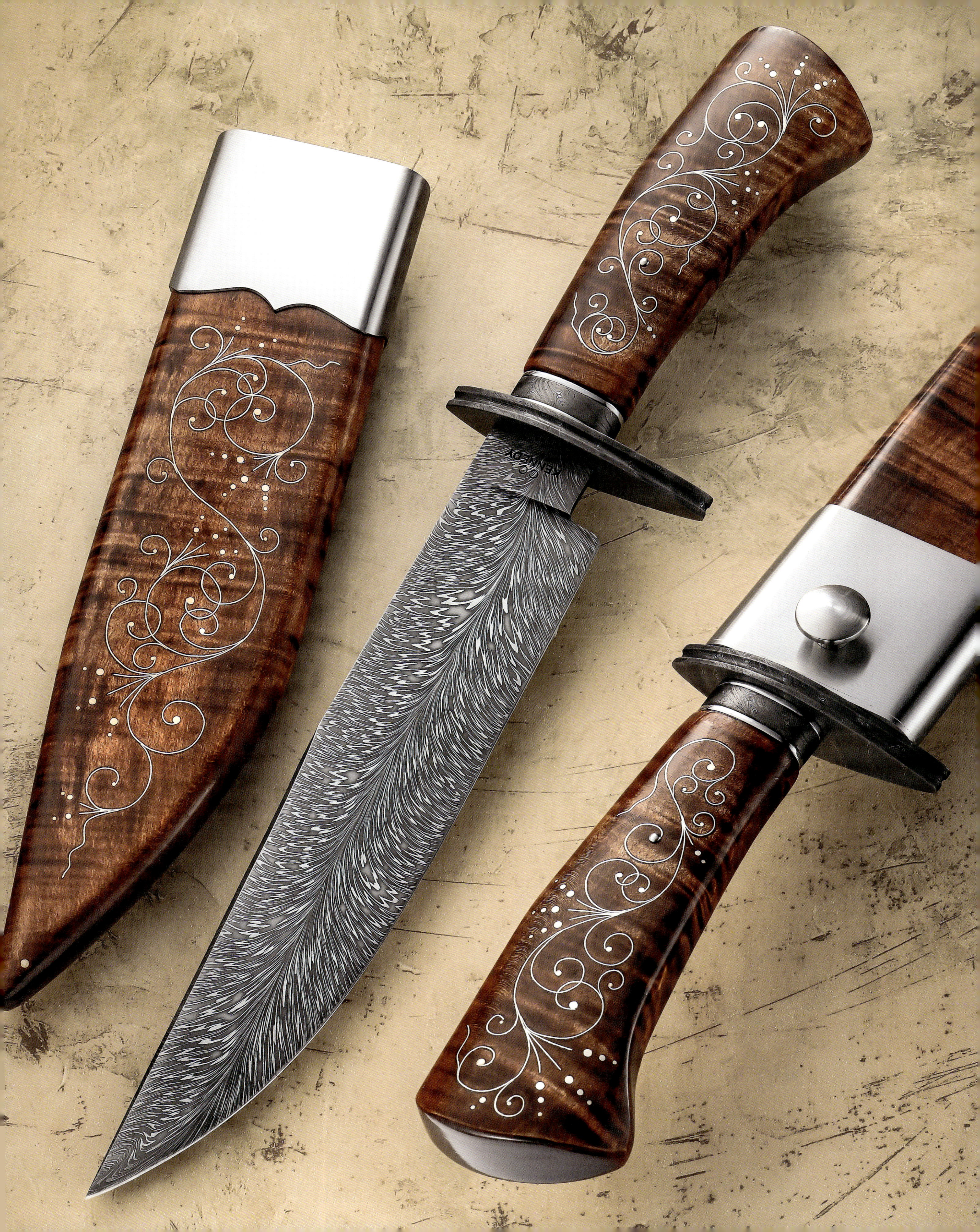

STUART KERR

Der australische Messermacher Stuart Kerr aus Salisbury in Queensland ist der Urheber dieses edlen Friction Folders. Seine Rasierklinge wurde von Bruce Barnett aus „Sharktooth"-Damast geschmiedet, bestehend aus den Stahlsorten 1084 und 15N20. Als Griffmaterial nahm Stuart „Raindrop Gold"-Kohlefaser. Einen zusätzlichen Hingucker bildet das blaue Distanzstück mit Wabenmuster am Griffende.

The Australian knifemaker Stuart Kerr from Salisbury, Queensland, is author of this noble friction folder. Its razor blade was made of "Sharktooth" damascus forged by Bruce Barnett from 1084 and 15N20 steel types. As handle material Stuart used „Raindrop Gold" carbon fiber. An additional eyecatcher is created by the blue backspacer with honeycomb pattern.

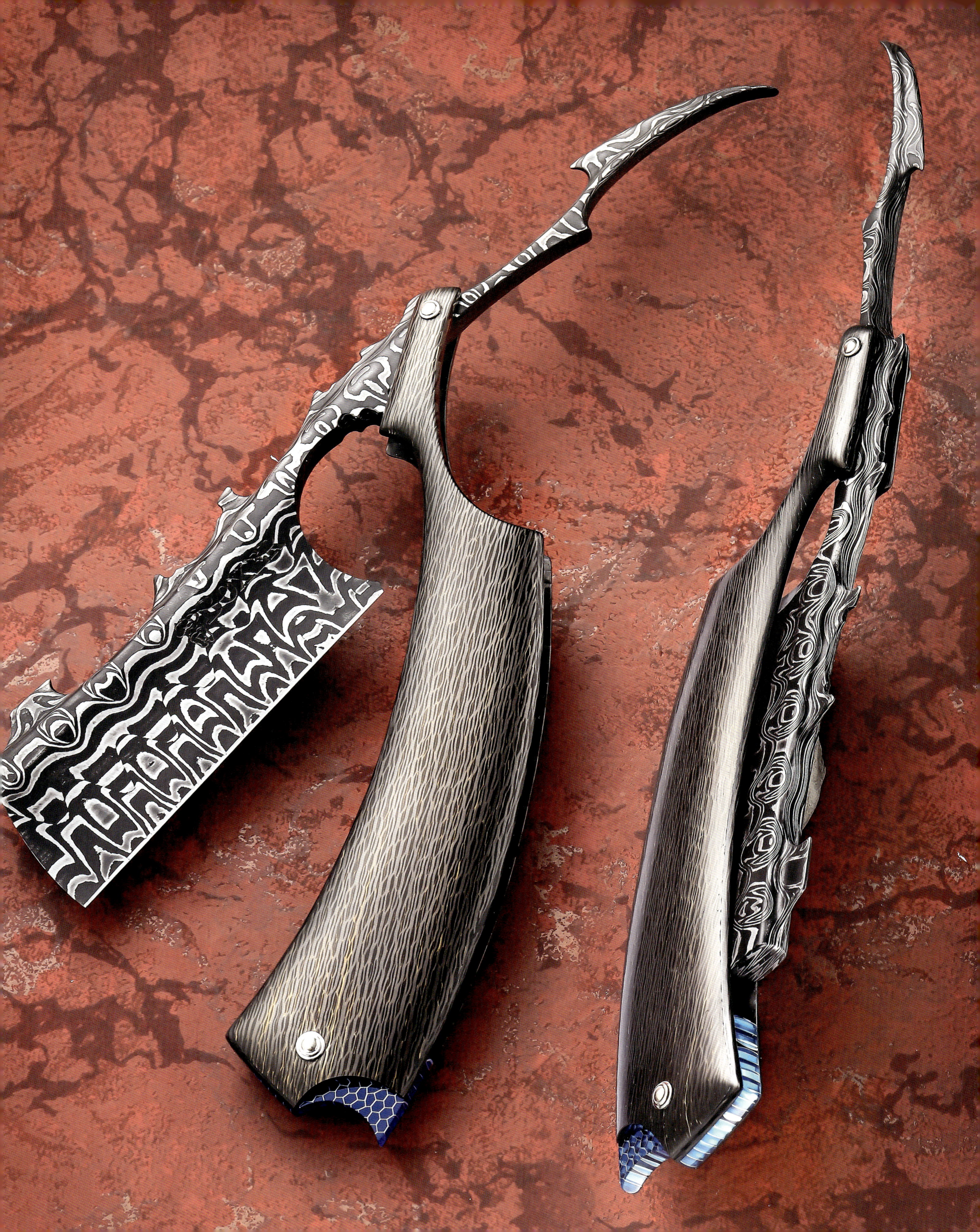

KEVIN KLEIN

Kevin Klein aus Portland, Maine, nennt dieses feststehende Kampfmesser *The Mule*. Trotz seines Namens besticht dieser „Dickkopf" mit seiner schlichten Eleganz. Der Damast, der sowohl für die Klinge als auch den knochenförmigen Griff zum Tragen kommt, wurde vom Messermacher selbst aus 1084 und 15N20 geschmiedet. Das Knocheninnere und die Scheide wurden aus Grenadill-Holz geformt.

Kevin Klein from Portland, Maine, called his fixed fighter *The Mule*. Despite its name, the knife intrigues by its simple elegance. The damascus for the blade as well as the bolsters and bone-shaped handle was forged by the maker himself from 1084 and 15N20 steels. The bone's interior and the sheath are crafted from African blackwood.

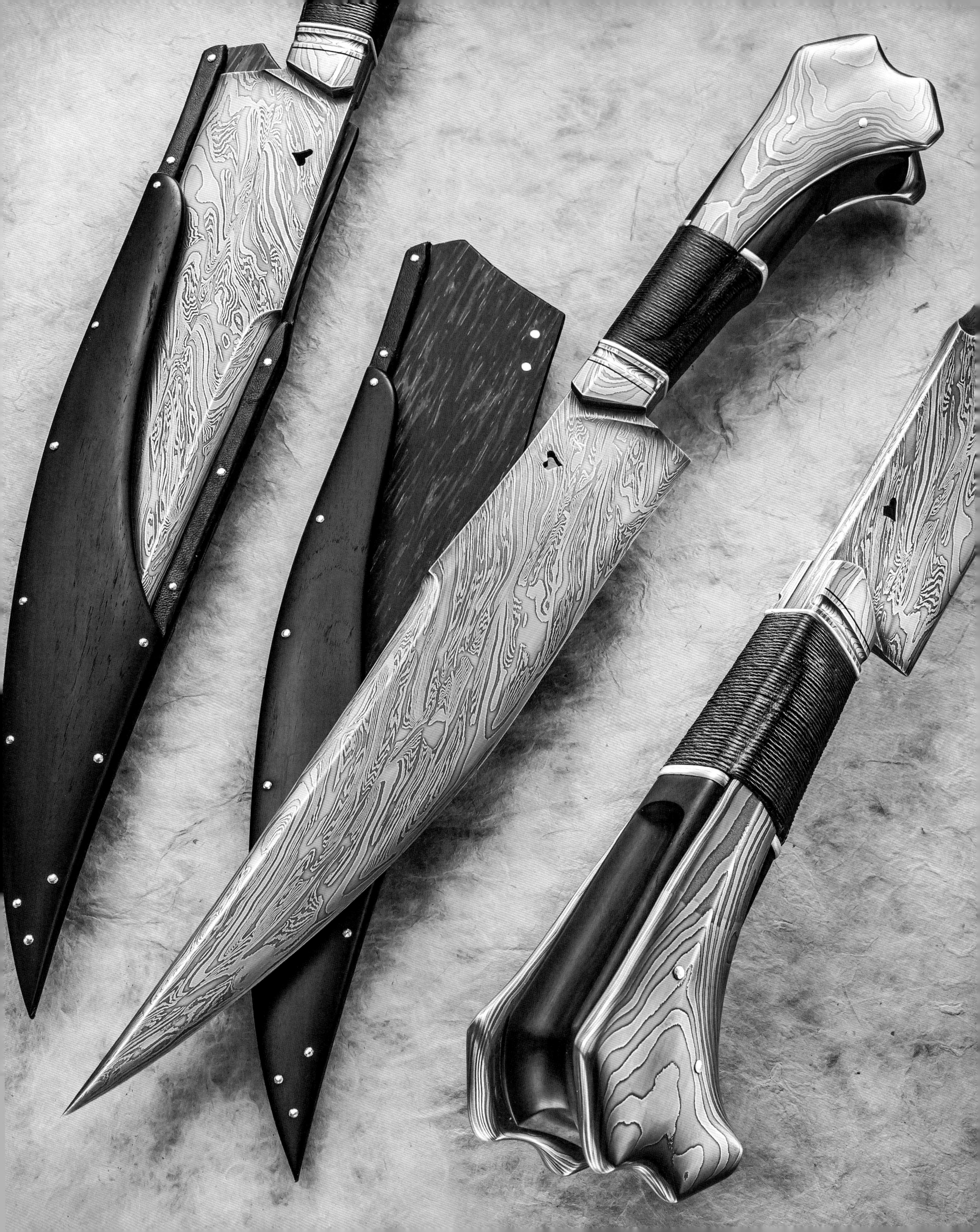

VLADIMIR KOLENKO

Hoffentlich geht niemand auf einen Kreuzzug mit diesem wunderschönen *Crusader*-Dolch. Der Mosaikdamast für die 10 Zoll lange Klinge wurde von Konstantin Lysenko geschmiedet. Vladimir Kolenko selbst, ein Messermacher aus Huntingdon Valley, Pennsylvania, erschuf alles Übrige einschließlich der gesamten Verzierungen aus Gold und Silber. Er vergaß auch nicht den Helm des Kreuzfahrers, der als Knauf dient.

Hopefully no one is going on a crusade with this beautiful *Crusader* dagger. The mosaic damascus for the 10"-blade was forged by Konstantin Lysenko. Vladimir Kolenko himself, a knifemaker from Huntingdon Valley, Pennsylvania, created all the rest with lots of gold and silver embellishments. He didn't even forget the crusader's helmet which serves as the pommel.

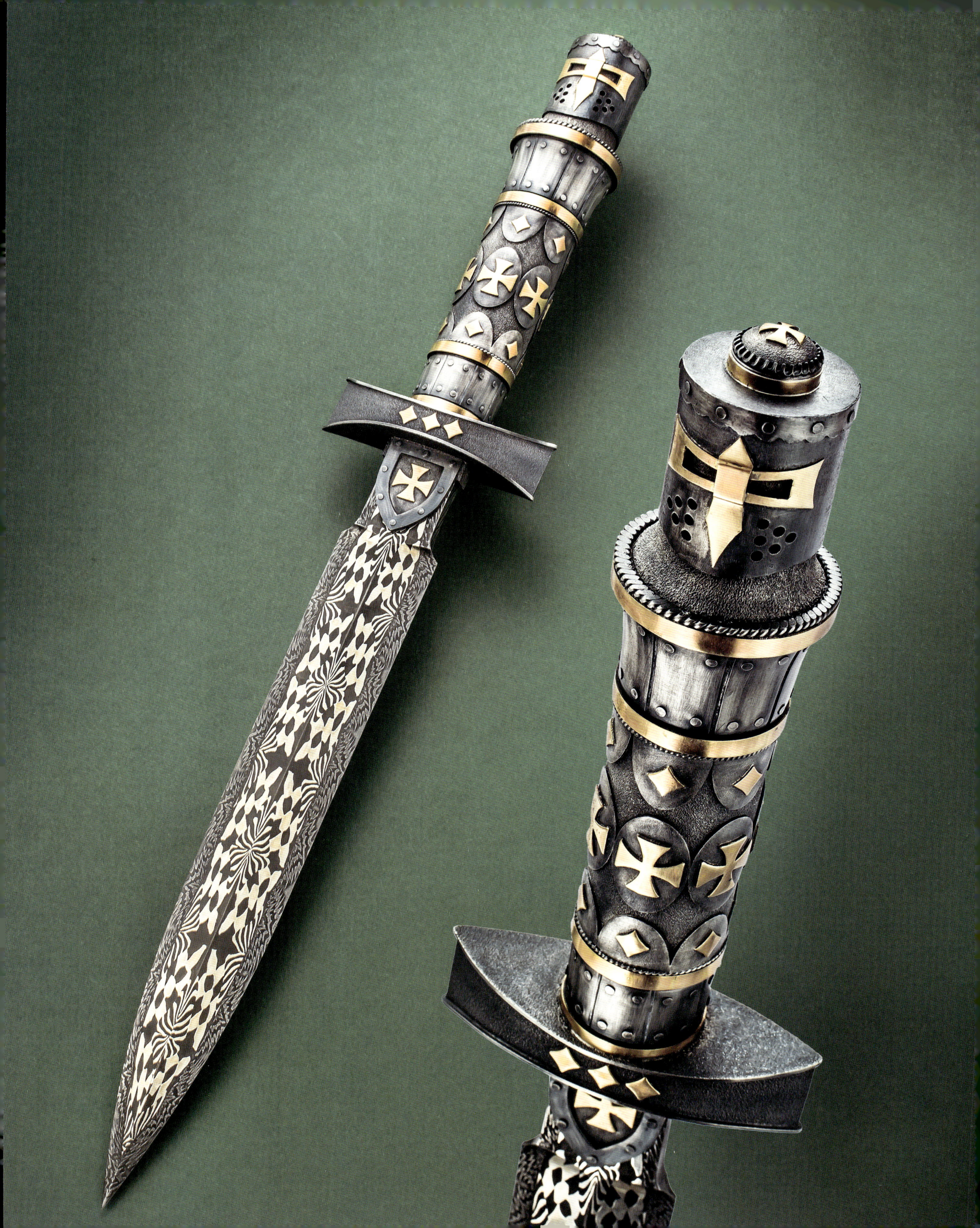

JAMIE LUNDELL

Jamie Lundell ist dem Leser vielleicht bekannt durch seinen Fernsehauftritt in „Forged in Fire – Wettkampf der Schmiede" auf dem History Channel. Dort zeigte er, wie man ein römisches Gladius macht. Hier ist nun das Gegenstück, ein römisches Pugio. Der Messermacher aus Wolcott, Connecticut, schmiedete das strahlenförmige Explosionsmuster des Damasts aus den Stahlsorten 15N20 und 1095. Der Griff besteht aus Elchgeweih und wird eingerahmt von Endstücken aus Ahorn-Maserknolle für Handschutz und Knauf. Beide Griffenden werden mit Bronzescheiben abgeschlossen.

Jamie Lundell may be familiar to the reader for his appearance in History Channel's „Forged in Fire". There he showed how to make a Roman gladius. Here now is its counterpart, the Roman pugio. The maker from Wolcott, Connecticut, forged the radial explosion pattern damascus from 15N20 and 1095 steels. The handle is made from moose antler, framed by pieces of maple burl for guard and pommel. Both ends of the handle are marked by spacers of bronze.

JAMIE LUNDELL

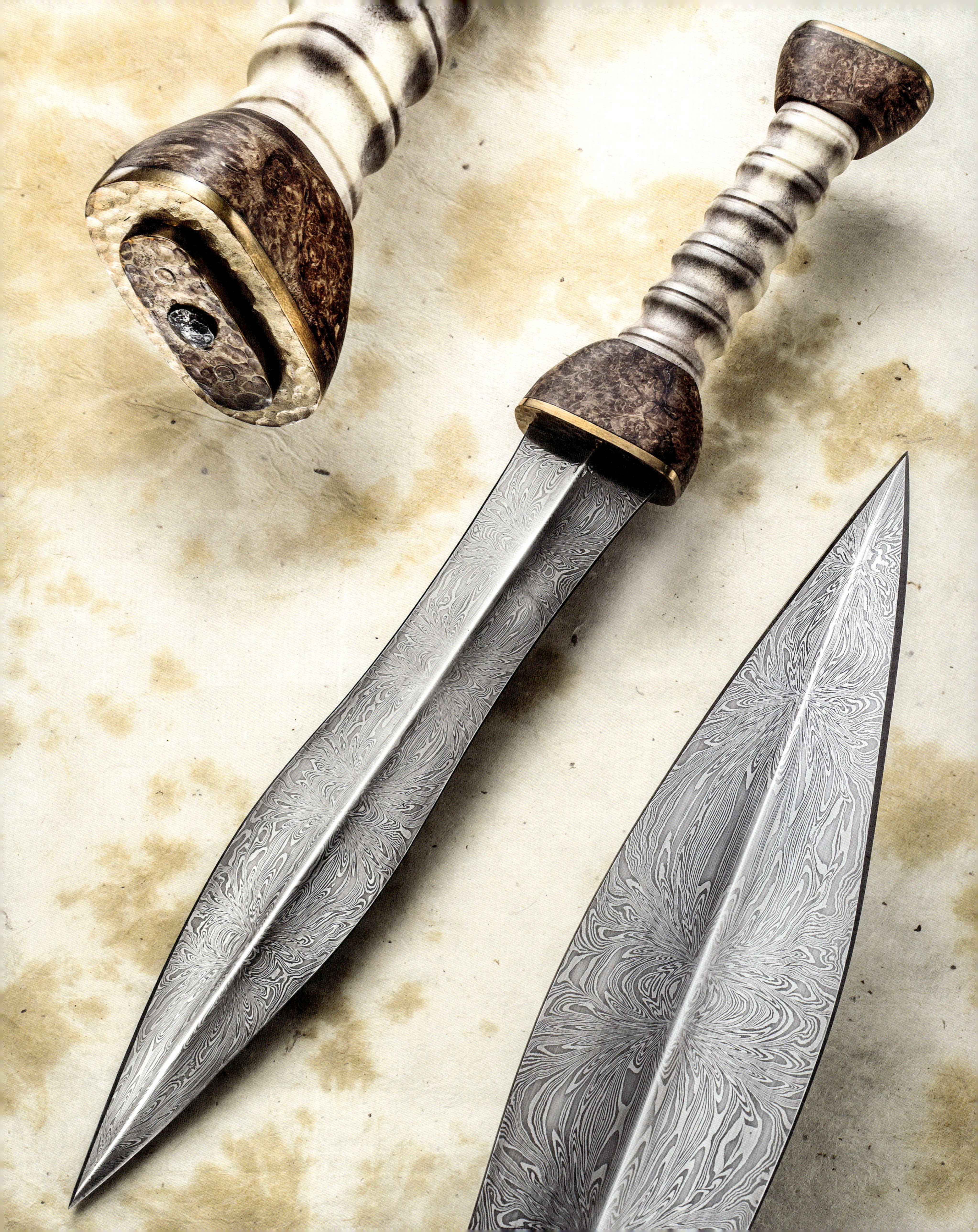

SAMUEL LURQUIN

Der belgische Messermacher und ABS-Meisterschmied Samuel Lurquin erschuf dieses kleine feststehende Messer als Teil eines Sets. Klinge und Zwinge sind eine integrale Konstruktion aus dem Leiterdamast des Meisters. Als Griffmaterial verwendete er exquisites Wüsteneisenholz mit besonders attraktiver Maserung. Die begleitende Lederscheide wurde von Jeremy Guillaume hergestellt und mit einer Einlage aus Haifisch-Haut und Zierknöpfen aus fossilem Walross-Stoßzahn versehen.

Belgian knifemaker and ABS Master Bladesmith Samuel Lurquin created this small fixed blade as part of a set. Blade and bolster are an integral construction from the master's ladder damascus. As handle material he used exquisite desert ironwood with especially attractive grain. The accompanying sheath was created by Jeremy Guillaume with an inlay of shark skin and studs of fossil walrus tusk.

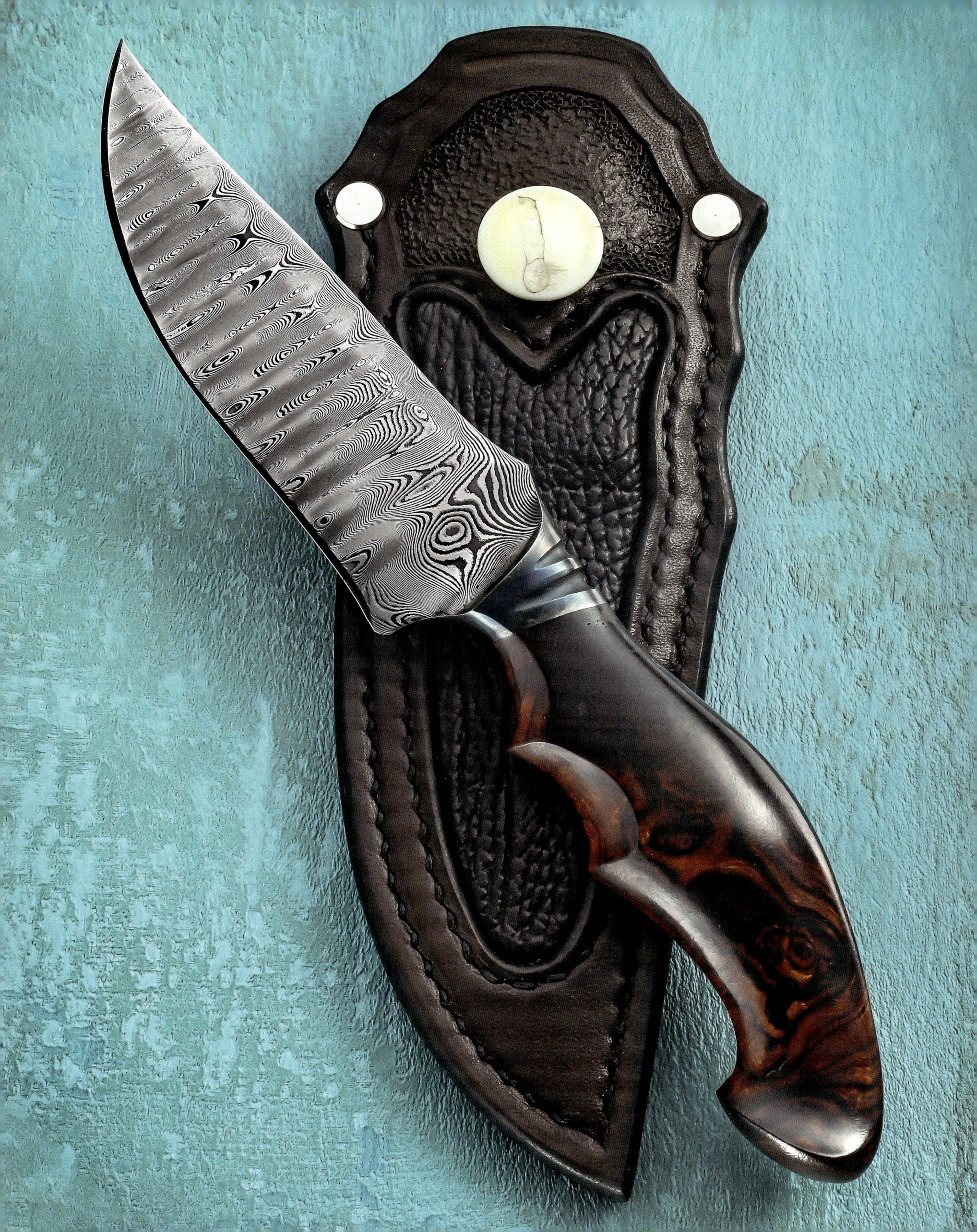

COLLIN MAGUIRE

Es sind wirklich zwei Messer und nicht nur eines, das vom Fotograf gespiegelt wurde. Der Schöpfer dieses edlen Paars ist Collin Maguire aus Foster, Rhode Island. Er schmiedete die feststehenden Messer aus zwei Barren seines „Firestorm"-Damasts und formte die Griffschalen aus Mastodon-Elfenbein. Zwischen Damast und Elfenbein befinden sich Platinen aus schwarzem 610-Werkzeugstahl.

Those are really two knives and not just one mirrored by the photographer. The maker of this elegant set is Collin Maguire from Foster, Rhode Island. He forged the fixed blades from two bars of his „Firestorm" damascus and shaped the handle scales of mastodon ivory. Between damascus and ivory are liners of black 610 tool steel.

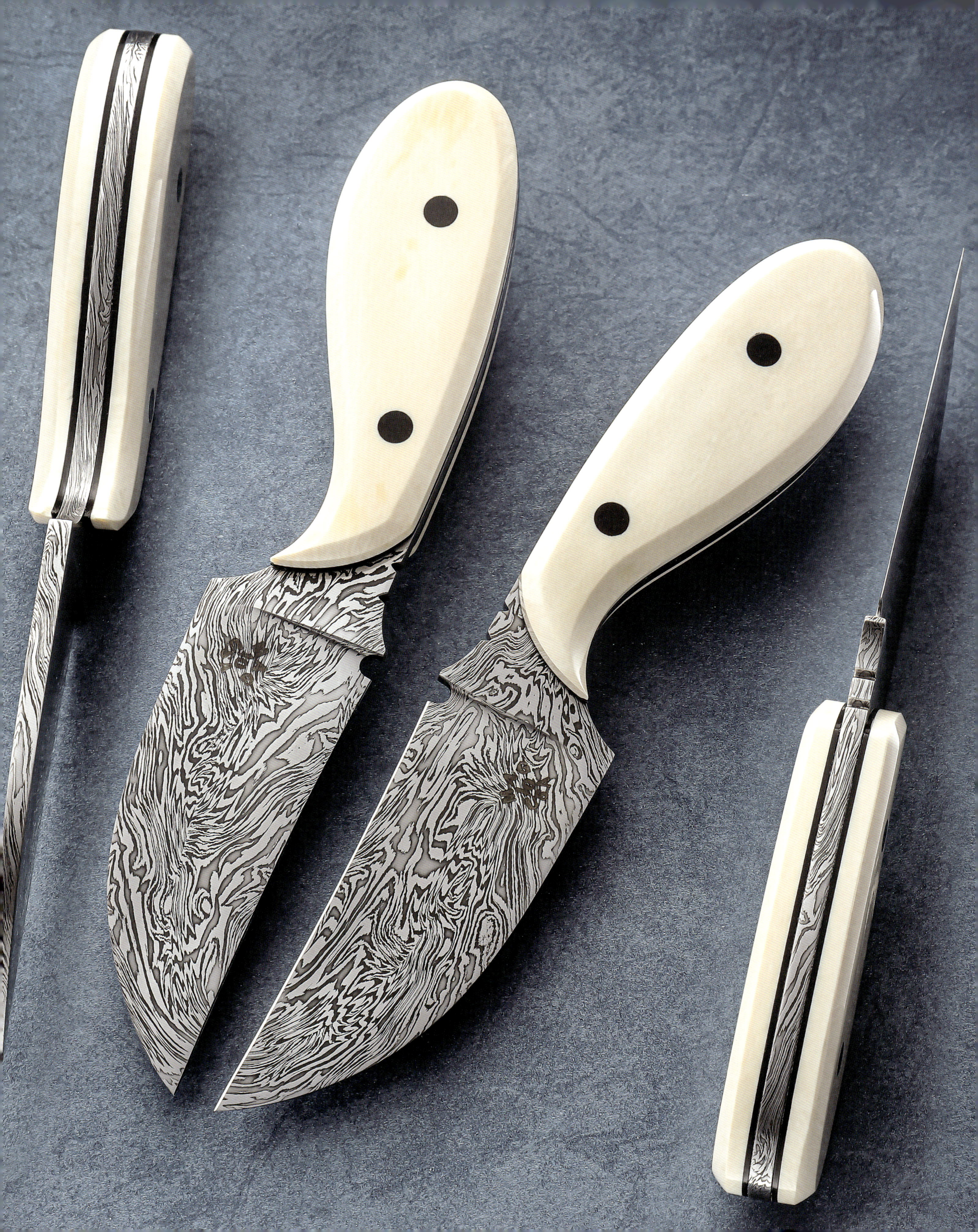

R. J. MARTIN

Dieses Klappmesser ist eine besonders hervorstechende Version von R. J. Martins Q36 Flipper, der den Preis als „Best Tactical Folder" auf der Blade Show 2007 erhielt. R. J. produzierte viele dieser Flipper aus allen möglichen Materialien von einfachem Stahl und Kohlefaser bis hin zum feinsten Damast und erlesenem Hirschhorn wie beim abgebildeten Messer. Vielleicht ist er dazu bereit, auch ein Exemplar für Sie in seiner Werkstatt in Bridgewater, Massachusetts, zu machen.

This folder is an outstanding variation on R. J. Martin's Q36 tactical flipper which won the award for „Best Tactical Folder" at the Blade Show 2007. R. J. made many of these with all kinds of materials from plain steel and carbon fiber up to the finest damascus and exquisite stag as with this one. He may still be willing to do just another one for you in his workshop in Bridgewater, Massachusetts.

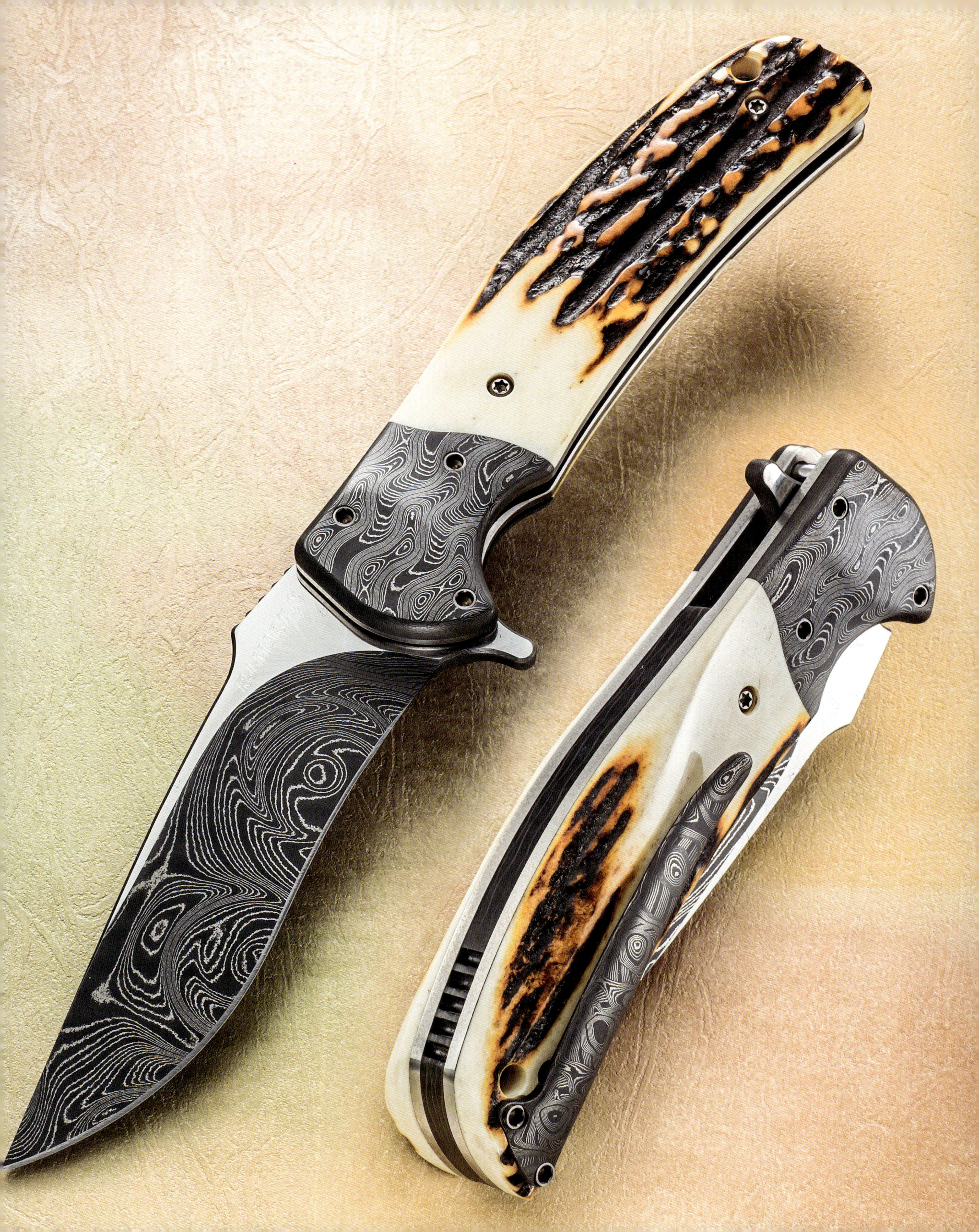

MAREKO MAUMASI

Mareko Maumasi aus Olympia, Washington, hat sich auf Küchenmesser von hoher Qualität spezialisiert. Dieses außergewöhnlich schöne Messer wurde aus dem „Acanthus"-Mosaikdamast des Messermachers geschmiedet. Zum Design mit integriertem Kropf wurde ein angenehm kurvig geformter Griff aus Maserknolle hinzugefügt.

Mareko Maumasi of Olympia, Washington, specializes in high-quality kitchen knives. This outstanding one was forged from the maker's „Acanthus Mosaic Damascus". To the design with integral bolsters, a nicely curved handle of burl was added.

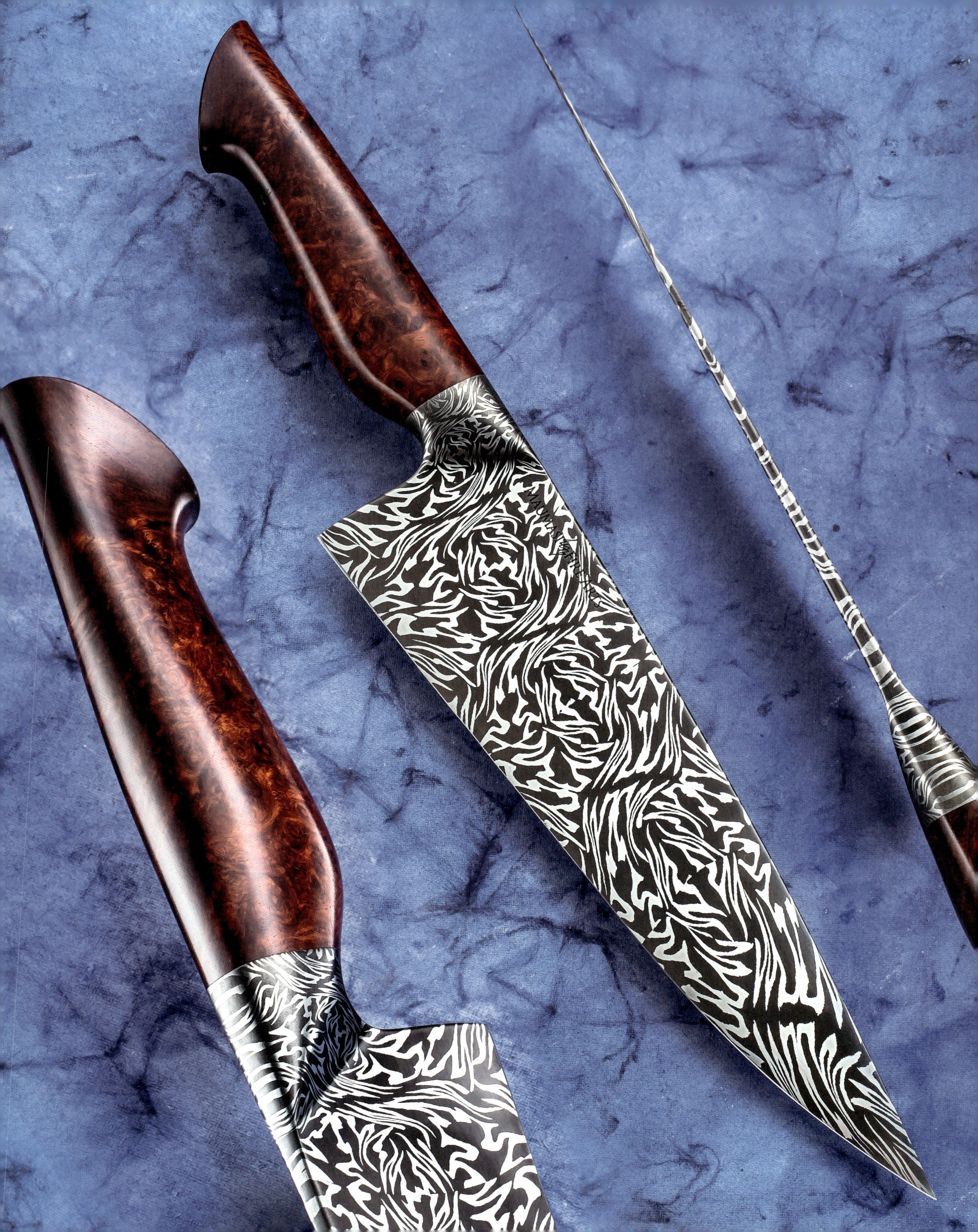

ANDREW B. MEERS

Das *Vulpecula* von ABS-Meisterschmied Andrew B. Meers ist ein wirklich außergewöhnlicher Dolch. Die Geschichte besagt, dass er eines Tages einen Fuchszahn fand und ein Freund diesen für ihn in ein Glasfläschchen einschloss. Dann entschied er sich dazu, ein Messer um diese Phiole zu bauen, als eine Art Reliquiar. Der Damast für das Messer wurde von Meers aus 1084 und 15N20 geschmiedet. Der Griff besteht aus Grenadill mit dem Glasfläschchen in der Mitte. Sowohl Klinge als auch Griff sind mit vielen goldenen Einlege- und Schnitzarbeiten versehen, die Motive mit Bezug auf den Fuchs zeigen. Auch die Lederscheide wurde von Andrew selbst hergestellt.

The *Vulpecula* by ABS Master Bladesmith Andrew B. Meers is really a stunning dagger. The story goes, he found a fox tooth one day and had it sealed in a glass vial by a friend. Then he decided to build a knife around it as a reliquary. The knife's damascus was forged by Meers himself of 1084 and 15N20 steels. The handle is made of African Blackwood with the glass vial in the center. Blade as well as handle are decorated with lots of golden inlays and carvings showing fox-related motifs. The matching leather sheath was made by Andrew, too.

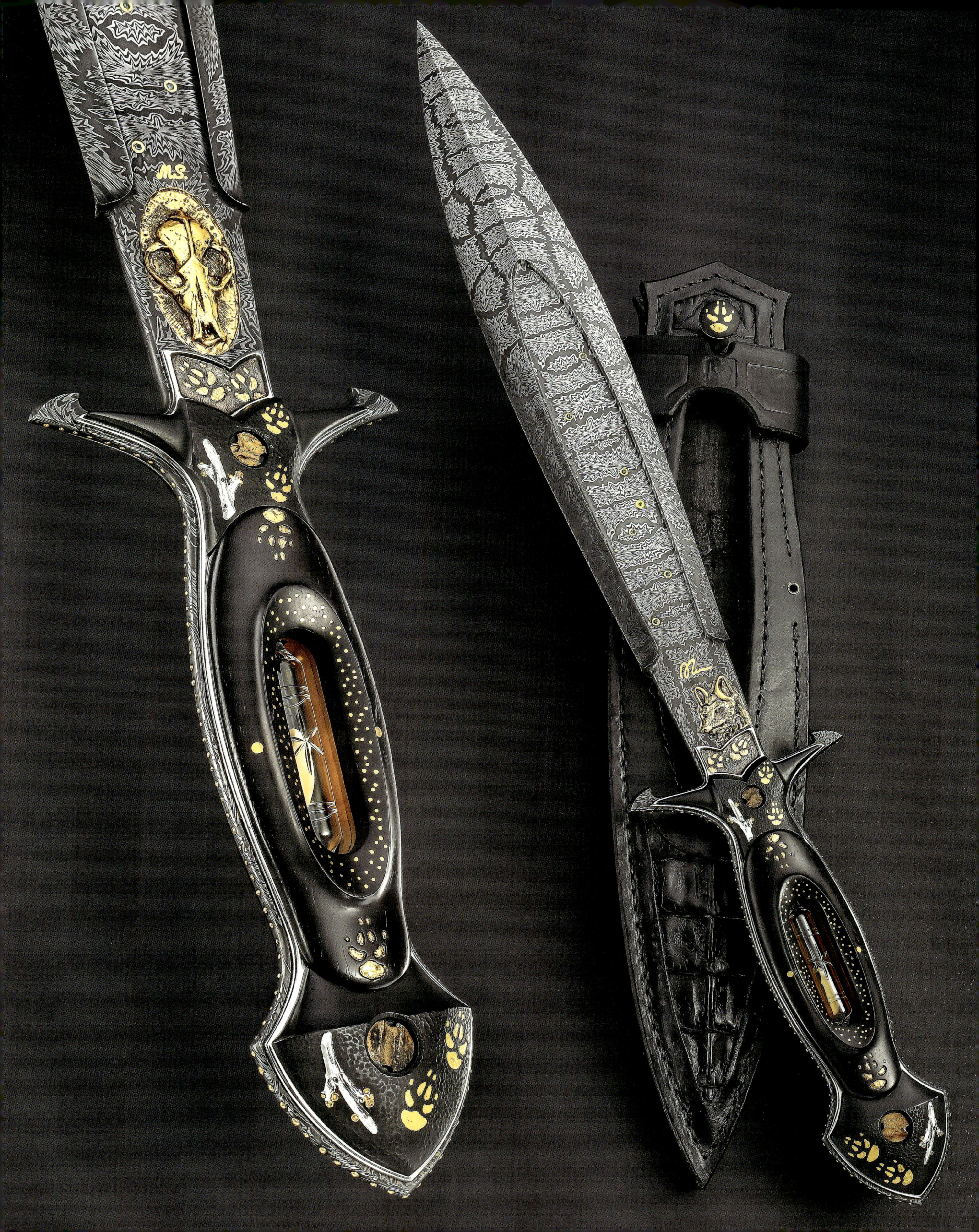

MARDI MESHEJIAN

Mardi Meshejian ist ein ABS-Journeyman-Schmied aus Santa Fe, New Mexico. Er ist auch der alleinige Schöpfer dieses schottischen Sgian-Dubh mit einer Gesamtlänge von 10 Zoll. Die Klinge selbst hat eine Länge von 6 Zoll und wurde aus 1080 und 15N20 geschmiedet. Ein dünnes Kupfer-Distanzstück trennt sie vom Griff aus Bloodwood (Satiné). Auch die Scheide wurde aus diesem Holz hergestellt.

Mardi Meshejian is an ABS Journeyman Smith from Santa Fe, New Mexico. He is also the sole author of this Scottish Sgian-Dubh with an overall length of 10". The blade itself has a length of 6" and was forged from 1080 and 15N20 steels. A thin copper spacer separates it from the bloodwood handle. The sheath is made of bloodwood as well.

MARDI MESHEJIAN

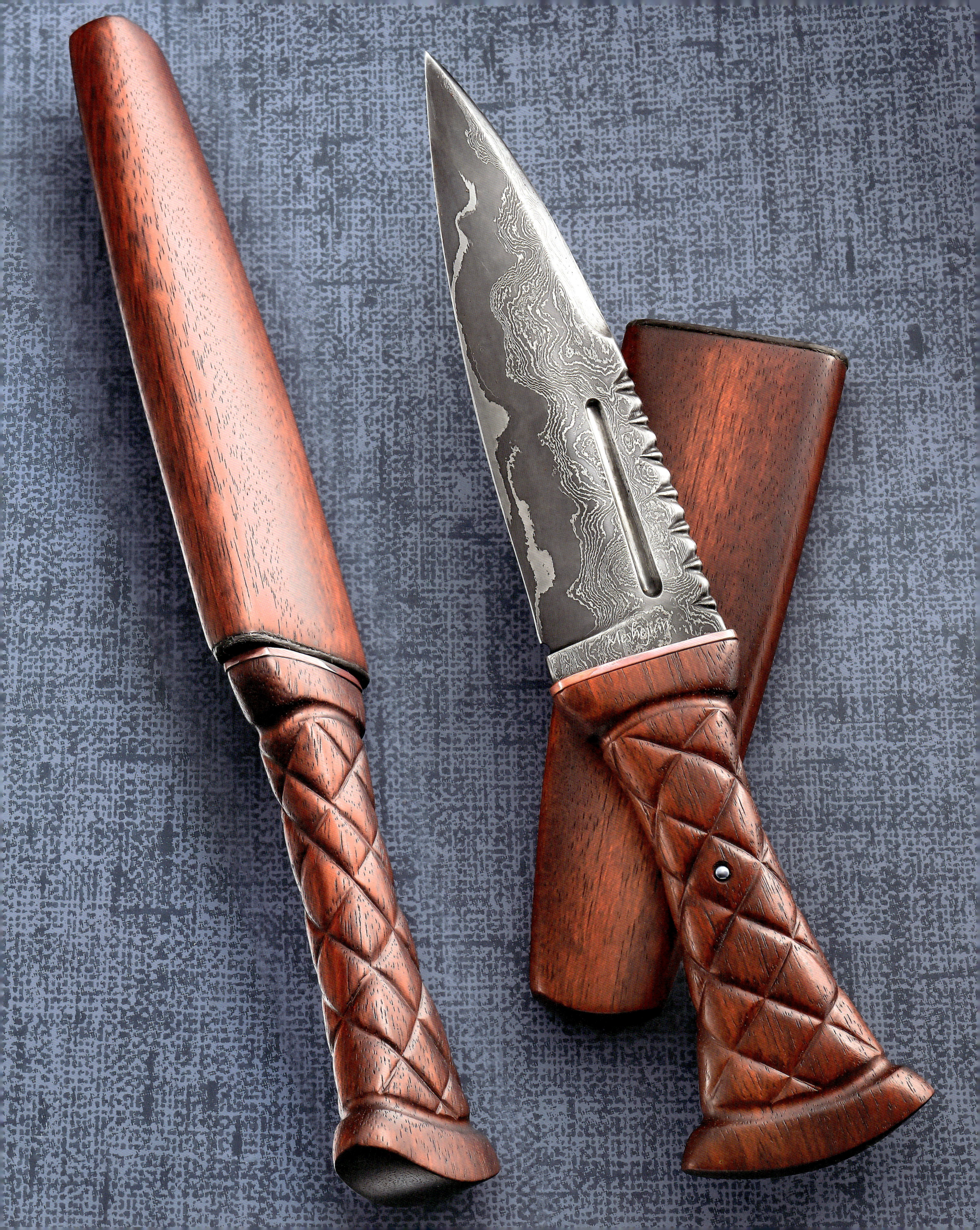
Meshejian

ADAM MILLÉ

Adam Millé aus Fort Smith, Arkansas, kreierte diesen Skinner, der gleichzeitig elegant und rustikal wirkt. Adam schmiedete den Damast für Klinge und Griffbacken aus 100 Lagen von 1084 und 15N20. Für den Griff nutzte er nicht nur Hirschhorn, sondern auch altes Micarta mit einem hübschen Braunton. Attraktive Akzente aus Kupfer und die begleitende braune Lederscheide vervollständigen dieses Kunstwerk.

Adam Millé from Fort Smith, Arkansas, created this skinner which looks both elegant and rustic at the same time. Adam forged the damascus for blade and guard from 100 layers of 1084 and 15N20 steels. For the handle he used not only stag, but also vintage micarta with a lovely brown hue. Attractive copper accents and the accompanying brown leather sheath complete this piece of art.

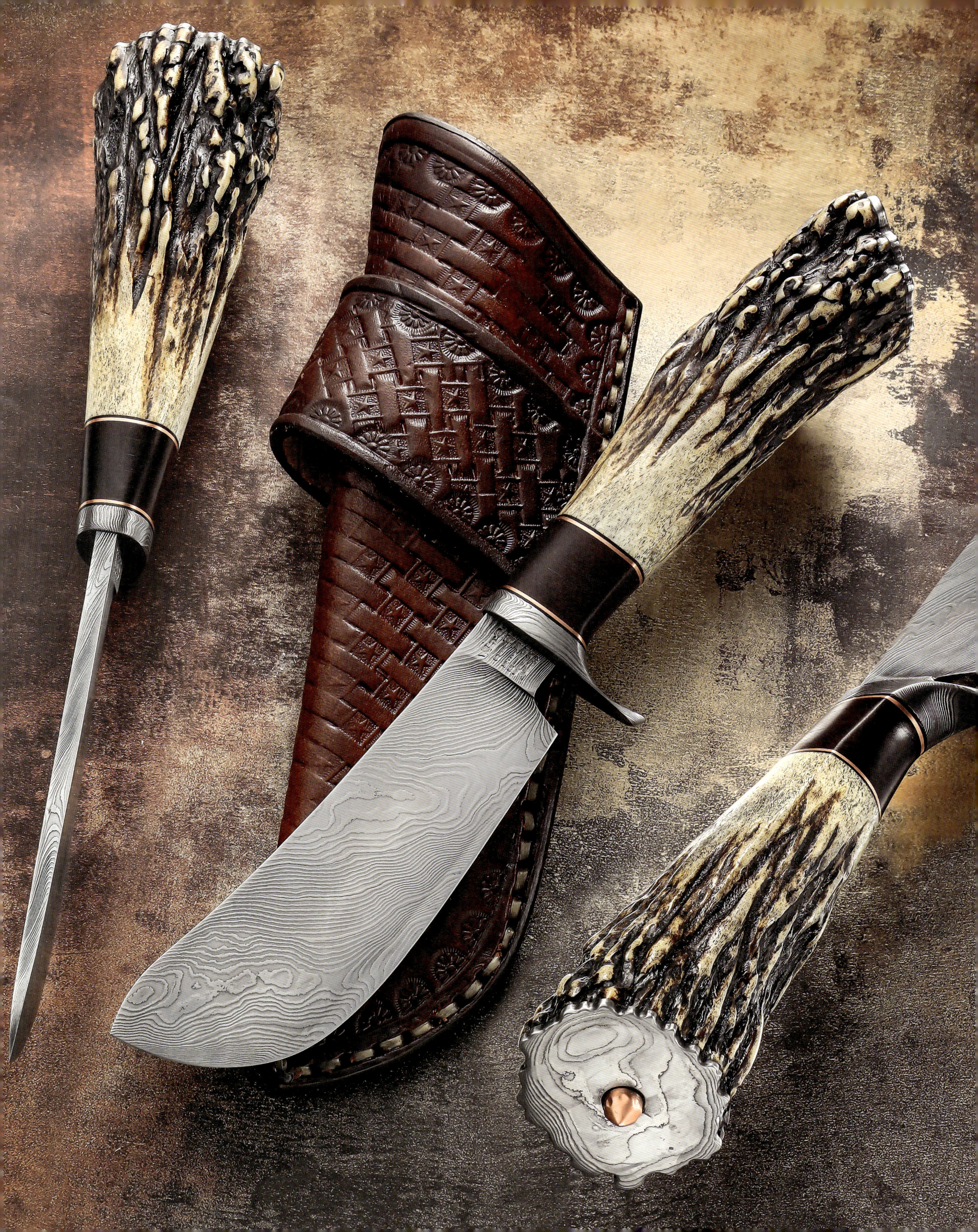

DAVID MIRABILE

David Mirabile aus Juneau, Arkansas, nennt dieses Messer *Aikuchi Carry Bowie*. Die Sandwich-Klinge aus Damast mit einem Kern aus rostträgem Stahl ist wie die eines Bowie-Messers geformt, während alles übrige wie ein traditionelles japanisches Aikuchi wirkt – ein kurzes Tanto oder Kampfmesser. Das kleine Tsuba (rundes Stichblatt) wurde aus „Lightning Strike"-Carbon hergestellt, der Griff ist im traditionell japanischen Stil umwickelt.

David Mirabile from Juneau, Arkansas, calls this knife *Aikuchi Carry Bowie*. Indeed, the sandwiched blade of damascus with a core of stainless steel is shaped like that of a Bowie knife while all the rest make it look like a traditional Japanese Aikuchi, a short tanto or fighter knife. Its small tsuba (rounded guard) is made of „Lightning Strike" carbon fiber. The handle is wrapped in traditional Japanese style.

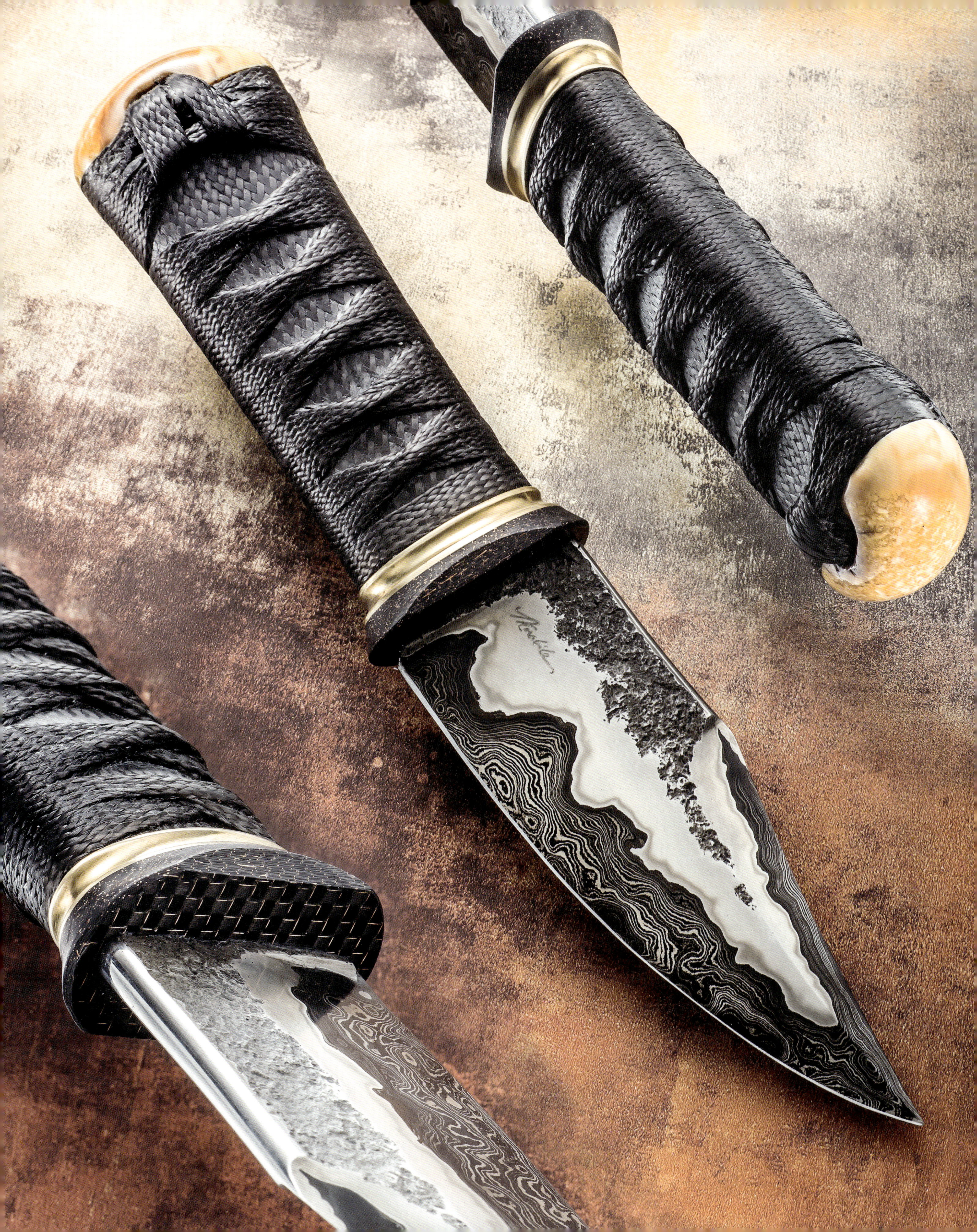

TREVOR MORGAN JR.

Dieses Küchenmesser von Trevor Morgan Jr. aus Apple Valley in Kalifornien ist wirklich ungewöhnlich. Als Ergebnis davon erhielt es den Preis „Best in Show" bei der Blade Show West 2022. Der Federdamast für die Klinge und die komplexen integrierten Griffbacken wurde von Trevor aus 1084 und 15N20 geschmiedet. Der Griff wurde aus stabilisiertem Eukalyptusholz geformt.

This chef's knife by Trevor Morgan Jr. from Apple Valley, California, is really unusual and as a result was awarded „Best in Show" and „Best Kitchen Knife" at the Blade Show West 2022. The feather damascus for blade and intricate integral bolsters was made by Trevor from 1084 and 15N20 steels. The handle was created of stabilized eucalyptus.

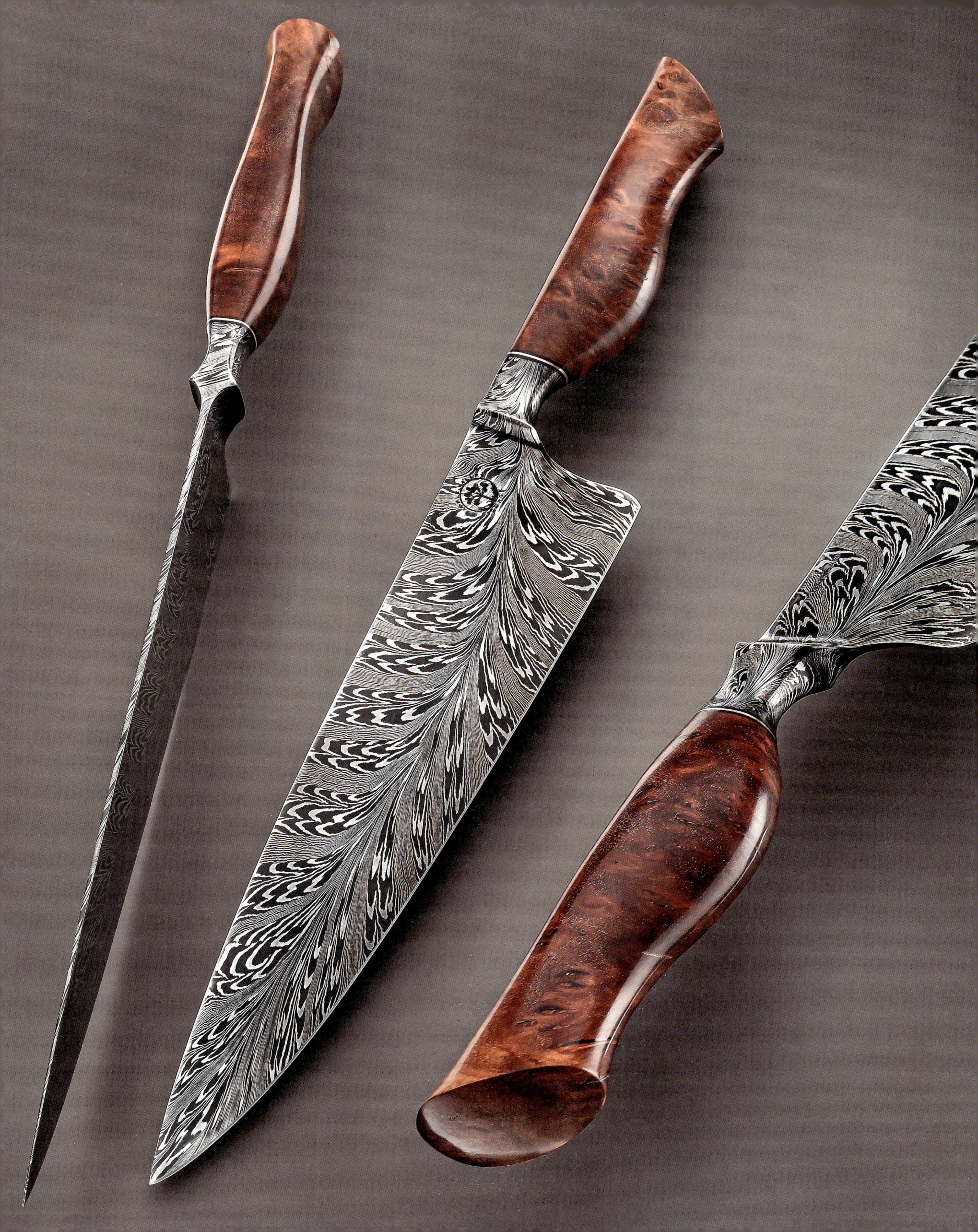

THEO NAZZ

Theo „Rock" Nazz aus New York City ist ein sehr vielseitiger Messermacher. Er macht so ziemlich alles von kleinen Messern bis zum großen Schwert. Das hier ist sein *Steampunk-mascus Bowie*. Für den Steampunk-Damast feuerverschweißte er allerlei Arten von Schraubenmuttern, Bolzen und andere Metallteile mit 1095-Stahl und Nickel und schmiedete das Ergebnis auf einen Kern aus Damast mit Zufallsmuster. Der Handschutz wurde zuerst mit dem 3D-Drucker erstellt, dann aus Bronze gegossen. Die Bronze-Medaillons auf dem Ebenholz Griff, die das Nazz-Logo verstecken, wurden auf dieselbe Weise hergestellt.

Theo „Rock" Nazz from New York City is a very versatile knifemaker. He makes virtually everything from small knives to big swords. This is his *Steampunk-mascus Bowie*. For the steampunk damascus he forge-welded all kinds of nuts and bolts and other metal things together with 1095 and nickel and then forged the outcome onto a core of random-pattern damascus. The guard was created first via 3D-printing, then cast of bronze. He did the same for the bronze medallions on the ebony handle with the Nazz logo hidden inside.

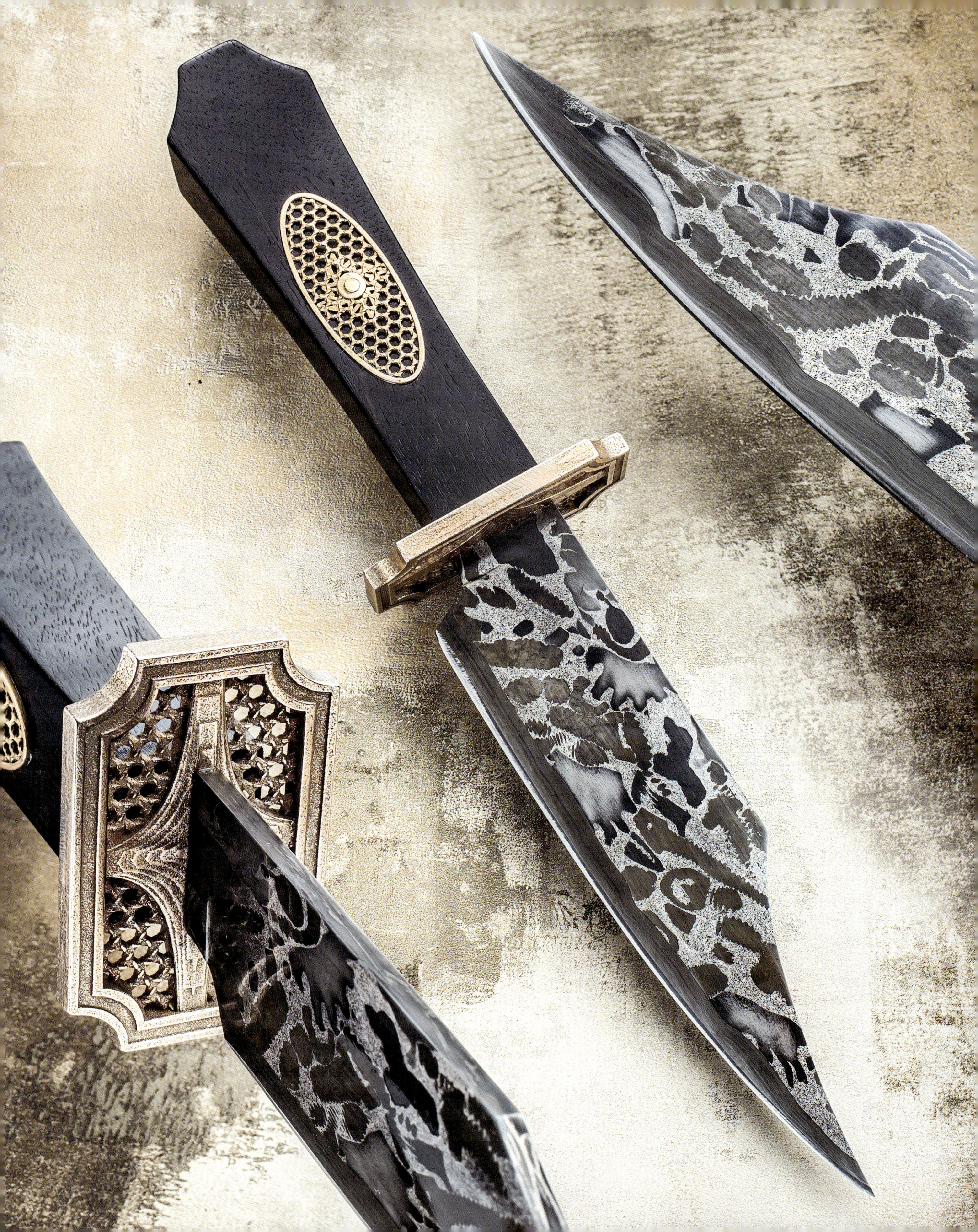

WILL NEWHAM

Messermacher Will Newham aus Howden in Tasmanien konstruierte dieses großartige Gyuto aus „Fafnir"-Damast von Damasteel. Distanzstücke und Beschläge bestehen aus Messing und schwarzem G-10, Griff und Scheide wurden aus Palisander geformt. Das Resultat von Wills hingebungsvollem Einsatz beim Bau dieses Messers war der Preis „Best Chef Knife" bei der Sydney Blade Show 2022.

Knifemaker Will Newham of Howden, Tasmania, made this gorgeous gyuto of „Fafnir" damascus from Damasteel. Spacers and fittings are of brass and black G-10, handle and sheath are shaped from rosewood. The result of Will's dedication to making this knife was the award „Best Chef Knife" at the Sydney Blade Show 2022.

WILL NEWHAM

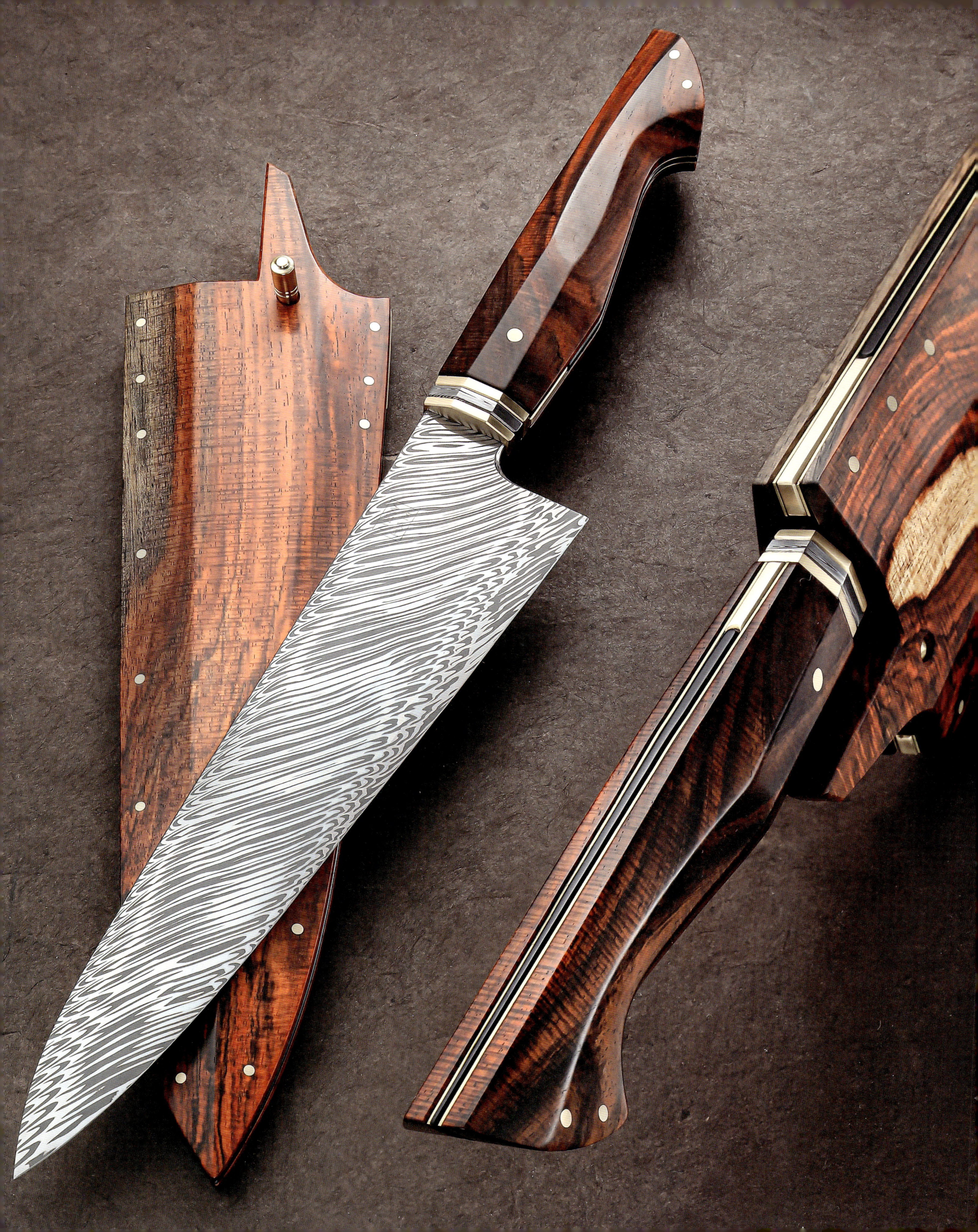

OLAMIC CUTLERY

Olamic Cutlery ist ein kleines, familiengeführtes Unternehmen aus Visalia, Kalifornien, und alle feststehenden Messer, die dort hergestellt werden, sind eine Kombination aus traditioneller Handwerkskunst mit modernen Materialien. Das hier abgebildete Messer besitzt eine Klinge aus Mokume-Damast. Olamic fertigte diesen auffälligen Damast aus sogenanntem „HCVD" (High Carbon Vanadium Damascus) mit Lagen aus Kupfer und Nickel. Diese Materialien wurden auch für das Parierelement, den Knauf und die Distanzstücke verwendet. Der Griff besteht aus Canvas-Micarta.

Olamic Cutlery is a small, family-owned business of Visalia, California, and all their fixed blades are made combining traditional manual work with modern materials. The one depicted here has a blade of mokume damascus. Olamic makes this eyecatching damascus from what they call „HCVD" (High Carbon Vanadium Damascus) with layers of copper and nickel. Those materials were also used for the guard, pommel and spacers. The handle is made of canvas micarta.

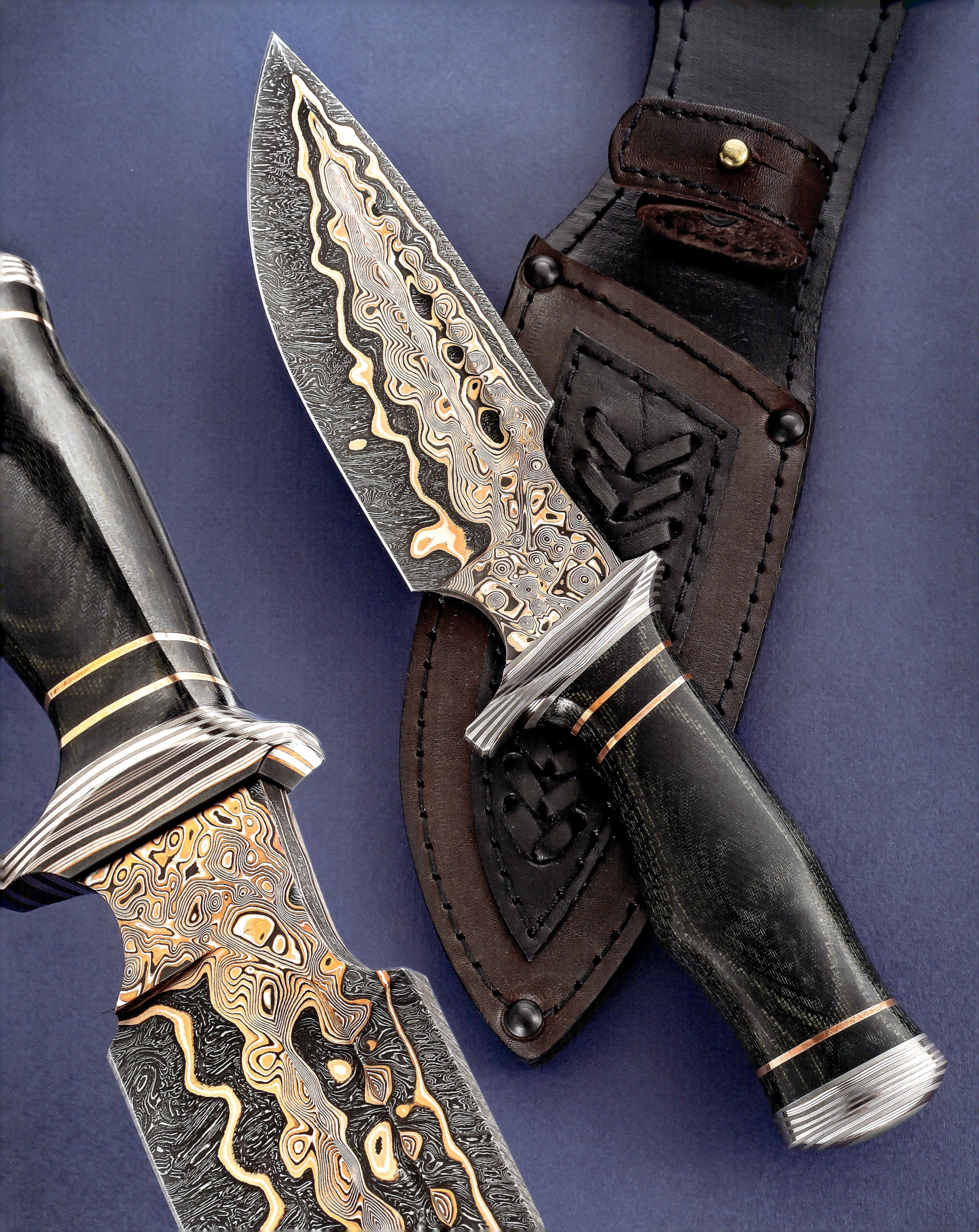

MATT PARKINSON

ABS-Journeyman-Schmied Matthew „Matt" Parkinson aus Wolcott, Connecticut, ist Miteigentümer der Dragon's Breath Forge, die er sich mit Jamie Lundell teilt. Sein *Damascus Dirk* ist ein Blickfang. Die Klinge wurde aus mehreren Damastbarren zusammengesetzt. Die Schneide besteht aus Torsionsdamast mit 340 Lagen. Derselbe Damast wurde auch für den Schlangen-Handschutz und die Spacer benutzt. Der Knauf besteht aus Mosaikdamast. Der Griff wurde mit Leder und Schnur umwickelt. Die Scheide besteht aus Pappelholz mit Lederwicklung. Der Dirk ist mit Schädeln und Karneolen verziert. Ein kleiner Schraubenschlüssel aus Damast erlaubt das Zerlegen.

ABS Journeyman Smith Matthew „Matt" Parkinson of Wolcott, Connecticut, is co-owner of the Dragon's Breath Forge which he shares with Jamie Lundell. His *Damascus Dirk* is an absolute eyecatcher. The blade was constructed of several damascus bars with the edge made of twisted damascus consisting of 340 layers. The same damascus was also used for the snake-guard and spacer. The pommel was created from mosaic damascus. The handle is wrapped with leather and cord. The scabbard is made of poplar with felt lining, steel fittings and a leather wrap on the outside. The dirk is decorated with skulls and carnelians. A small damascus wrench allows its complete takedown.

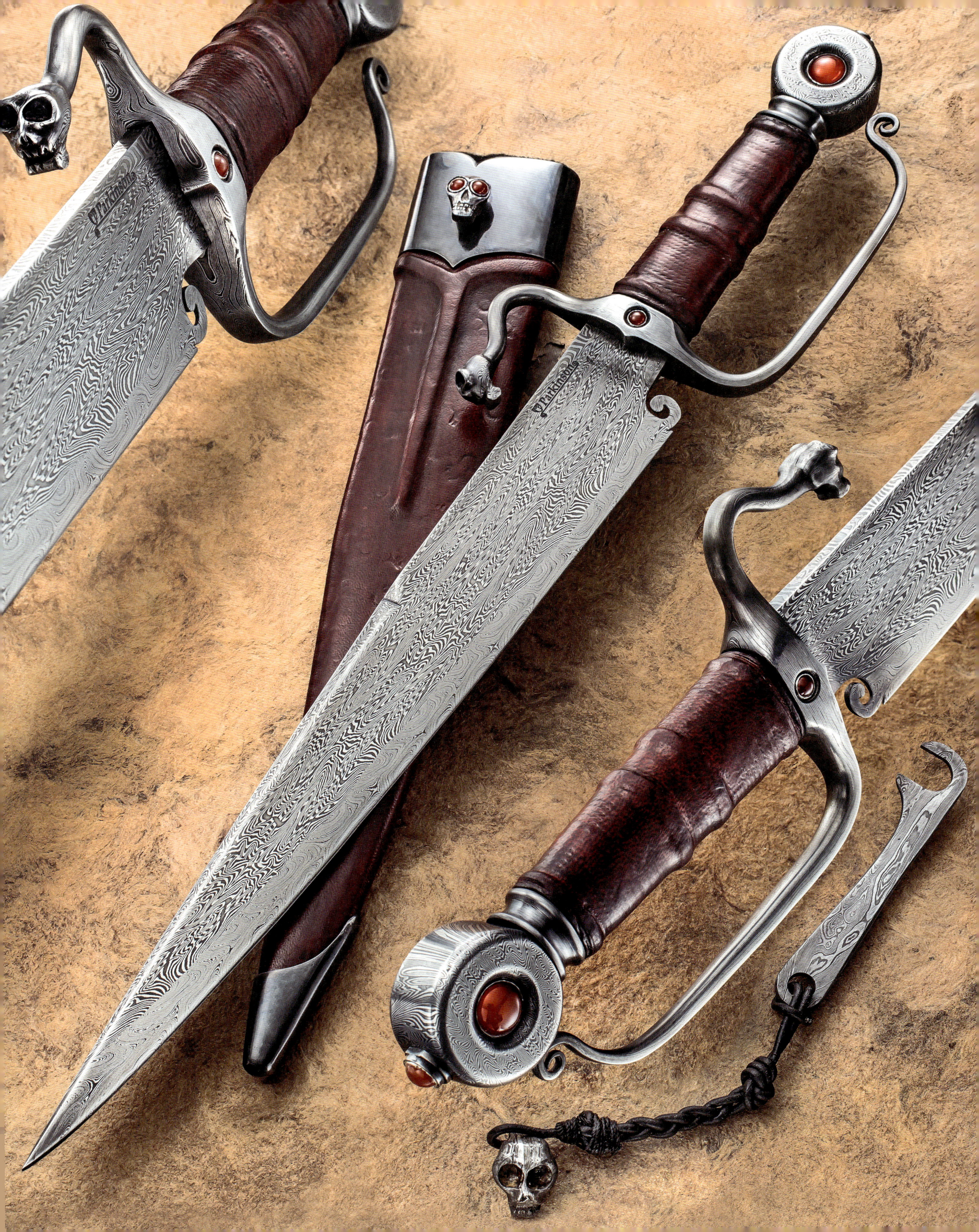
Parkinson

LOGAN PEARCE

Logan Pearce aus De Queen, Arizona, erlernte das Messermachen von seinem Großvater. So wie er kreiert auch Logan seine Messer immer noch aus Alltagsgegenständen. Sein feststehendes Messer *Leros* ist allerdings sehr viel eleganter als seine Messer aus Nägeln von Eisenbahnschienen. Die 4½ Zoll lange Klinge besteht aus Torsionsdamast, das Parierelement aus rostfreiem Stahl, und der Griff wurde aus gefärbtem und stabilisiertem Eschenahorn-Holz gefertigt.

Logan Pearce of De Queen, Arizona, learned knifemaking from his grandfather. Like him, Logan still creates knives from everyday objects. However, this *Leros* fixed blade is far more elegant than his railroad spike knives. The 4½"-blade is forged of twisted damascus, the guard is made of stainless steel and the blue handle is shaped of dyed and stabilized boxelder burl.

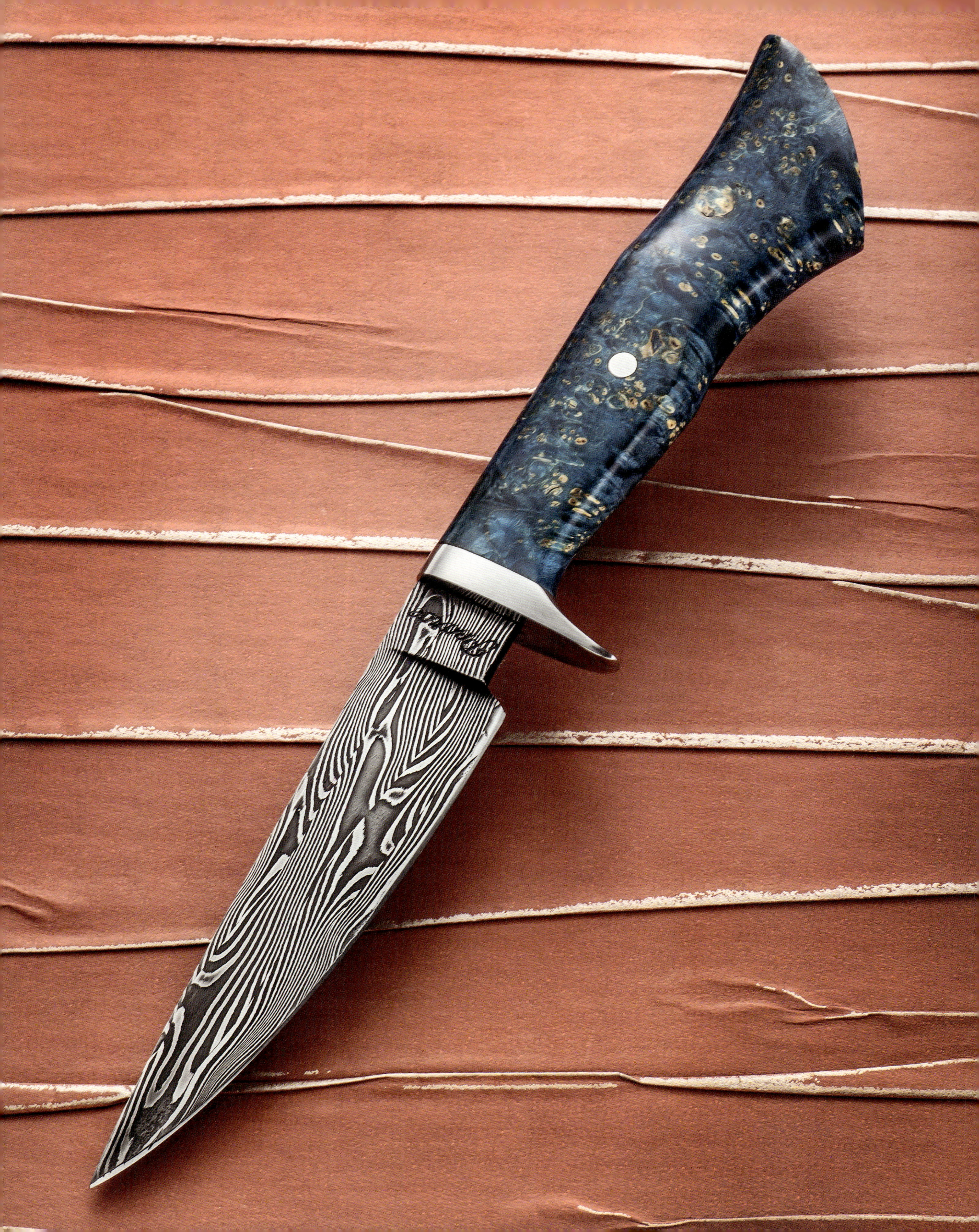

BEN PITTMAN

Messermacher Ben Pittman aus Montpelier, Virginia, ist der Schöpfer dieses eleganten Kunstwerks. Mit diesem Bowie gewann er auch den Preis für den besten Damast bei der Blade Show Texas 2022. Die feuerverschweißten Bahnen und Lagen seines „Firestorm"-Mosaikdamasts sind in der Tat umwerfend. Hier wurden sie für alles außer dem Griff aus Walross-Elfenbein benutzt.

Knifemaker Ben Pittman of Montpelier, Virginia, is the creator of this elegant piece of art. He won the award for „Best Damascus" at the Blade Show Texas 2022 with this Bowie. The forge-welded bars and layers of his „Firestorm" mosaic damascus are indeed mind-boggling. Here, it was used for everything but the handle of walrus ivory.

BEN PITTMAN

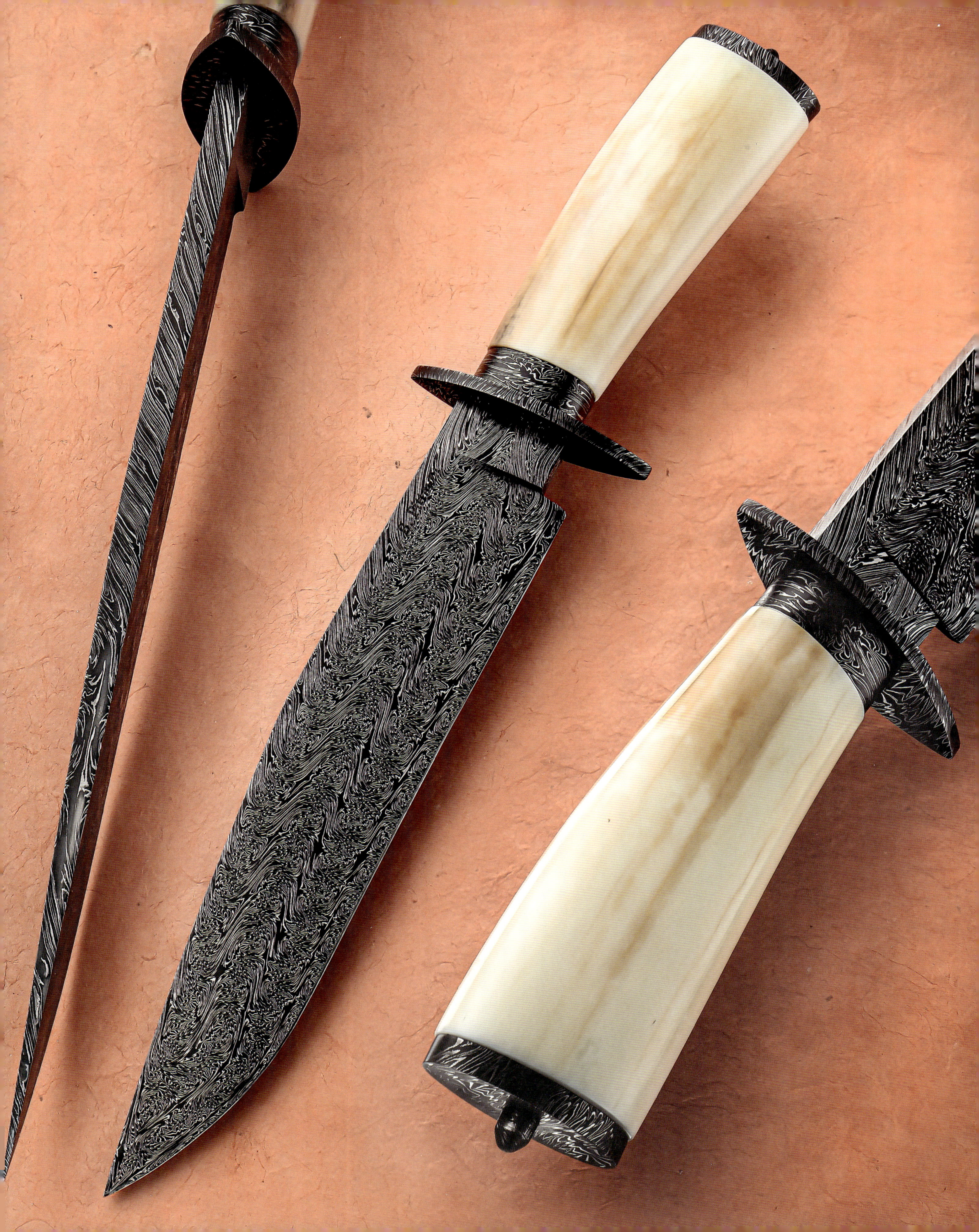

BILL POOR

Bill Poor aus Tuscola, Texas, nennt dieses bedrohlich-wirkende Bowie seinen *Dragon Slayer* (Drachentöter). Also, Drachen seid auf der Hut! Bill schmiedete den Drachen-Mosaikdamast aus 1080, 15N20 und pulvermetallurgischem Stahl mit hohem Nickelanteil. Handschutz und Parierelement wurden ebenfalls aus 1080 und 15N20 geschmiedet. Der Griff mit den Drachenschuppen ist aus Pappelholz geschnitzt.

Bill Poor of Tuscola, Texas, calls this menacing Bowie his *Dragon Slayer*. So, dragons beware! Bill forged the dragon mosaic damascus out of 1080, 15N20 and powder steel with high nickel content. The guard was also forged from 1080 and 15N20 steels. The dragon-scale handle is shaped from poplar.

BILL POOR

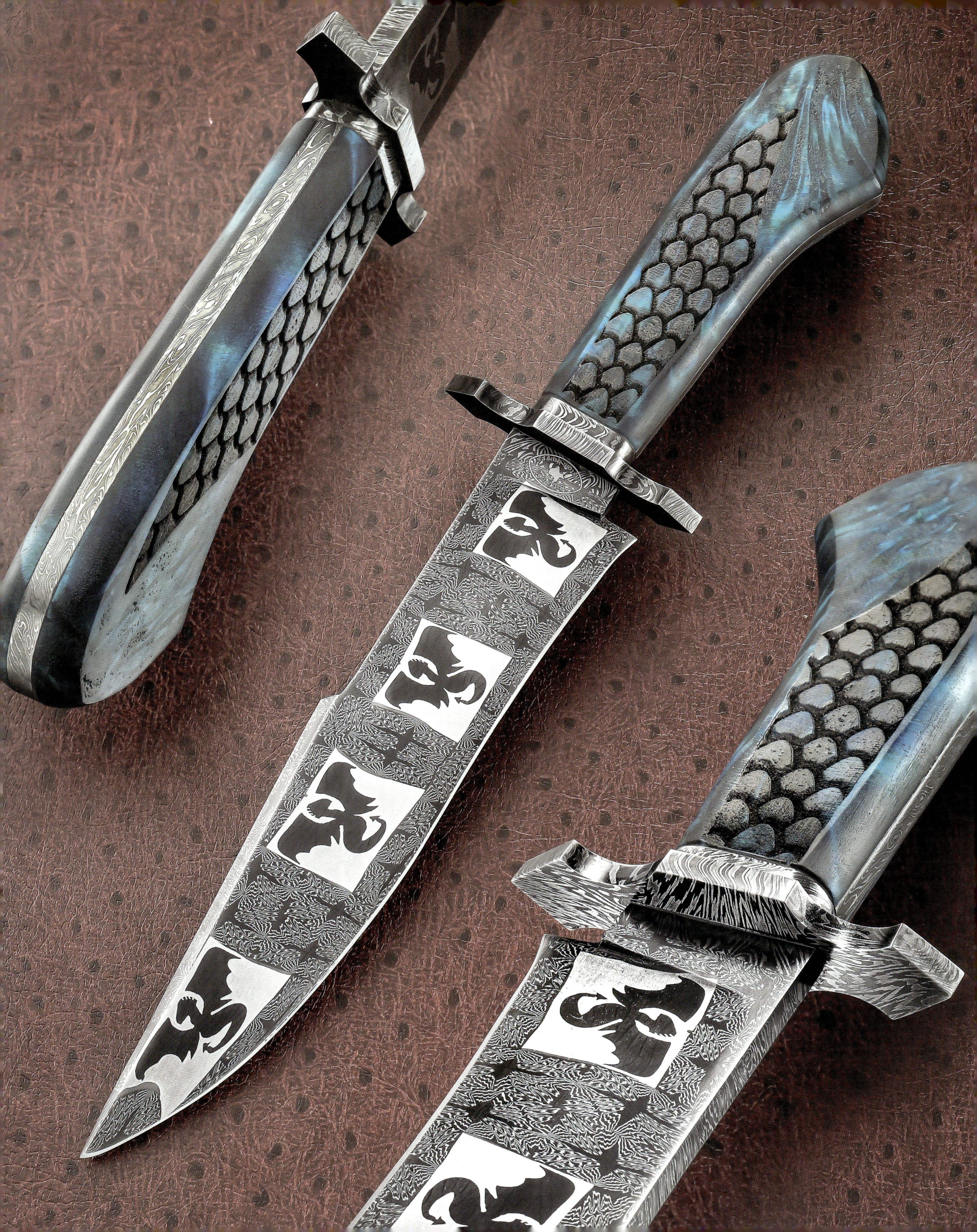

JEAN-PIERRE POTVIN

Was für ein musikalisches Messer! Ein Notenschlüssel auf dem Ricasso, eine Schnecke als Knauf und Noten auf dem Griff: *El Violin de Vulcano* wurde erschaffen vom kanadischen Messermacher Jean-Pierre Potvin aus Saint-Sauveur, Quebec. Er schmiedete den Damast für diese herausragende Integral-Konstruktion aus den Stahlsorten 1070 und 15N20. Die Griffschalen wurden aus Mammut-Elfenbein geschnitzt. Jean-Pierre stellte dieses meisterhafte Kunstwerk auf der Nashville Custom Knife Show 2022 aus.

What a musical knife! A clef on the ricasso, a scroll forming the pommel and musical notes on the handle: *El Violin de Vulcano* was created by Canadian knifemaker Jean-Pierre Potvin from Saint-Sauveur, Quebec. He forged the damascus for this outstanding integral construction of 1070 and 15N20 steels. The handle scales are carved from mammoth ivory. Jean-Pierre exhibited this masterful piece of art at the Nashville Custom Knife Show 2022.

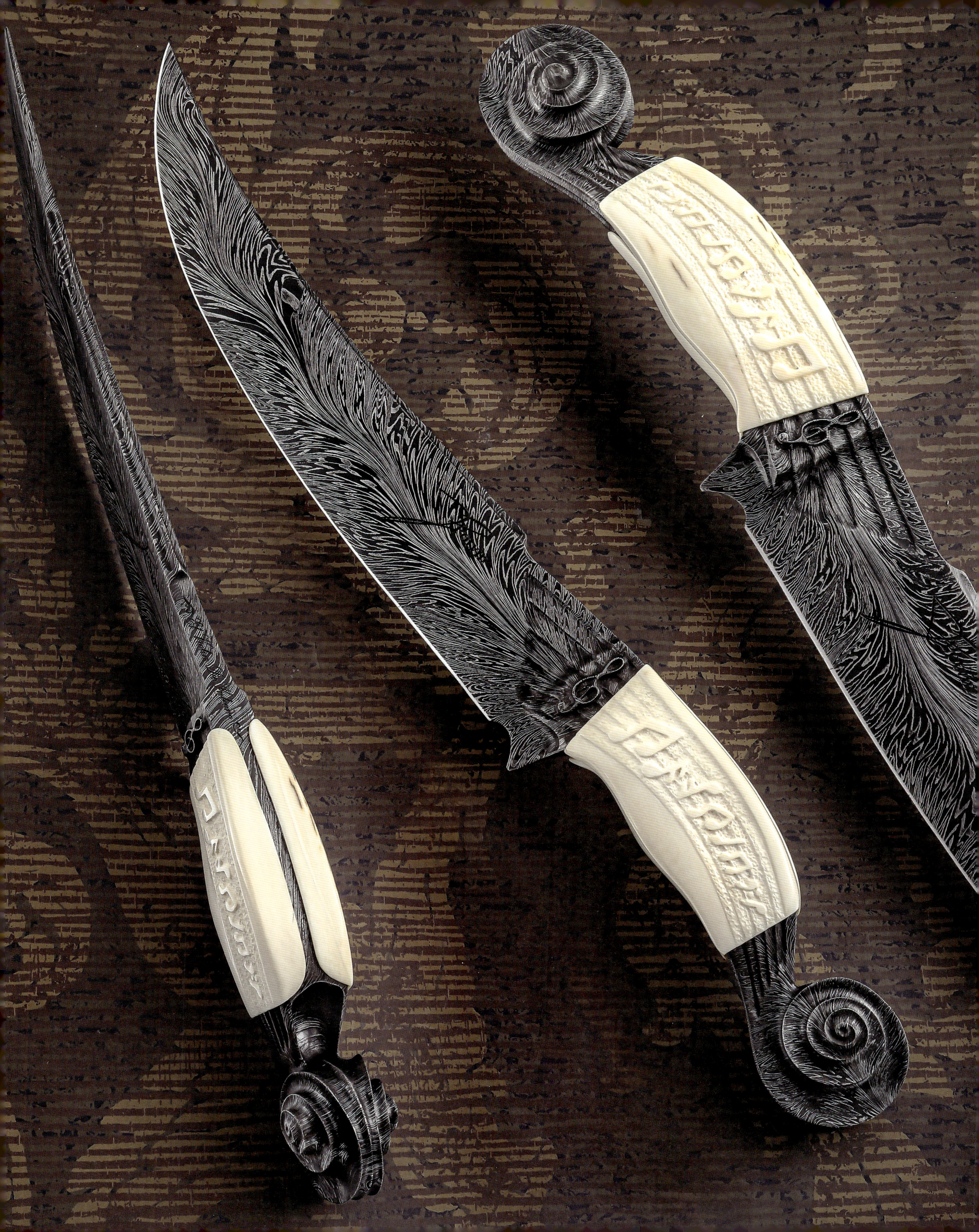

JOSHUA PRINCE

Joshua Prince aus Barrington, Rhode Island ist der Schöpfer einiger ziemlich ungewöhnlicher und kunstvoller Messer. Sie haben auch ungewöhnliche Namen. Die Klinge seines *Both Sides Now* besitzt einen Kern aus 80CrV2-Kohlenstoffstahl mit einer eingeschweißten Damastscheibe als „Stöpsel". Noch mehr Damast wurde im San-Mai-Stil auf beiden Seiten hinzugefügt mit einer hellen Linie, die wie ein Hamon wirkt. Der Griff ist aus Ziricote geformt.

Joshua Prince of Barrington, Rhode Island, is the maker of some quite unusual and artistic knives. They have unusual names as well. The blade of his *Both Sides Now* has a core of 80CrV2 carbon steel containing a plug-welded damascus disk. Further damascus was cladded on both sides in a San Mai style with a bright line looking like a hamon. The handle was shaped from ziricote.

JOSHUA PRINCE

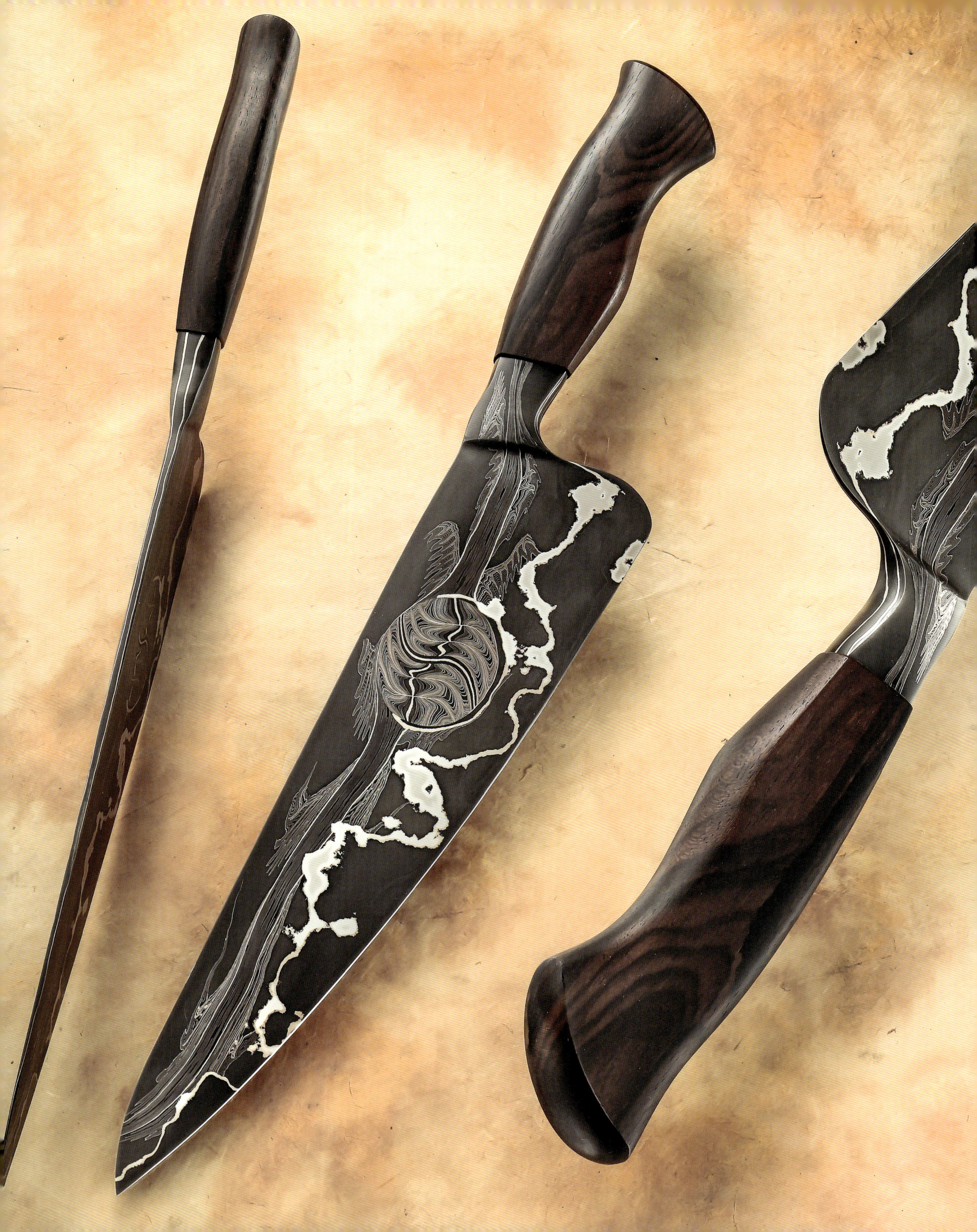

MIKE QUESENBERRY

Dies ist ein exquisiter Dolch von ABS Master Bladesmith Mike Quesenberry aus Blairsden, Kalifornien. Mike schuf nicht nur den Mosaikdamast für die Klinge, sondern übernahm auch die Wärmebehandlung, die Einlagen aus 24-karätigem Gold und fügte das Perlmutt in Ausstellungsqualität für die Griffschalen hinzu.

This is an exquisite dagger created by ABS Master Bladesmith Mike Quesenberry from Blairsden, California. Mike created not only the mosaic damascus for the blade, but also did the heat-treatment, made the 24k gold inlays and added the exhibition-grade mother-of-pearl for the handle scales.

MIKE QUESENBERRY

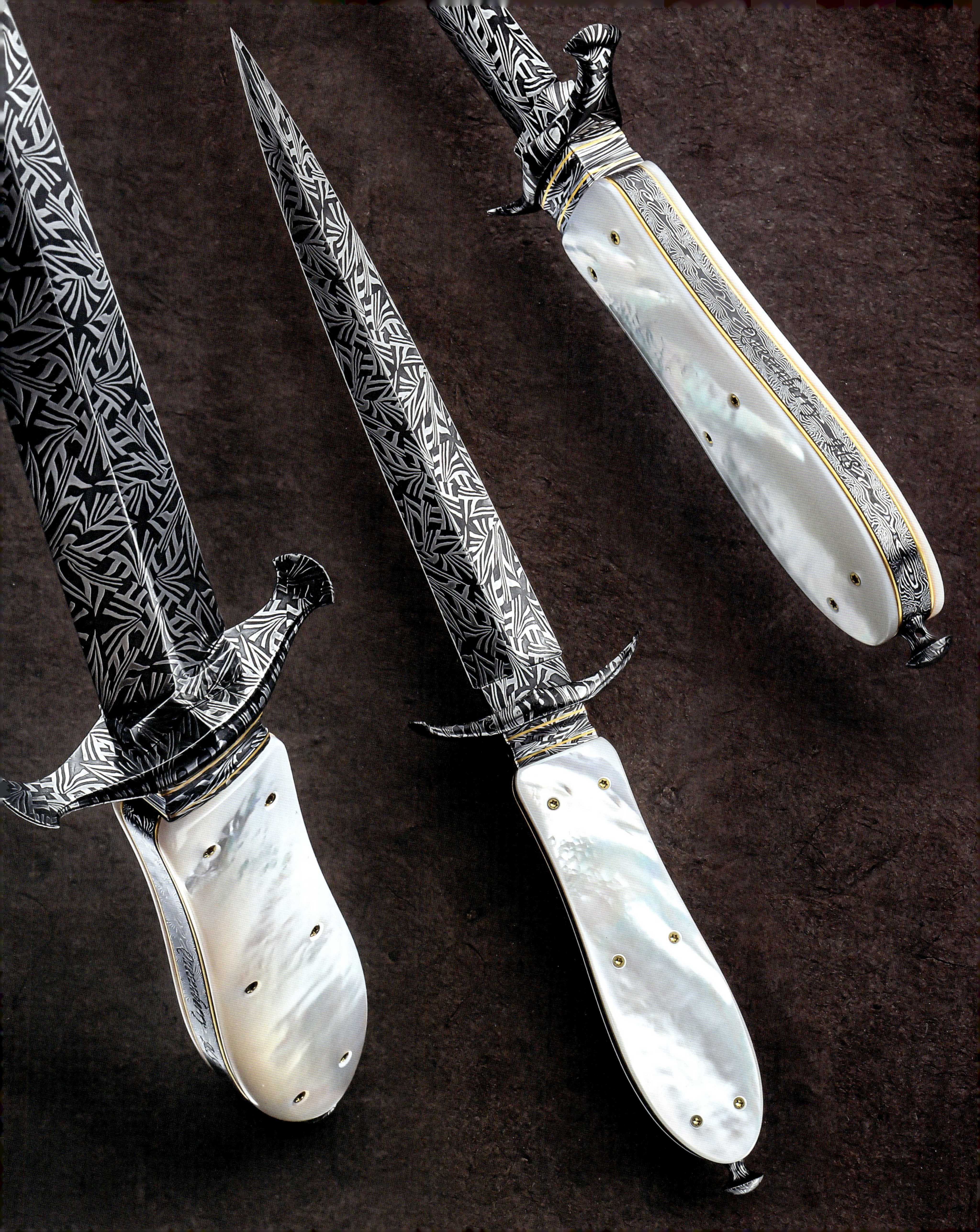

LIN RHEA

Einer von den Messermachern, die alles selbst machen, ist ABS-Meisterschmied Lin Rhea aus Prattsville, Arkansas. Er ist auch berühmt dafür, viele Schneidwettbewerbe bei der Blade Show und anderswo mit seinen handgemachten Messern gewonnen zu haben. Dieses traditionelle Bowie wurde als ein Steckangelmesser entworfen und aus 1084 und 15N20 geschmiedet. Dazu kommt ein Hirschhorngriff. Der D-förmige Handschutz wurde aus rostfreiem Stahl geformt.

One of the makers who do everything themselves is ABS Master Bladesmith Lin Rhea from Prattsville, Arkansas. He is also famous for winning many cutting contests at the Blade Show and elsewhere with his handmade knives. This traditional Bowie was made as a hidden tang knife from ladder damascus of 1084 and 15N20 steels with a stag handle. The D-guard was shaped of stainless steel.

LIN RHEA

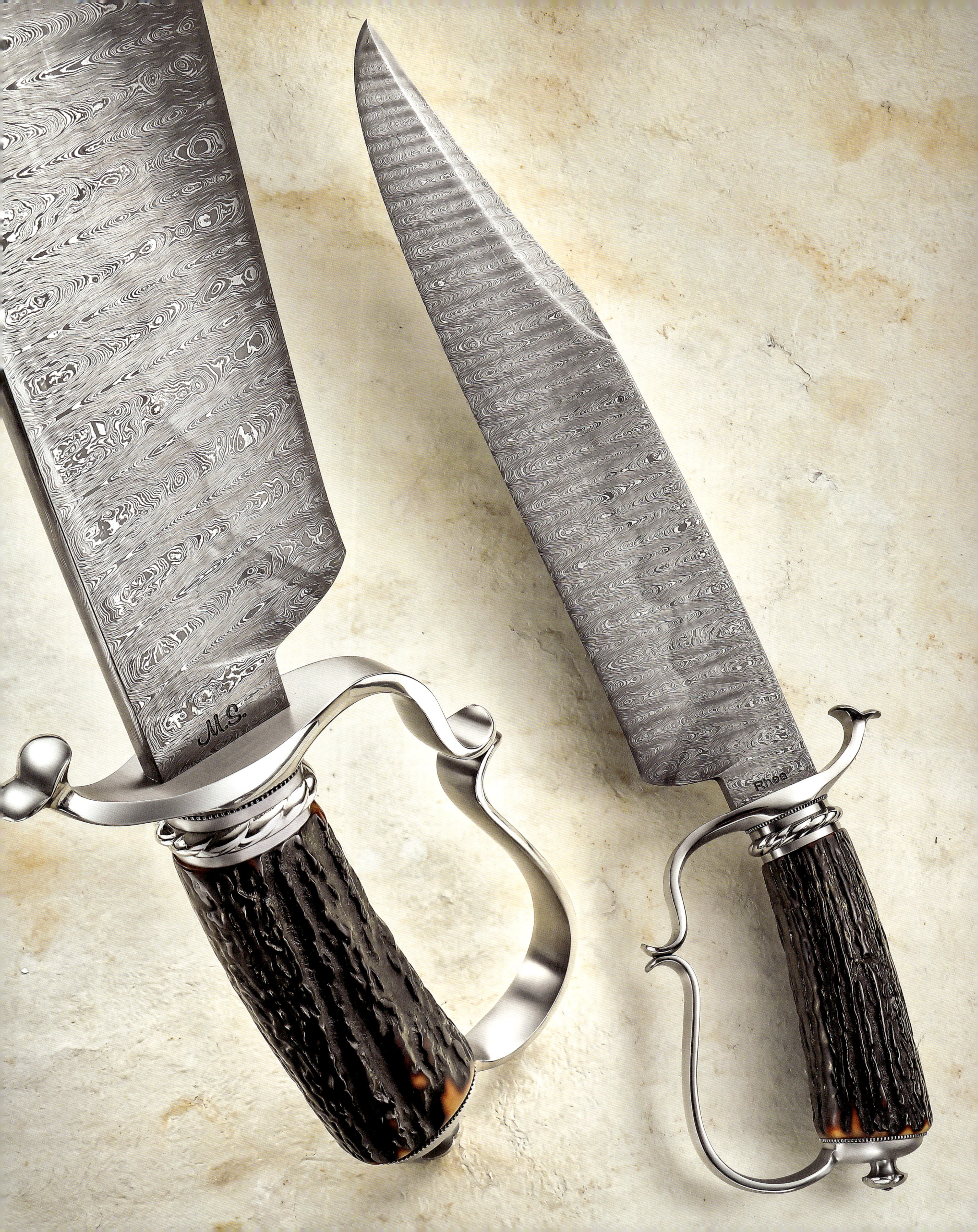
M.S.
Rhea

BERTIE RIETVELD

Bertie Rietveld aus Magalienburg, Südafrika, ist wahrscheinlich mehr bekannt für seinen herausragenden Damast als dafür, attraktive Messer zu machen. Nichtsdestotrotz ist sein *Pugio Legacy 2* mehr als nur ein Beweis für seine Fähigkeiten als exzellenter Messermacher. Die Klinge dieses Dolches im römischen Stil besteht aus Berties „Nebula"-Damast. Handschutz und Knauf bestehen aus Titan mit eingravierten Adlern und Akanthus-Blättern von Jonathan Knoesen. Der Griff wurde mit einem Mittelstück aus Picasso-Marmor gemacht, das von vier Stücken schwarzer Jade umgeben ist, die durch Titanringe getrennt sind.

Bertie Rietveld from Magaliesburg, South Africa, is probably more famous for his outstanding damascus than for making beautiful knives. Nevertheless, his *Pugio Legacy 2* is more than just proof of his abilities as an excellent knifemaker. The blade of this Roman-type dagger is created of Bertie's „Nebula" damascus. The guard and pommel are of titanium, engraved with acanthus leaves and eagles by Jonathan Knoesen. The handle is made with a centerpiece of Picasso marble surrounded by four pieces of black jade separated by titanium spacers.

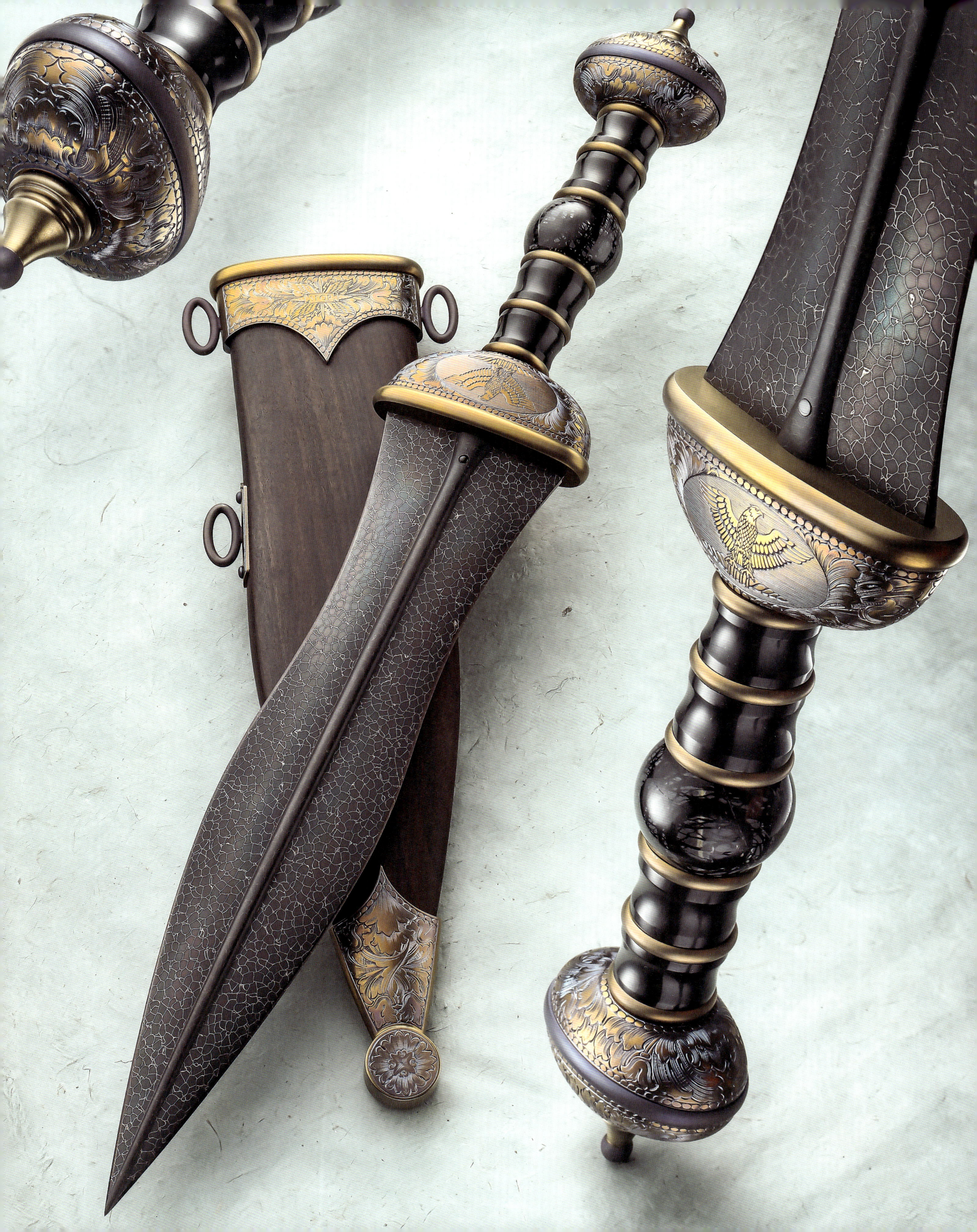

JAVAN ROBERTS

Das *Siren*, ein Back-Lock-Taschenmesser von Javan Roberts aus Milton, Florida, ist beinahe zu schön, um überhaupt daran zu denken, es für irgendwelche Schneidaufgaben zu benutzen. Die Damastklinge wurde durch Schleifen geformt, so wie auch der Griff aus rostfreiem 416er-Stahl. Der Griff wurde dann von Tyler Prince mit der namensgebenden Sirene graviert und mit vielen Schnörkeln und Blättern verziert.

The *Siren* lockback folder by Javan Roberts from Milton, Florida, is almost too beautiful to even think about using for any cutting task. The damascus blade was shaped by stock removal as is the case with the handle of stainless 416 steel. The handle then was engraved with the name-giving siren and lots of scrolls and leaves by Tyler Prince.

JAVAN ROBERTS

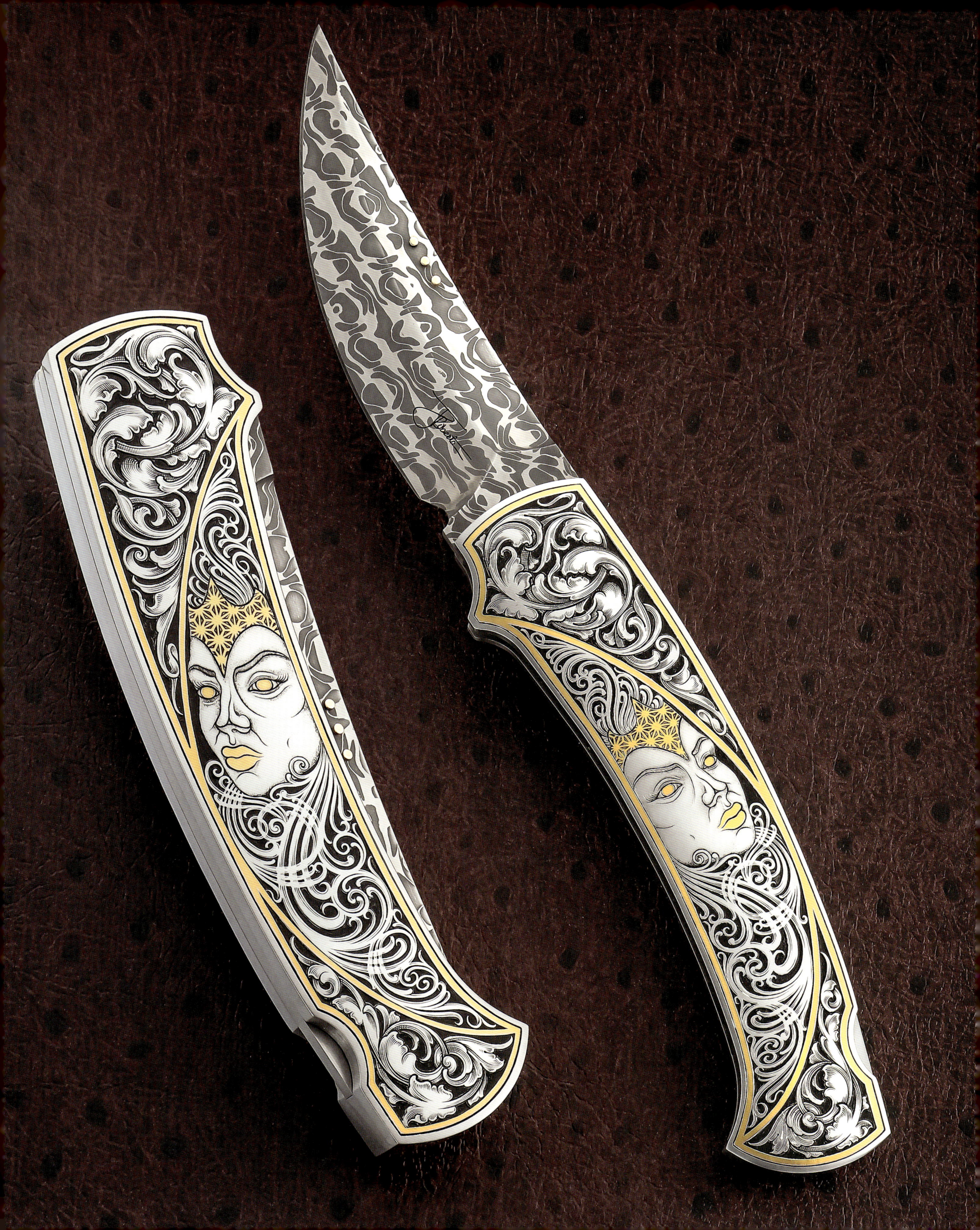

CHARLES RODDENBERRY

Messermacher Charles Roddenberry aus Live Oak, Florida, hat sich auf kleine, feststehende Messer spezialisiert. Der *Lime Cutter* ist eines seiner Lieblingsdesigns. Er hat schon viele verschiedene Versionen davon hergestellt. Für die Klinge dieses Exemplars verwendete er „Damascus Oh Mai", den er aus den Stahlsorten 1095 und 15N20, Kupfer und Nickel schmiedete. Die Griffschalen bestehen aus „Lightning Strike"-Kohlefaser. Die Scheide wurde von seiner Frau Jordan Medley genäht.

Knifemaker Charles Roddenberry from Live Oak, Florida, specializes in small fixed blades. The *Lime Cutter* is one of his favorite designs and he has created many different versions of it already. For this piece's blade he used „Damascus Oh Mai" forged from 1095 and 15N20 steels, copper and nickel. The handle scales are made from silver „Lightning Strike" carbon fiber. The sheath was sewn by his wife Jordan Medley.

CHARLES RODDENBERRY

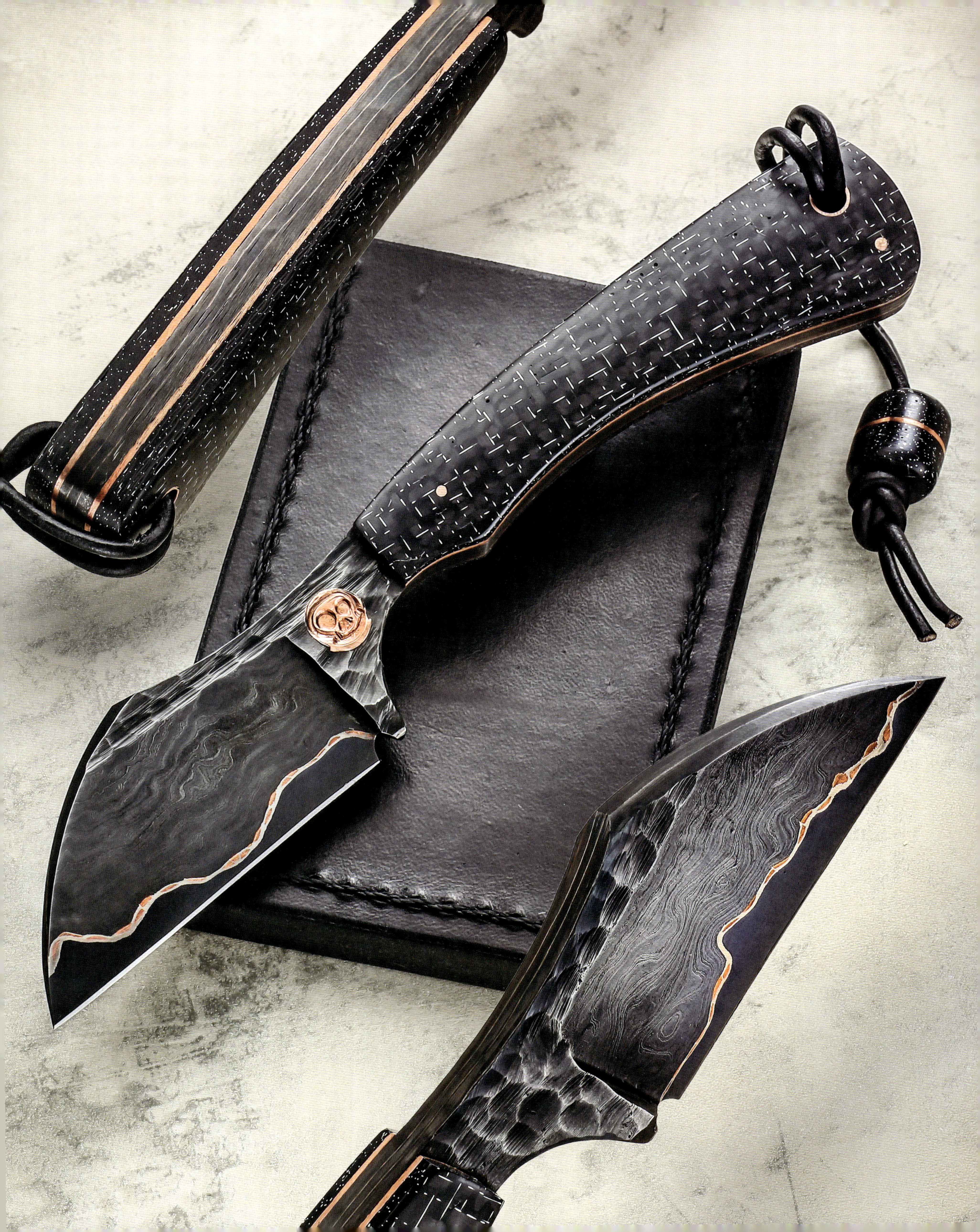

KYLE ROYER

ABS-Meisterschmied Kyle Royer aus Clever, Missouri, ist der Schöpfer dieses fantastischen *Fortitude*. Seine innere Stärke bezieht dieses Messer aus dem Mosaikdamast, der vom Meister selbst geschmiedet wurde. Handschutz und Griffrahmen bestehen aus Stahl mit einer schwarzen Hochglanzpolitur, durch eingelegten Golddraht hervorgehoben. Die Griffschalen sind aus erlesenem Perlmutt gefertigt.

ABS Master Bladesmith Kyle Royer from Clever, Missouri, is the maker of this fantastic *Fortitude*. Its inner strength comes from the knife's mosaic damascus forged by the master himself. The guard and handle frame are shaped of steel with a black mirror finish outlined with inlaid gold wire. The handle scales are made of exquisite mother-of-pearl.

KYLE ROYER

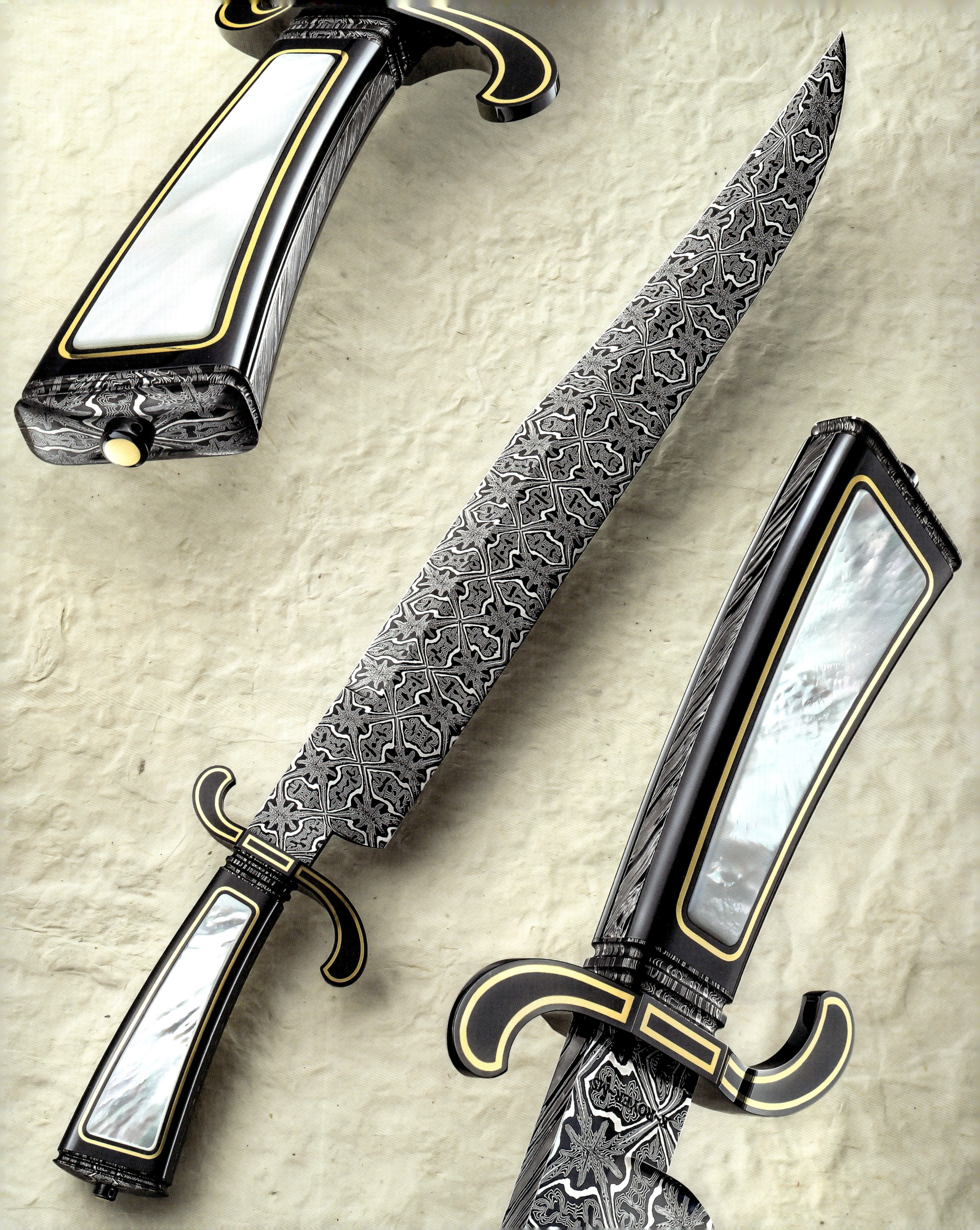

BRIAN SELLERS

Brian Sellers aus Cottonwood, Alabama, ist bekannt für hervorragende Bowies und gewann auch den Preis für den „Best Fighter" auf der Blade Show 2019. Das hier abgebildete Bowie besitzt eine 10 Zoll lange Klinge aus feinem Leiterdamast und wurde vom Messermacher selbst geschmiedet. Auch der Handschutz wurde aus Brians Damast geformt. Als Griffmaterial benutzte er Horn von einem Moschusochsen.

Brian Sellers from Cottonwood, Alabama, is a maker of fine Bowies and also won the award for „Best Fighter" at the Blade Show 2019. The one depicted here has a 10"-blade of fine ladder damascus forged by the knifemaker himself. The guard was also shaped of the maker's damascus. As handle material, he used horn from a musk ox.

BRIAN SELLERS

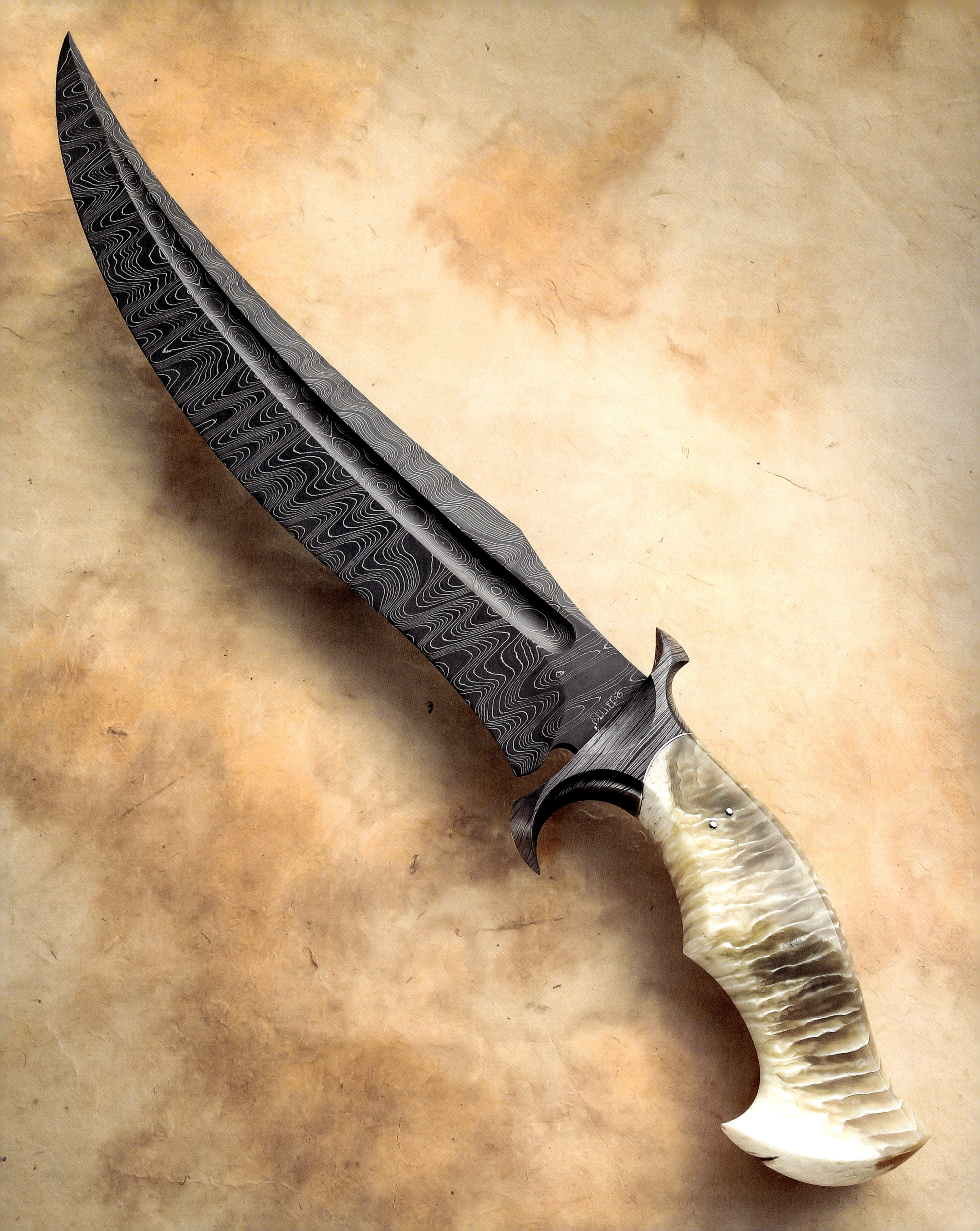

CHRIS SHARP

Chris Sharp aus Oxford, Ohio, ist spezialisiert auf Slipjoint-Klappmesser. Die beiden Klingen dieses Trappers sind aus Mosaikdamast hergestellt, den der Messermacher selbst aus 1075 und 15N20 schmiedete. Die Griffbacken, die Platinen und das Wappenschild wurden aus rostfreiem 416 gemacht. Typisch für Chris, ist das Schild als Loch ausgeführt anstelle der häufig verwendeten Metallplakette.

Chris Sharp from Oxford, Florida, is specialising in slipjoint folders. The two blades of this trapper were forged from the maker's own mosaic damascus, created from 1075 and 15N20 steels. The handle scales are of exquisite mammoth ivory bark. The bolsters, liners and the shield are made of stainless 416 steel. Typically for Chris, the shield is designed as a hole in the handle instead of the common plate.

CHRIS SHARP

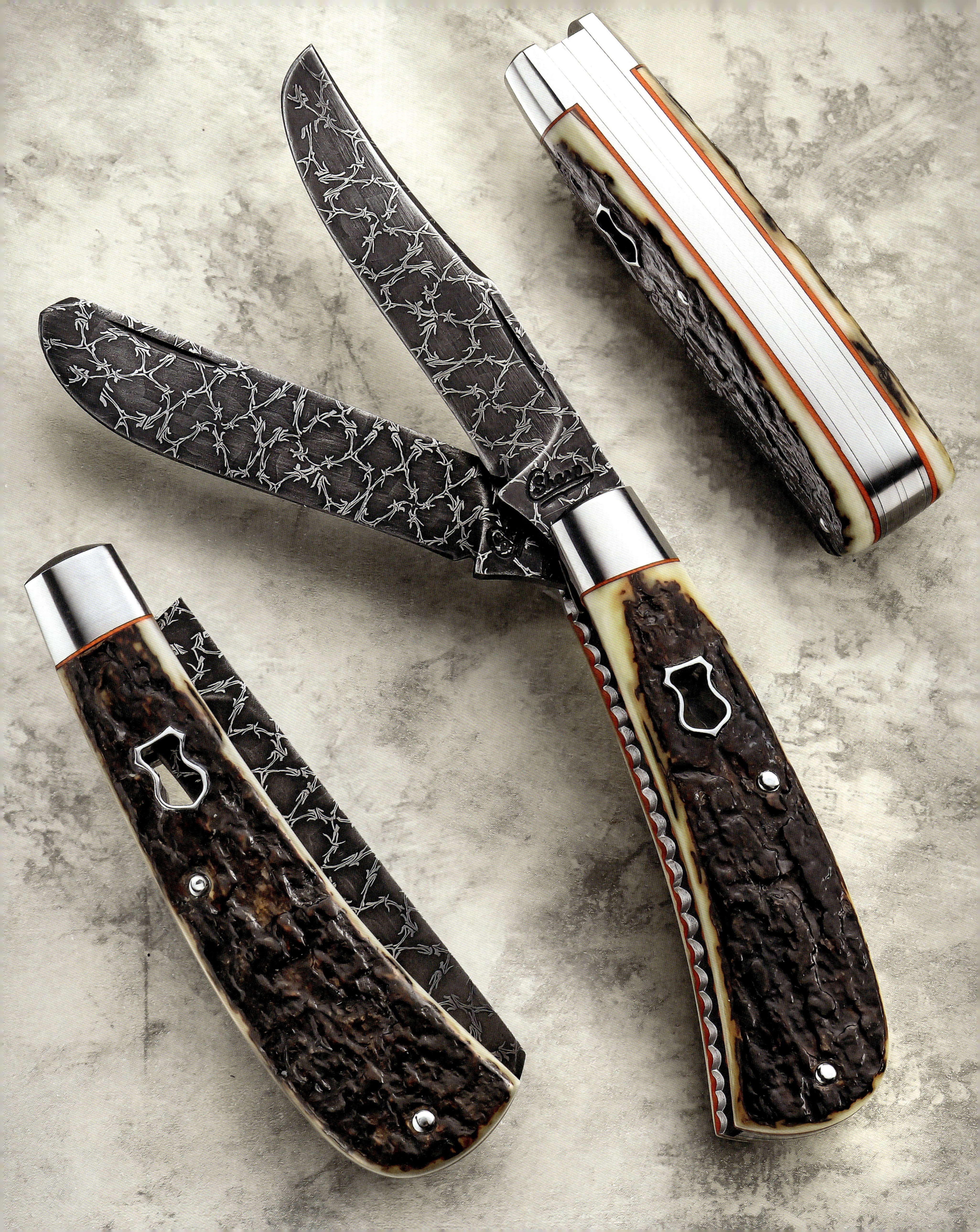

STEVEN SKIFF

Der *Culprit* ist ein Framelock-Klappmesser von Steven Skiff Sr. und Jr. aus Broadalbin, New York. Der „Angeklagte" ist auch schuld daran, dass die beiden mit dem „Best in Show" bei der NCCA (National Cutlery Collectors Association) Show 2022 ausgezeichnet wurden. Das Duo aus Vater und Sohn formte die Klinge für dieses eindrucksvolle Taschenmesser aus rostfreiem „Fafnir"-Damast von Damasteel. Der mit Rillen versehene Griff besteht aus Titan. Akzente aus Zirkon und anodisierte Schrauben im Farbton „Seafoam" bilden zusätzliche Highlights.

The *Culprit* is a frame lock folder made by Steven Skiff Sr. and Jr. from Broadalbin, New York. The Culprit is also to blame for winning them „Best in Show" at the NCCA (Northeast Cutlery Collectors Association) Show 2022. This duo of father and son shaped the blade for this impressive folder from Damasteel's stainless „Fafnir" damascus. The fluted handle is made from titanium with zirconium accents and „seafoam" anodized screws adding to its beauty.

STEVEN SKIFF

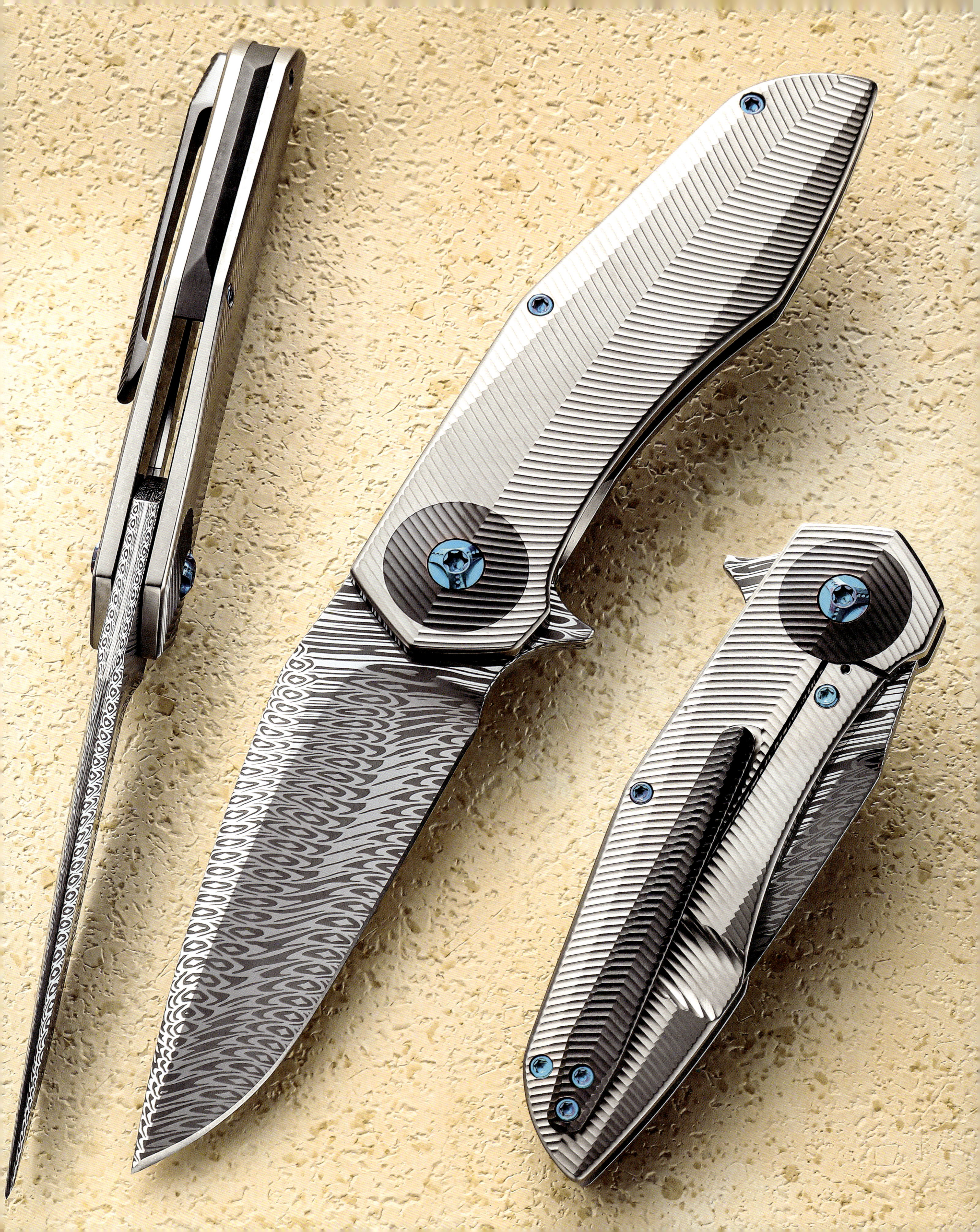

ANDREW K. SMITH

Andrew K. Smith aus Gonzales, Louisiana, schmiedete den Federdamast für dieses hübsche Kochmesser selbst. Das Muster fließt von den integralen Griffbacken herunter auf die Klinge und bis nach vorne zur Spitze. Der schön geschwungene Griff wurde aus Amboina-Maserknolle geformt und liegt sehr komfortabel in der Hand. Er ist nur durch einen Bronzering von der Damastklinge getrennt.

Andrew K. Smith from Gonzales, Louisiana, forged the feather damascus for this lovely chef knife himself. The pattern flows from the integral bolsters down onto the blade and up to its tip. The nicely curved handle is shaped from amboyna burl and surely rests comfortably in one's hand. It is separated from the damascus blade by a spacer of bronze.

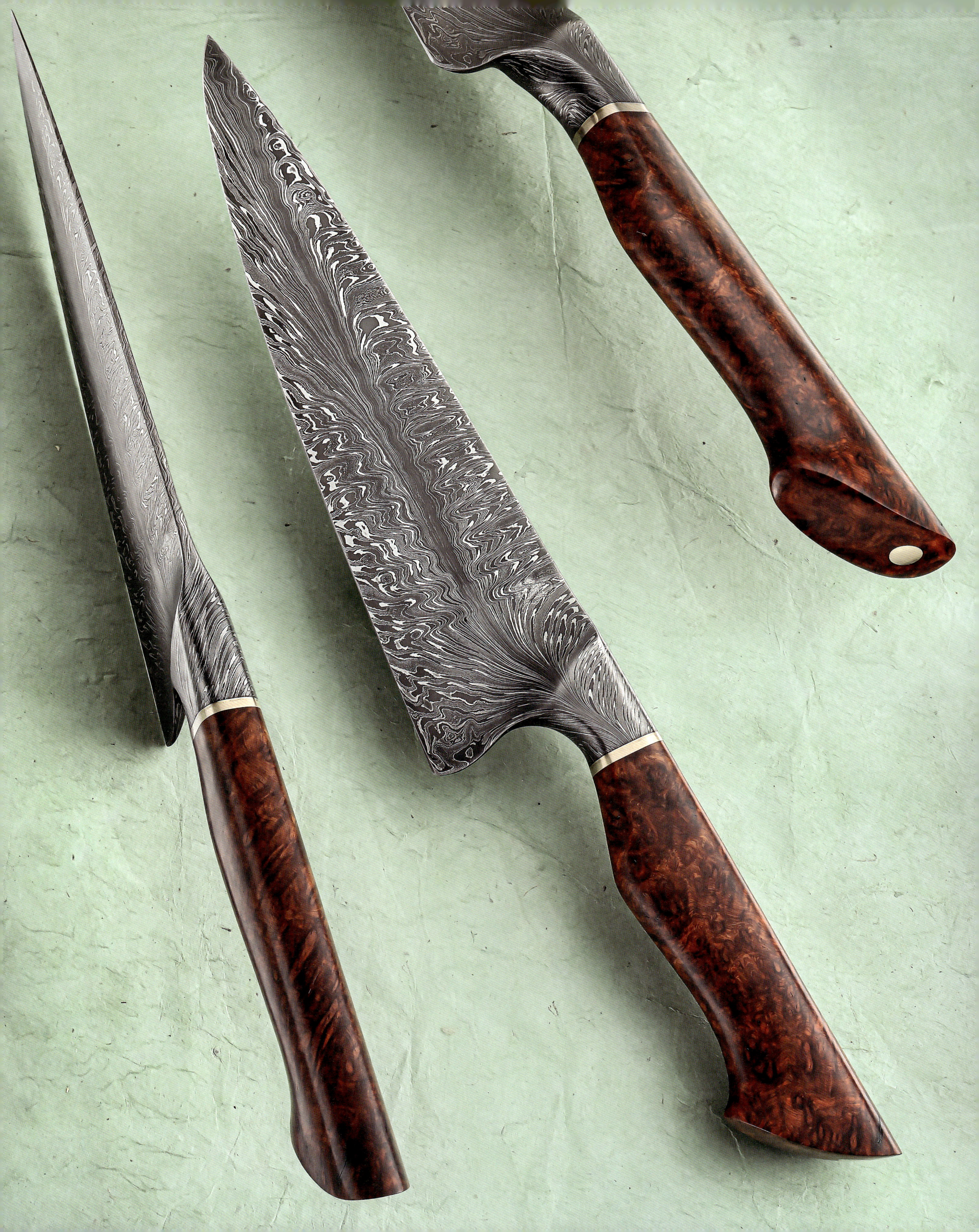

STUART SMITH

Stuart Smith ist ein ABS Journeyman Smith aus Blairgowrie, Südafrika. Seine Spezialitäten sind Puukkos und Bowies. Die Klinge des hier abgebildeten Messers wurde aus den Stahlsorten 1095 und 15N20 mit Zwischenlagen aus Kupfer geschmiedet. Der Handschutz ist aus Mokume geschmiedet, ebenfalls mit einem hohen Kupferanteil, der farblich auf die Klinge abgestimmt ist.

Stuart Smith is an ABS Journeyman Smith from Blairgowrie, South Africa. His specialty are puukko and Bowie knives. The blade depicted here was forged from 1095 and 15N20 steels with intermediate layers of copper. The guard is forged from mokume with a high copper content to match the blade's color scheme.

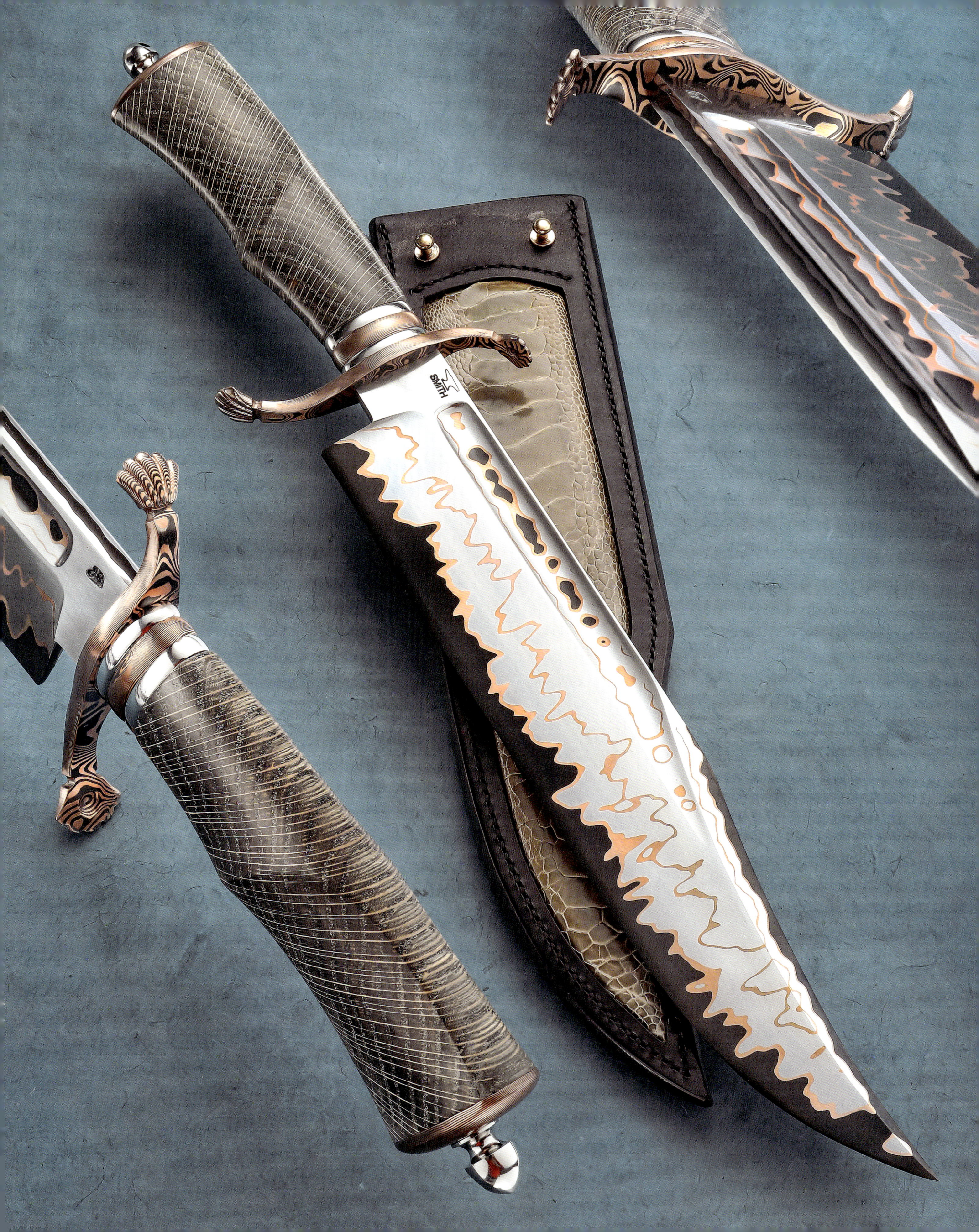
SMITH

SOBRAL BROTHERS

Claudio, Ariel und Marcelo Sobral sind drei Brüder aus Buenos Aires, Argentinien, die zusammen am Design und der Herstellung von erlesenen und individuellen Messern arbeiten. Cas Knives – wie sie sich selbst nennen – schmiedete den hier abgebildeten *Mustang* und gab ihm einen Griff aus Hirschhorn, einen Handschutz aus rostfreiem Stahl und eine passende Lederscheide.

Claudio, Ariel and Marcelo Sobral are three brothers from Buenos Aires, Argentina, who collaborate in designing and making fine custom knives. Cas Knives – that's what they call themselves – forged the *Mustang* depicted here and provided it with a handle of stag, a guard of stainless steel and a fitting leather sheath.

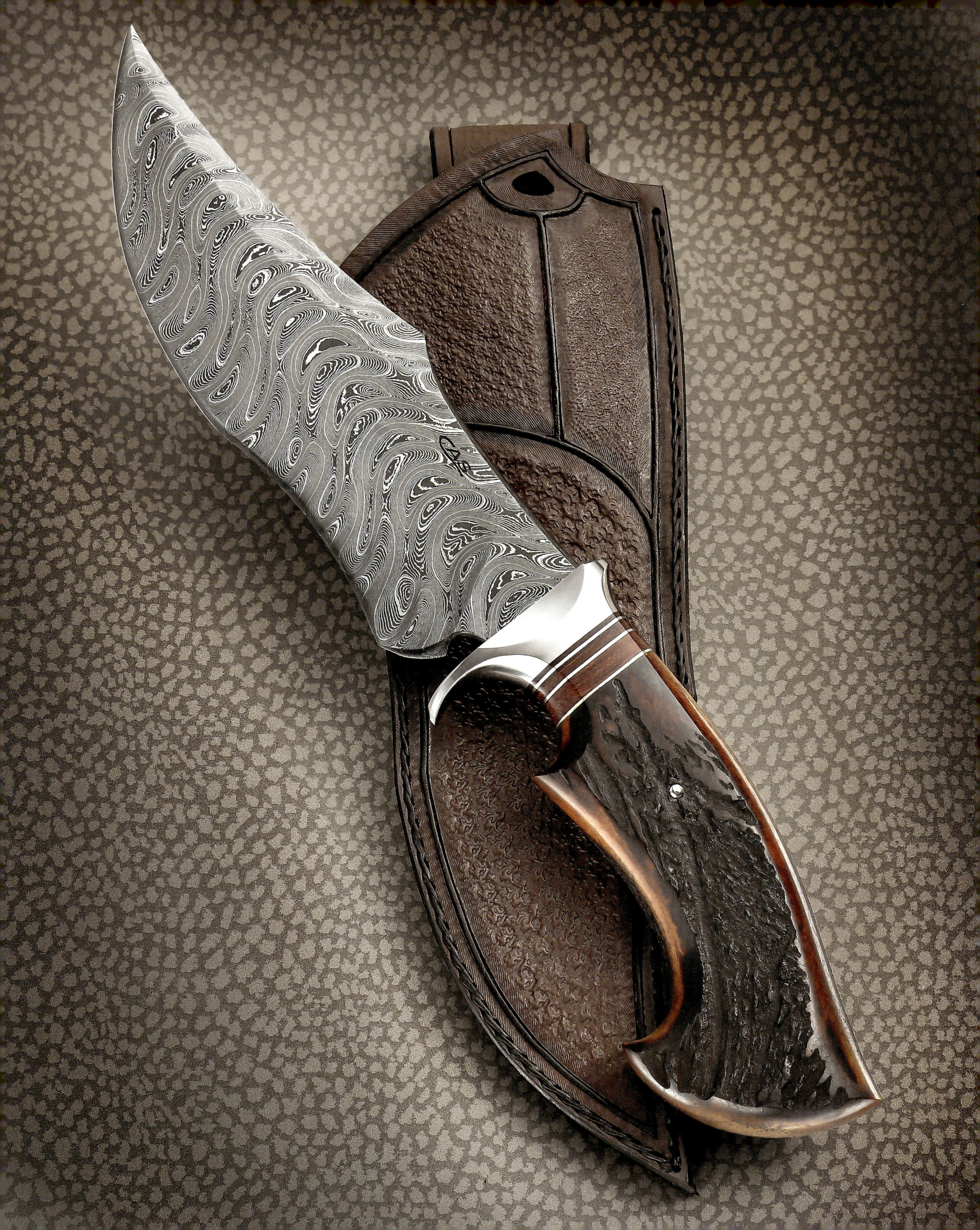

TIM K. STEINGASS

Tim K. Steingass ist ein Messermacher aus Bucksport, Maine. Obwohl er seine Klingen hauptsächlich aus Flachmaterial schleift, schmiedet er ab und zu auch seinen eigenen Damast, so wie bei diesem *Vest Bowie*. Die Klinge stellt ansprechenden Federdamast zur Schau, während der Griff uns stolz sein Mammut-Elfenbein präsentiert. Da das Messer für die Arbeit gedacht ist, wird es von einer einfachen, aber praktischen Scheide begleitet.

Tim K. Steingass is a knifemaker from Bucksport, Maine. Although he mainly makes knives using stock removal, he occasionally forges his own damascus as with this *Vest Bowie*. The blade exhibits an appealing feather damascus while the handle proudly presents mammoth ivory. Since the knife is meant for work, it is accompanied by a simple but practical leather sheath.

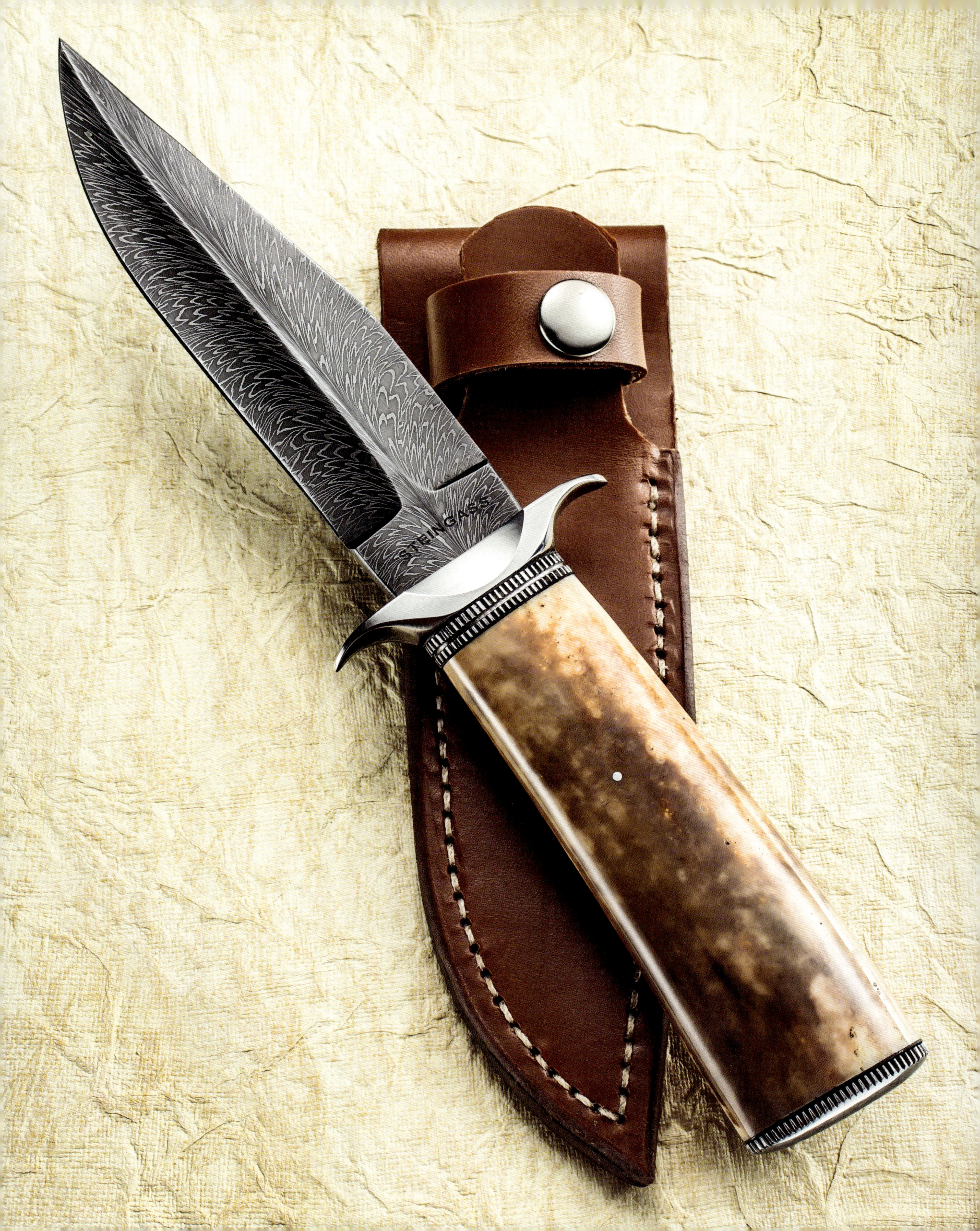
STEINGASS

WILL STELTER

ABS-Journeyman-Schmied Will Stelter aus Manhattan, Montana, begann schon mit 13 Jahren Messer zu machen. Er ist immer noch ziemlich jung, weiß aber bereits, wie man qualitativ hochwertige Messer mit selbst geschmiedeten Damastklingen herstellt. Dieses hervorragende Integral-Jagdmesser wurde von ihm 2022 aus Torsionsdamast einem Griff aus versteinertem Walross-Elfenbein gefertigt.

ABS Journeyman Smith Will Stelter of Manhattan, Montana, started knifemaking at age 13. He is still quite young, but already knows how to make high-end knives with his own forged damascus blades. This outstanding integral hunter was made in 2022 from twisted damascus with a handle of fossilized walrus ivory.

WILL STELTER

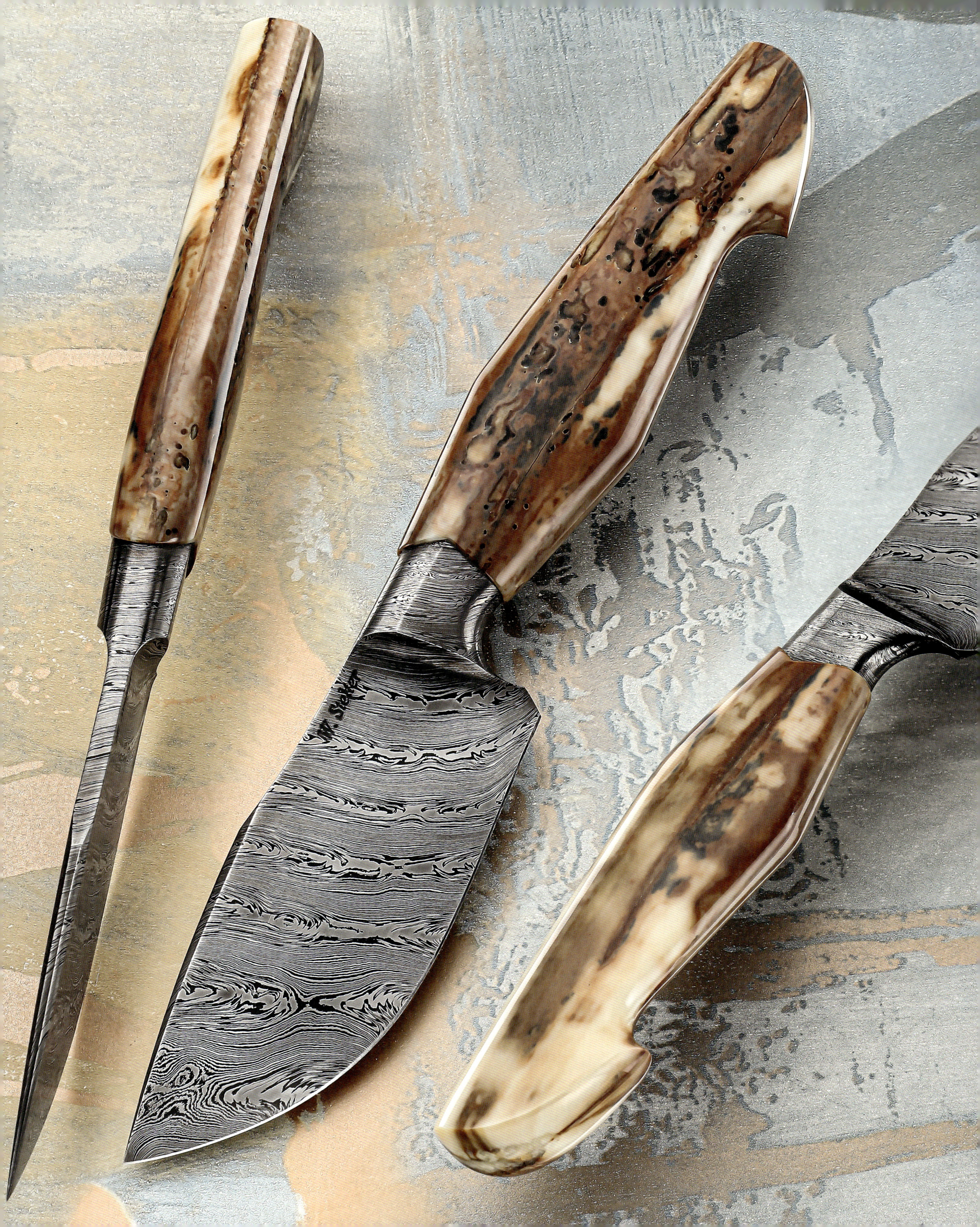

JOHNNY STOUT

Dieses Kunstwerk wurde von Johnny Stout aus New Braunfels, Texas, geschaffen. Er ist bekannt für seine exquisiten Gentleman-Taschenmesser. Das hier abgebildete Exemplar besitzt eine Klinge aus „River of Fire"-Damast, geschmiedet von Bill Burke. Die länglichen Griffbacken bestehen aus rostfreiem 416-Stahl und wurden von Marianne Kelly graviert. Die geschnitzten Griffschalen aus Horn von einem Moschusochsen bringen deren Schönheit noch mehr zur Geltung. Der Griffrücken ist ebenfalls graviert und von Platinen aus farbenfrohem Titan mit Feilmuster eingerahmt.

This masterful piece of art was created by Johnny Stout of New Braunfels, Texas. He is famous for his exquisite dress folders. The one depicted here has a blade made from „River of Fire" damascus forged by Bill Burke. The elongated bolsters are made of stainless 416 steel and engraved by Marianne Kelly. Carved handle scales of musk ox horn add to their beauty. The backspacer is engraved as well and framed by colorful fileworked titanium.

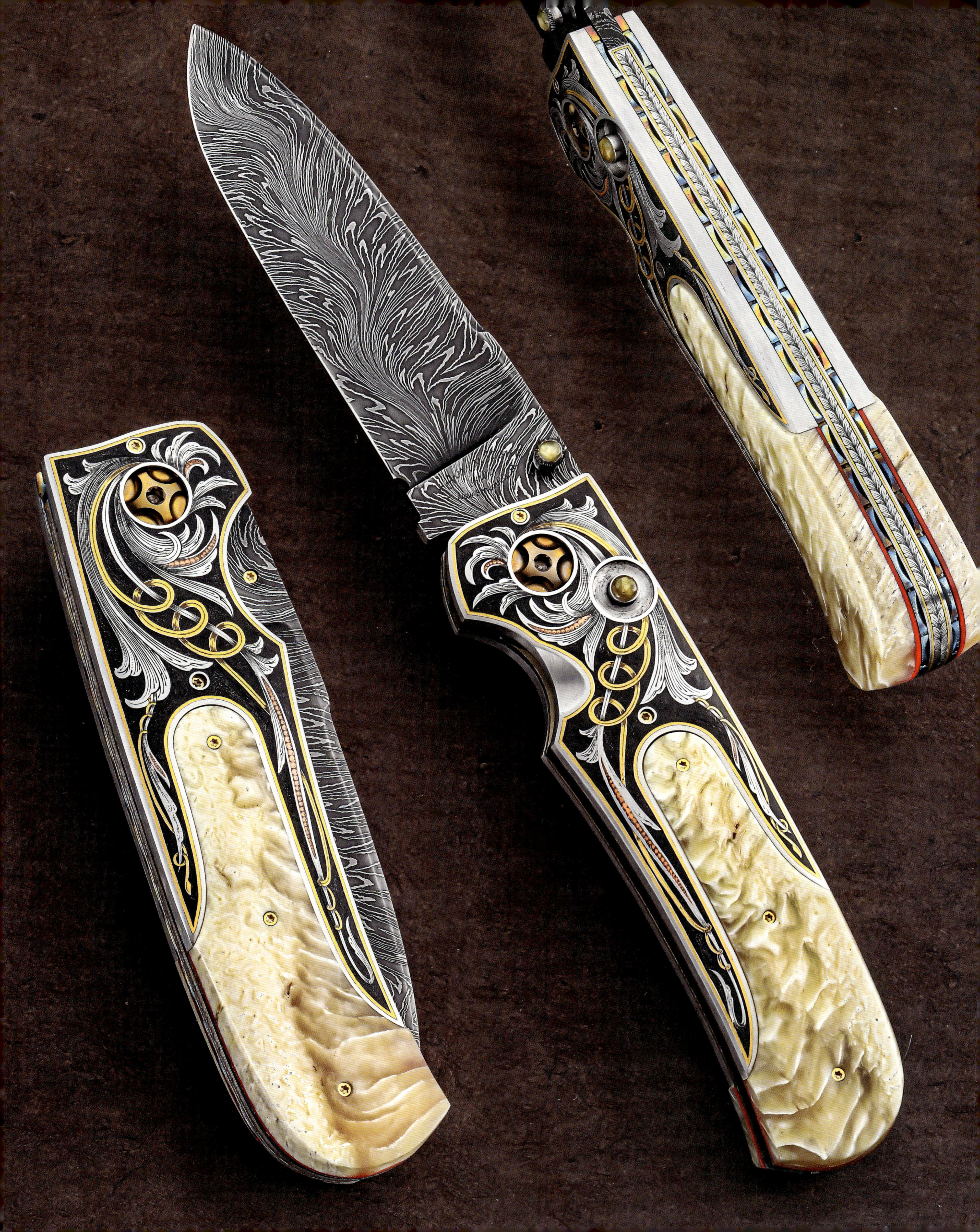

PETER SWARZ-BURT

Ein Cinquedea ist ein mittelalterlicher Dolchtyp aus Norditalien, dessen Klinge die Breite einer menschlichen Hand an der Stelle hat, an der die Klinge den Handschutz berührt. Dieses hier wurde von Peter Swarz-Burt gefertigt, einem Messermacher aus Waimea, Hawaii. Peter schmiedete den „Moustache Wolf's Tooth"-Damast für die Klinge des Cinquedea, den Handschutz und den Knauf aus den Werkzeugstählen O1 und L6. Beim Griffmaterial handelt es sich um geschnitztes Elchgeweih.

A cinquedea is a medieval type dagger originating from Northern Italy whose blade is as wide as a human hand at the point it joins the guard. This one was created by Peter Swarz-Burt, a knifemaker from Waimea, Hawaii. Peter forged the „Moustache Wolf's Tooth" damascus for the Cinquedea's blade, guard and pommel from O1 and L6 tool steels. The handle material is carved moose antler.

PETER SWARZ-BURT

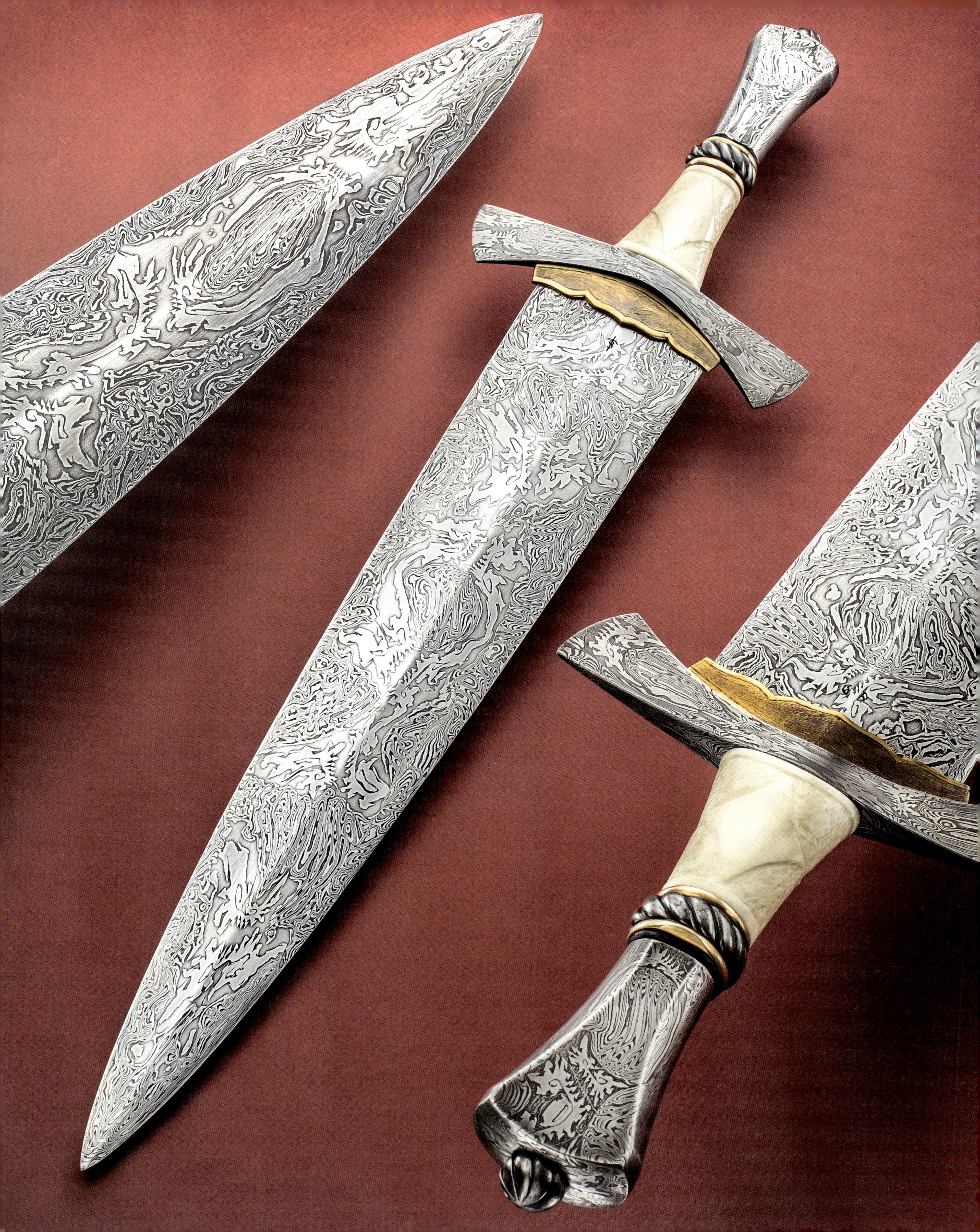

ANDRÉ & MARIETJIE THORBURN

Der preisgekrönte Messermacher André Thorburn aus Südafrika ist den meisten Messer-Enthusiasten wohlbekannt. Er ist der Schöpfer von sehr edlen Gentleman-Taschenmessern wie dem hier gezeigten *L36 M Eagle*. Der Adler auf diesem Messer wurde von Andrés Frau Marietjie kreiert. Die passenden Federn auf der Klinge bestehen aus Zladinox ZDI-1016 Federdamast. Die Griffschalen bestehen aus antikem Westinghouse-Elfenbein-Micarta, das auf einen Rahmen aus gebläutem und mit Feilmuster versehenem Ti6Al4V-Titan montiert wurde.

Award-winning knifemaker André Thorburn from South Africa is well-known to most knife enthusiasts. He creates very noble gent's folders such as this one, the *L36 M Eagle*. The eagle here was crafted by André's wife Marietjie. Its feathers on the blade are of Zladinox ZDI-1016 feather damascus. The handle scales are made of Westinghouse antique ivorite micarta mounted on a frame of blued and fileworked Ti6Al4V titanium.

ANDRÉ & MARIETJIE THORBURN

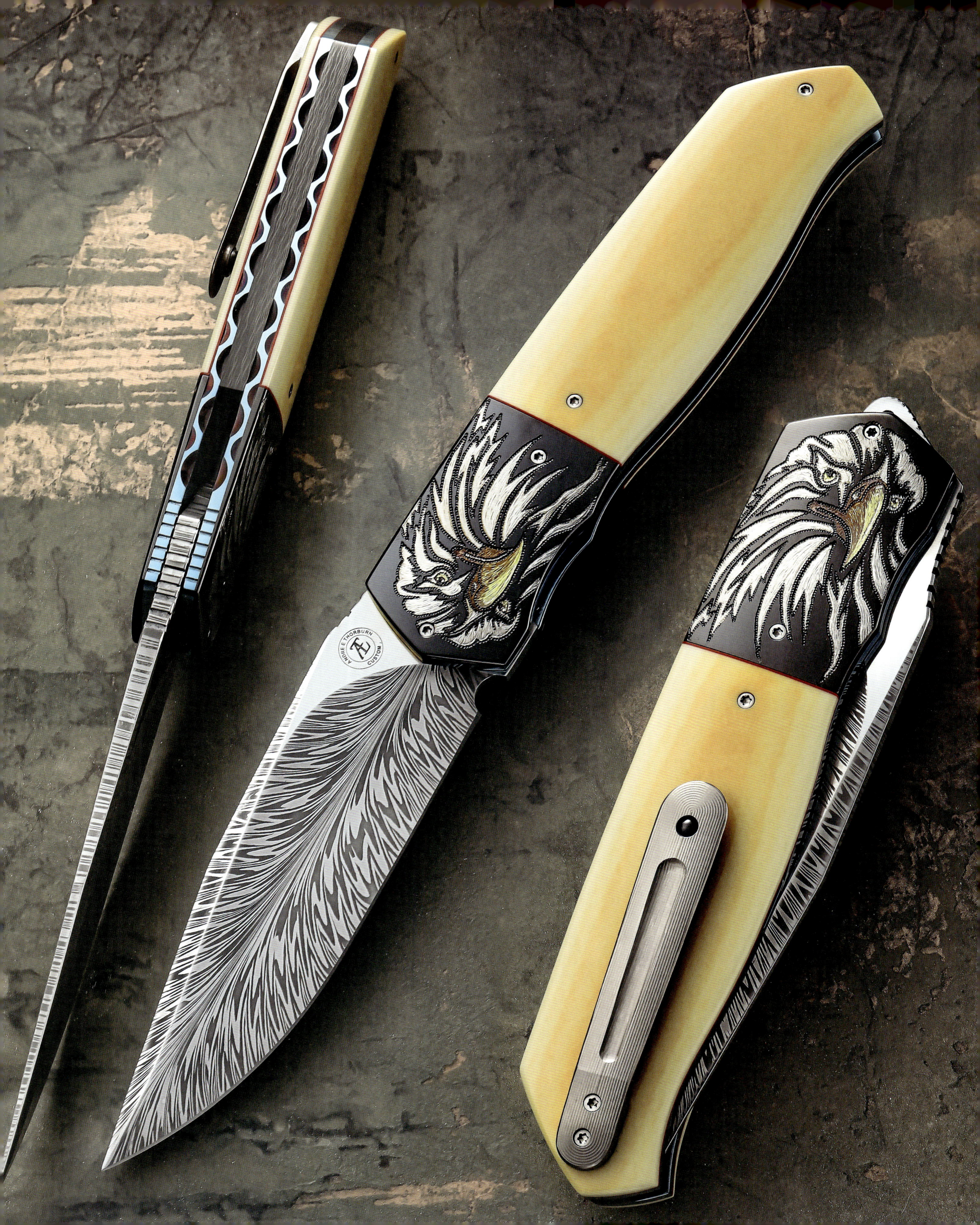
ANDRE E THORBURN CUSTOM

BRIAN TIGHE

Ein anderer berühmter und preisgekrönter Messermacher ist der Kanadier Brian Tighe. Seine ausgezeichneten Kunstwerke können in vielen Magazinen, Büchern und auch im Internet bewundert werden. Diese Version seines bekannten *Tighe Down*, einem Flipper mit Button-Lock, besitzt eine Klinge aus Damasteel. Der Griff besteht aus Titan mit Einlagen aus „Arctic Storm"-Kohlefaser der Firma Fatcarbon Materials aus Litauen.

Another famous and award-winning knifemaker is the Canadian Brian Tighe. His superb pieces of art can be seen in many magazines, books and in the internet as well. This version of his familiar *Tighe Down*, a button-lock flipper folder, has a blade of Damasteel. The handle is made of titanium with „Arctic Storm" carbon fiber inlays by Fatcarbon Materials, a Lithuania-based company.

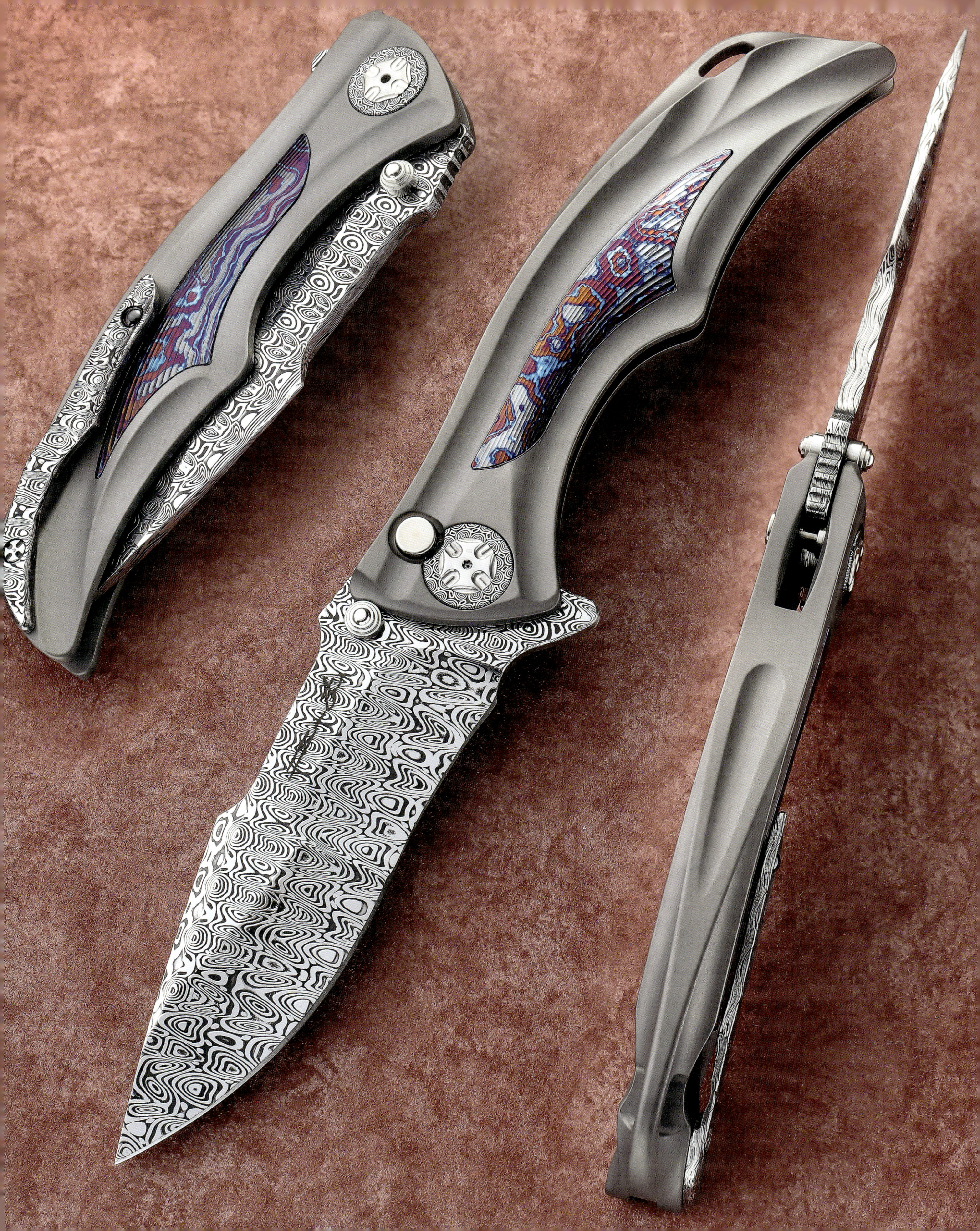

CORIN URQUHART

Der Australier Corin Urquhart aus Picton, New South Wales, ist in erster Linie ein Anbieter von Material für Messermacher und erst in zweiter Linie selbst ein Messermacher. Dieses Fassmesser wurde mit Mosaikdamast von Ian Stewart gestaltet. Die Damastklinge ist an einem Bronzerahmen befestigt. Das eigentliche Fass besteht aus „Greenstone Mallee Burl" (Holz einer buschig-wachsenden Eukalyptusart) mit Griffbacken aus Sterling-Silber.

The Australian Corin Urquhart from Picton, New South Wales, is primarily a supplier and is a knifemaker only secondly. This barrel knife was made with mosaic damascus by Ian Stewart. The damascus blade is fixed to a frame of bronze. The barrel itself is made of greenstone mallee burl (a bushy species of eucalyptus) with bolsters of sterling silver.

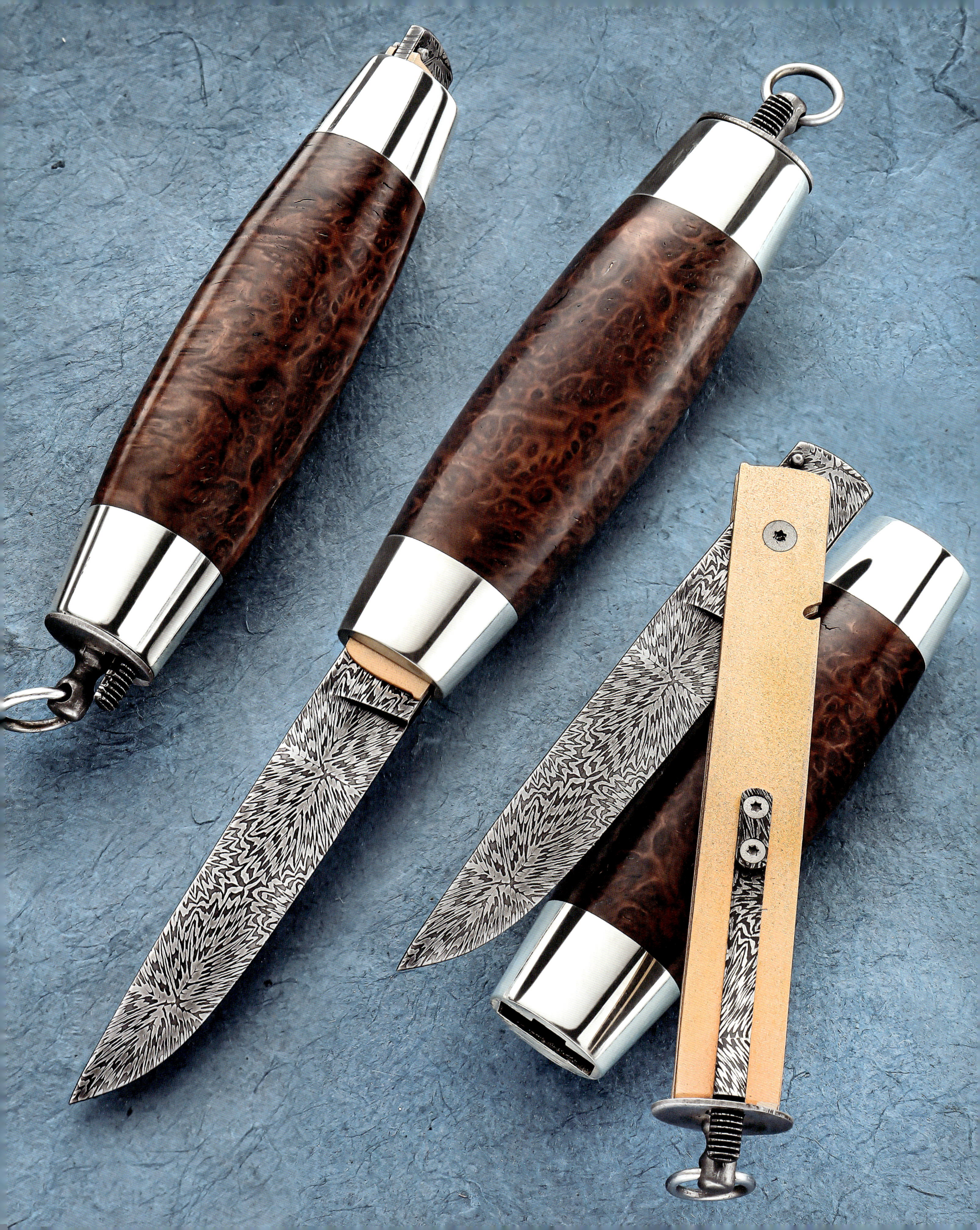

NOAH VACHON

Noah Vachon aus Stanstead, Quebec, baut hochwertige feststehende Messer. Für dieses Bowie verwendete er Damast aus Stahlsorten mit hohem Kohlenstoffgehalt. Das attraktive Damastmuster der Klinge harmoniert mit dem gefärbten Mangoholz und der Redwood-Maserknolle des Griffs. Der Handschutz wurde aus Baustahl geformt. Die passende Lederscheide wurde ebenfalls von Noah gefertigt.

Noah Vachon from Stanstead, Quebec, is a maker of high-quality fixed blades. For this Bowie, he used damascus from steels with high carbon content. The beautiful damascus pattern of the blade corresponds to the dyed curly mango and the redwood burl of the handle. The guard was shaped from mild steel. The accompanying leather sheath was also made by Noah.

NOAH VACHON

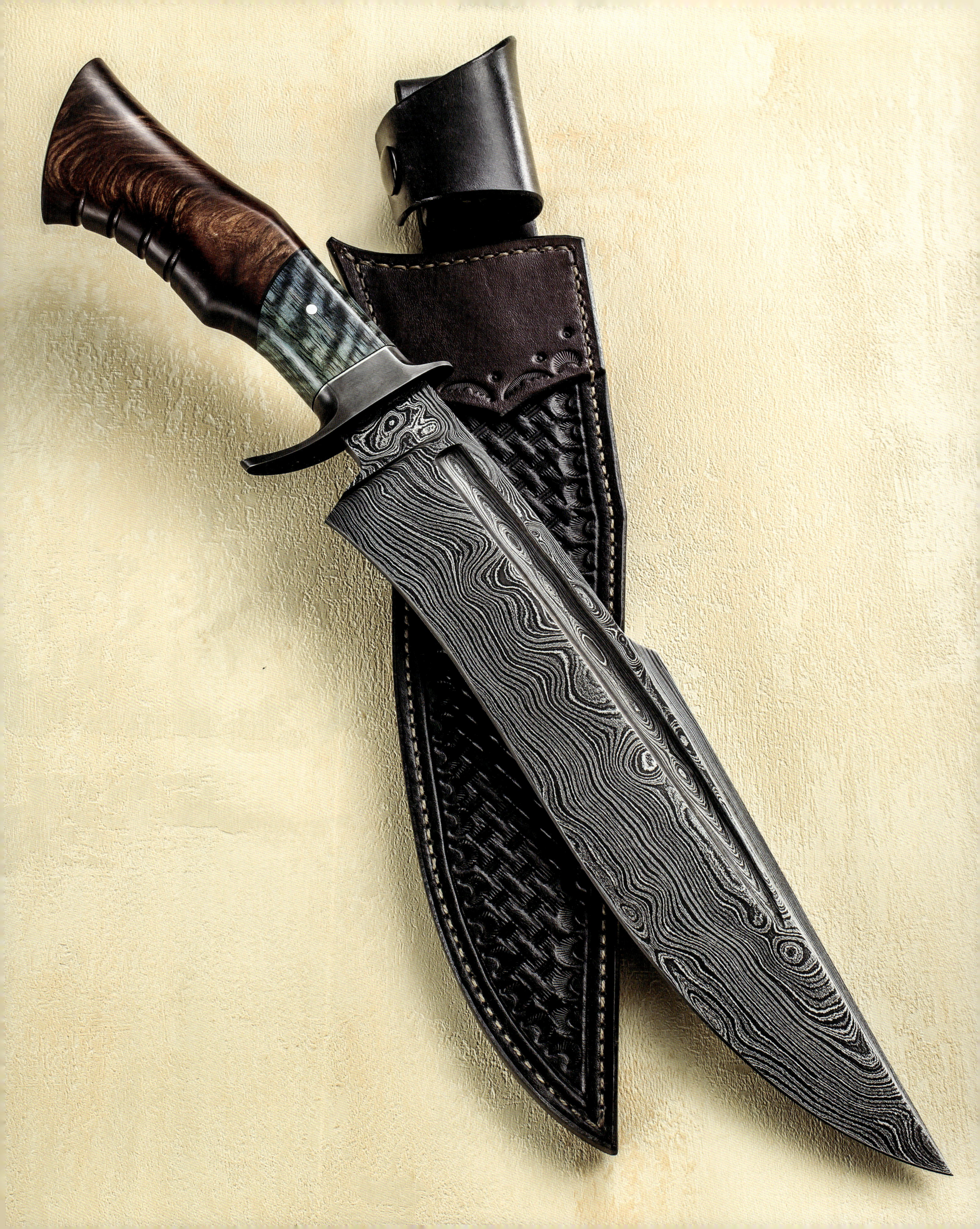

KELLY VERMEER-VELLA

ABS Journeyman Smith Kelly Vermeer-Vella aus Oakdale, Kalifornien, ist eine der wenigen Frauen unter den Klingenschmieden und Messermachern. Diesen *Oosik Fighter* ziert ihr hinreißender „Riptide"-Damast. Der daran anschließende Handschutz wurde aus brüniertem Baustahl hergestellt, gefolgt von einer Damastzwinge, die von zwei gefeilten Titanringen flankiert wird. Der Griff selbst ist aus Oosik geformt. Das Kampfmesser kann komplett auseinandergenommen werden. Die zugehörige Lederscheide wurde von Paul Long gemacht.

ABS Journeyman Smith Kelly Vermeer-Vella from Oakdale, California, is one of the few women among the bladesmiths and knifemakers. This *Oosik Fighter* sports her most gorgeous „Riptide" damascus. The adjacent guard is made of hot-blued mild steel followed by a damascus bolster sandwiched between fileworked titanium spacers. The handle itself is made of oosik. The fighter is built as a take-down construction. The accompanying sheath was created by Paul Long.

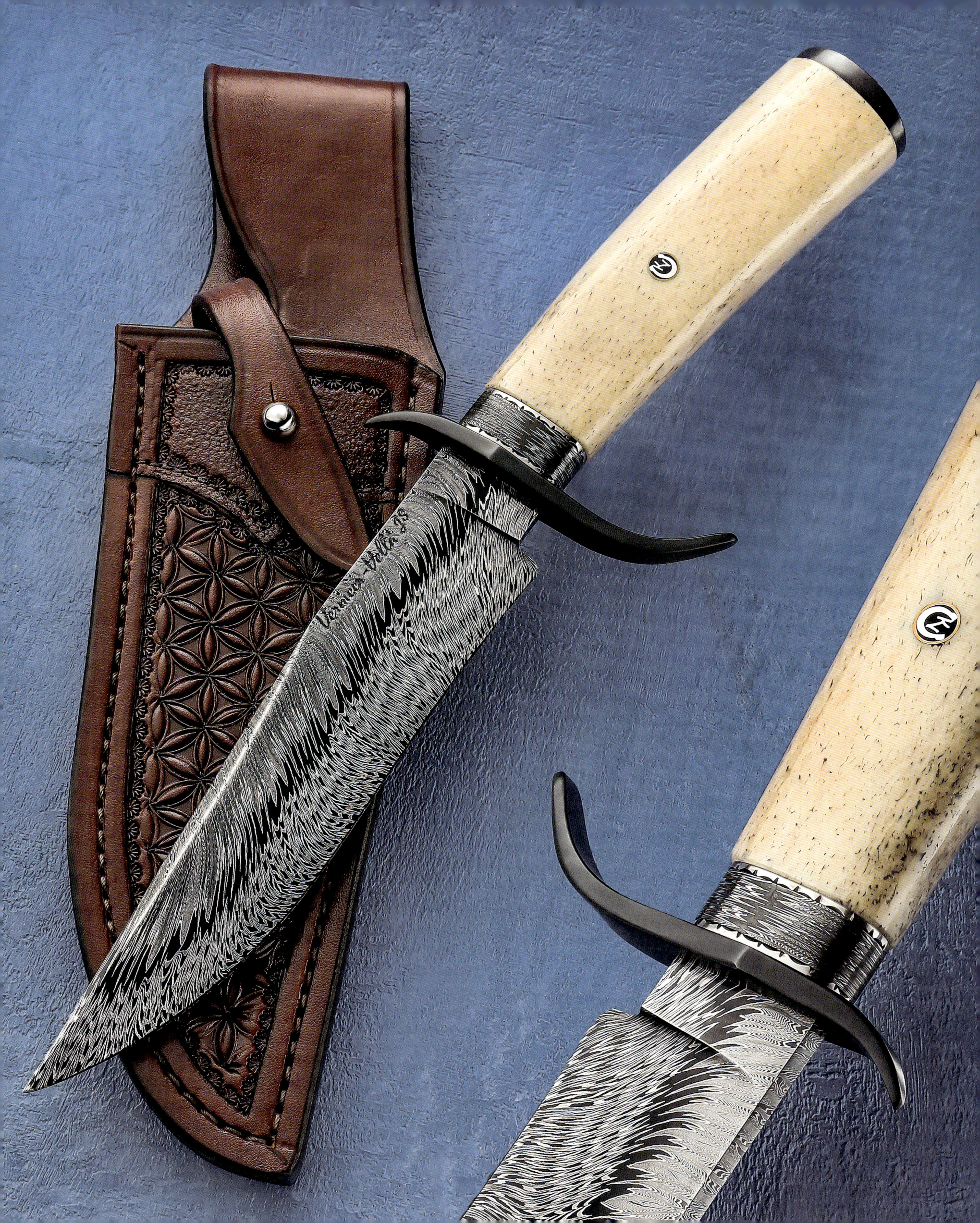

JAVIER VOGT

Dieser elegante Klappdolch wurde vom argentinischen Messermacher Javier Vogt aus Villa Elisa bei Buenos Aires geschaffen. Er nannte ihn *Daga Celta de Noël* – „keltischer Weihnachtsdolch". Seine Schönheit sowie seine Konstruktion als Springmesser mit Auslösung durch den Handschutz wurden belohnt mit der Auszeichnung „Best Folder" auf der Blade Show 2022. Die Klinge besteht aus Damast mit „Turkish Lace"-Muster, geschmiedet von Doug Ponzio. Die Backen aus Damast mit Zufallsmuster von Leo Marutti wurden mit 24-karätigem Golddraht verziert, der Handschutz aus hitze-koloriertem Stahl geformt. Die Griffschalen bestehen aus Mammut-Elfenbein. Passend dazu sind die teilweise mit Feilarbeit verzierten Platinen aus gebläutem Titan gemacht.

This elegant folding dagger was created by Argentinean knifemaker Javier Vogt of Villa Elisa, Buenos Aires. He named it *Daga Celta de Noël* – celtic Christmas dagger. Its beauty, as well as its construction as an automatic knife with guard release, were rewarded by winning „Best Folder" at the Blade Show 2022. The blade is of damascus with a „Turkish Lace" pattern forged by Doug Ponzio. The bolsters are made of random pattern damascus created by Leo Marutti and inlaid with 24k gold wire. The guard was shaped of hot-blued steel. The handle scales are of exquisite mammoth ivory of an appealing blue hue. Correspondingly, the partly fileworked liners are of blued titanium.

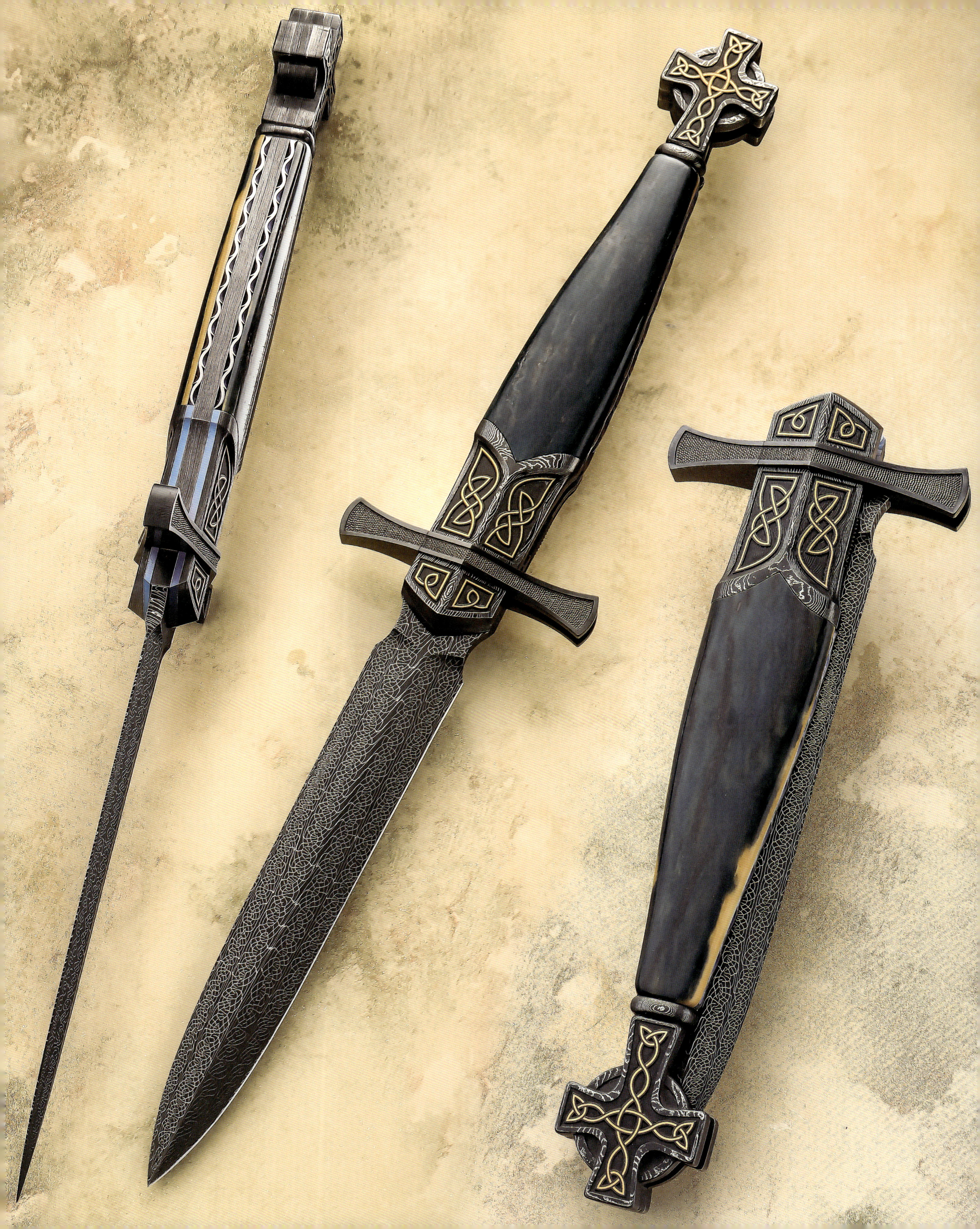

MICHAEL WALKER

Michael Walker aus Taos, New Mexico, ist nicht nur einer der bekanntesten Messermacher, sondern gilt als Erfinder der Liner-Lock-Arretierung. Die Klinge dieses extravaganten *Double Zipper* wurde nicht nur aus Torsionsdamast geschmiedet, sondern stellt auch Walkers „Zipper"-Konstruktion aus anodisiertem Stahl zur Schau. Der Arretierungsmechanismus ist in diesem Fall ein „Round Button Lock", von denen nur wenige von Walker gemacht wurden. In den Griff aus Titan sind Intarsien eingelegt.

Michael Walker of Taos, New Mexico, is not just a well-known knifemaker, but also the inventor of the famous and quite common linerlock. The blade of this extravagant *Double Zipper* is not only created out of twisted damascus, but also exhibits Walker's „Zipper" construction of anodized steel. The locking mechanism in this case is an assisted opening Round Button Lock, of which only very few were made by Walker. The handle, made of titanium, features damascus, mokume, and gold inlays.

MICHAEL WALKER

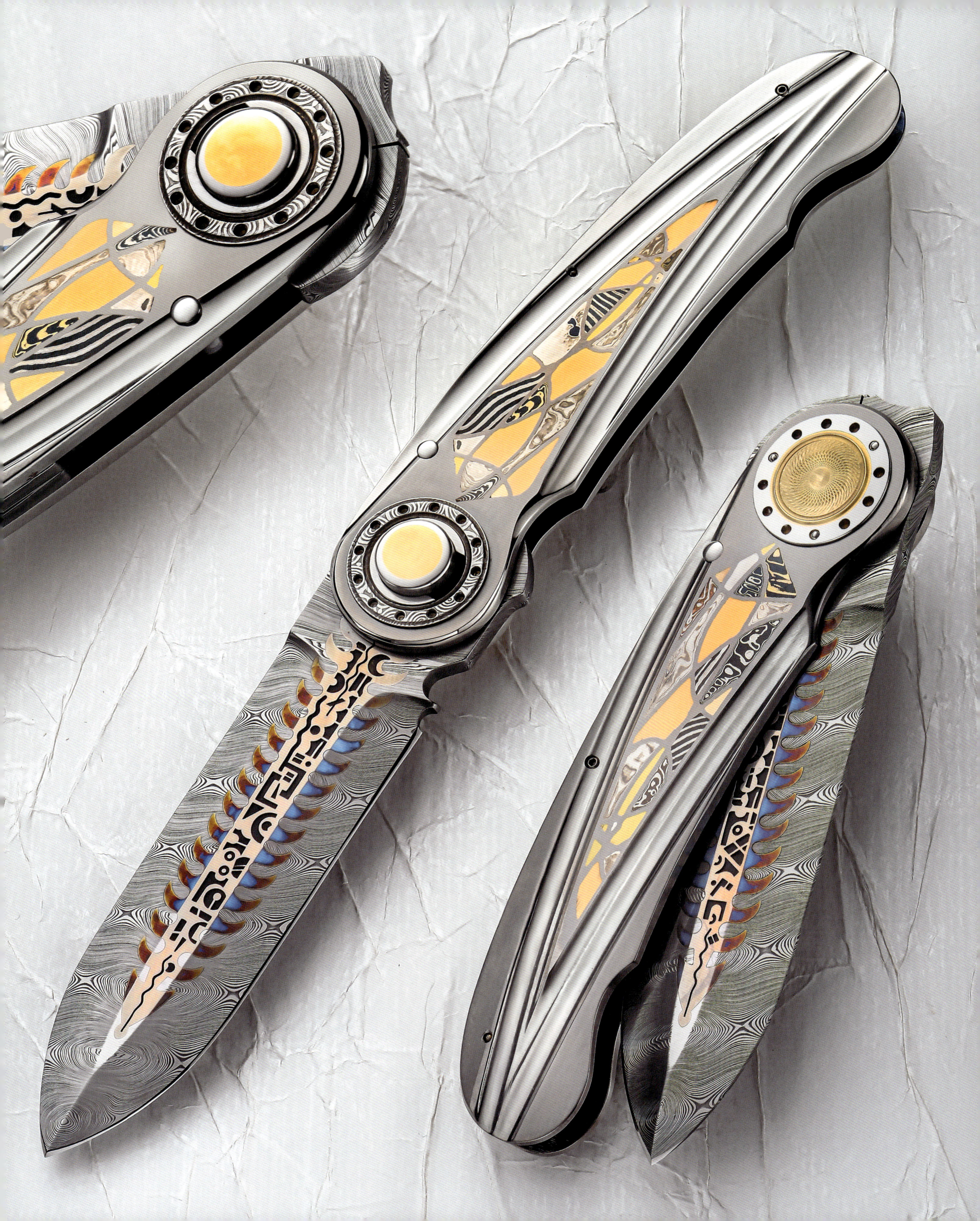

AARON WILBURN

ABS-Meisterschmied Aaron Wilburn aus Idaho Falls kreierte dieses elegante Bowie mit einer Klinge aus seinem eigenen Mosaikdamast, den er aus den Stahlsorten 1084 und 15N20 schmiedete. Der Handschutz besteht aus Schmiedeeisen. Der Messermacher formte die Rille des Bronze-Spacers und färbte das Distanzstück durch Erhitzen. Links und rechts davon befinden sich zwei schmale Ringe aus Neusilber. Der attraktive Griff ist aus altem Walross-Elfenbein gemacht. Die Scheide wurde ebenfalls von Wilburn selbst angefertigt.

ABS Master Bladesmith Aaron Wilburn, from Idaho Falls, Idaho, created this elegant Bowie with a blade of his own mosaic damascus, which he forged from 1084 and 15N20 steels. The guard was made of wrought iron. The maker fluted and heat-colored the bronze spacer which is accompanied by two small rings of nickel silver. The handsome handle is shaped from ancient walrus ivory. The sheath was also crafted by the master himself.

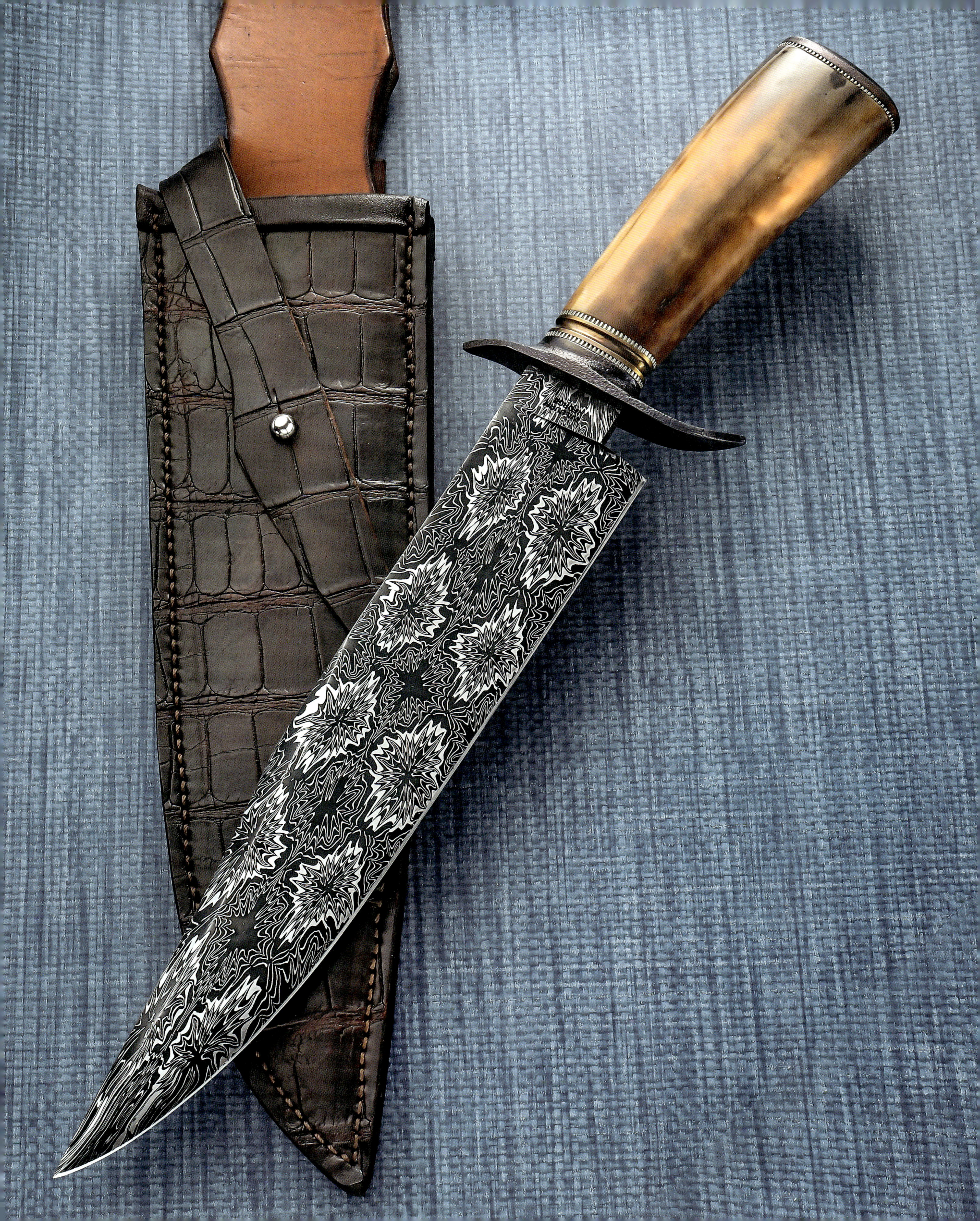

HENNING WILKINSON

Hier ist einer von Henning Wilkinsons hervorragenden *Keyhole Hunters*. Der erfahrene Designer und Messermacher – das Magazin „Blade" nannte ihn „Magier unter den südafrikanischen Messermachern" – hat schon viele verschiedene Varianten dieses Integraldesigns geschaffen, mit verschiedenen Materialen für Klinge und Griff. Das abgebildete Exemplar mit „Schlüsselloch-Rahmen" ist aus Wilkinsons „Kaleidoscope"-Mosaikdamast gefertigt. Das eigentliche Schlüsselloch besteht aus afrikanischer Akazie.

Here is one of Henning Wilkinson's excellent *Keyhole Hunters*. This skilled designer and knifemaker from South Africa – Blade Magazine called him „Magician of South African Knifemaking" – has already created various versions of his own integral design with different materials for the blade and handle. The one depicted here has a blade and „keyhole frame" made of the maker's own „Kaleidoscope" mosaic damascus while the keyhole itself is made from African acacia.

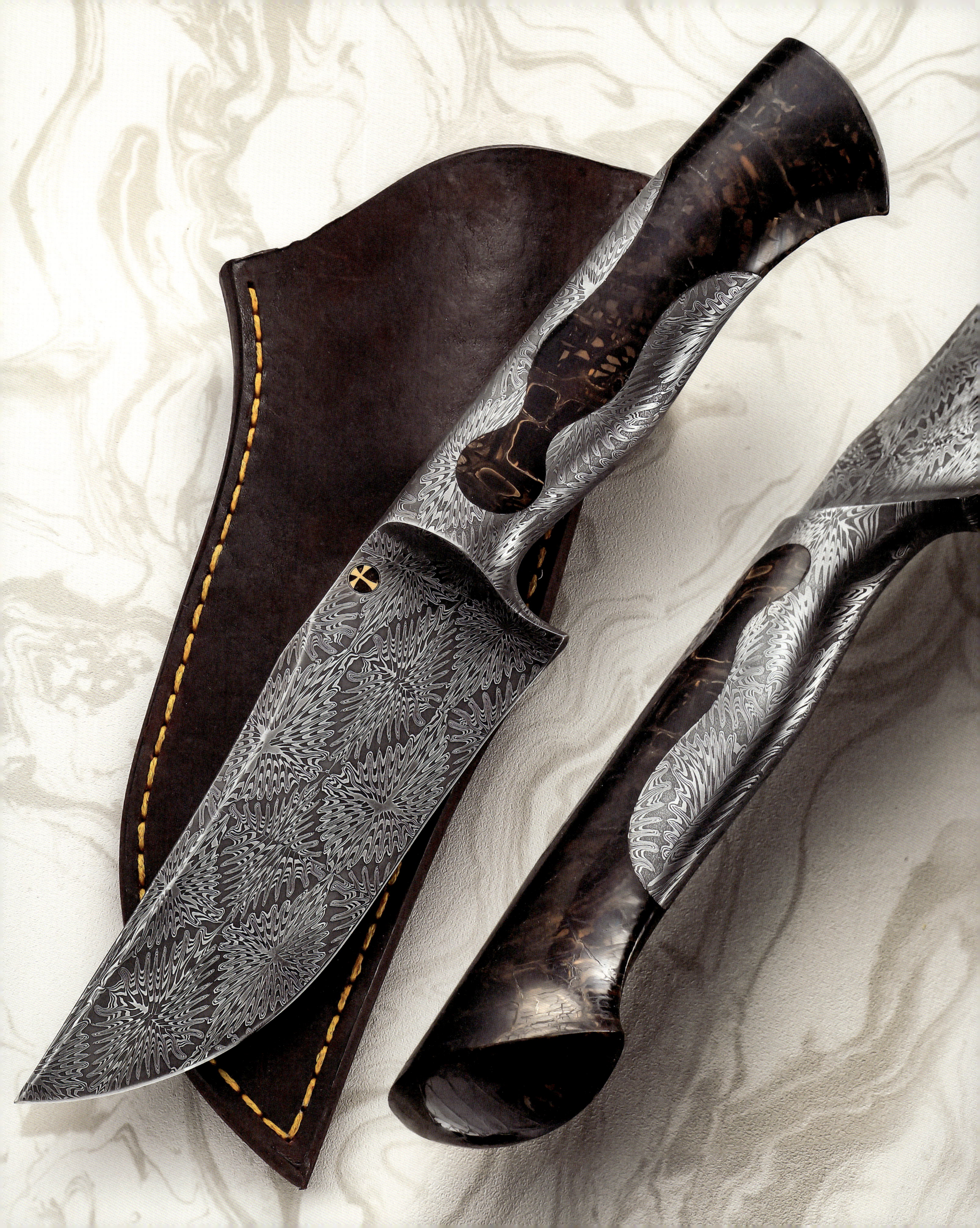

JOSH WISOR

ABS-Journeyman-Schmied Josh Wisor aus Port Republic, Virginia, ist der Schöpfer dieses bemerkenswerten persischen Kampfmessers. Josh schmiedete die Klinge aus seinem „türkischen" Torsionsdamast. Griff und Scheide wurden aus einem einzigen Stück Wüsteneisenholz hergestellt. Dabei wird der Verlauf der Maserung nur durch die Beschläge aus künstlich gealterter Bronze unterbrochen.

ABS Journeyman Smith Josh Wisor of Port Republic, Virginia, is the maker of this remarkable Persian fighter. Josh forged the blade with his „Turkish twist" damascus. Handle and scabbard were shaped from a single piece of desert ironwood so the flow of its grain is only interrupted by the fittings of antiqued bronze.

JOSH WISOR

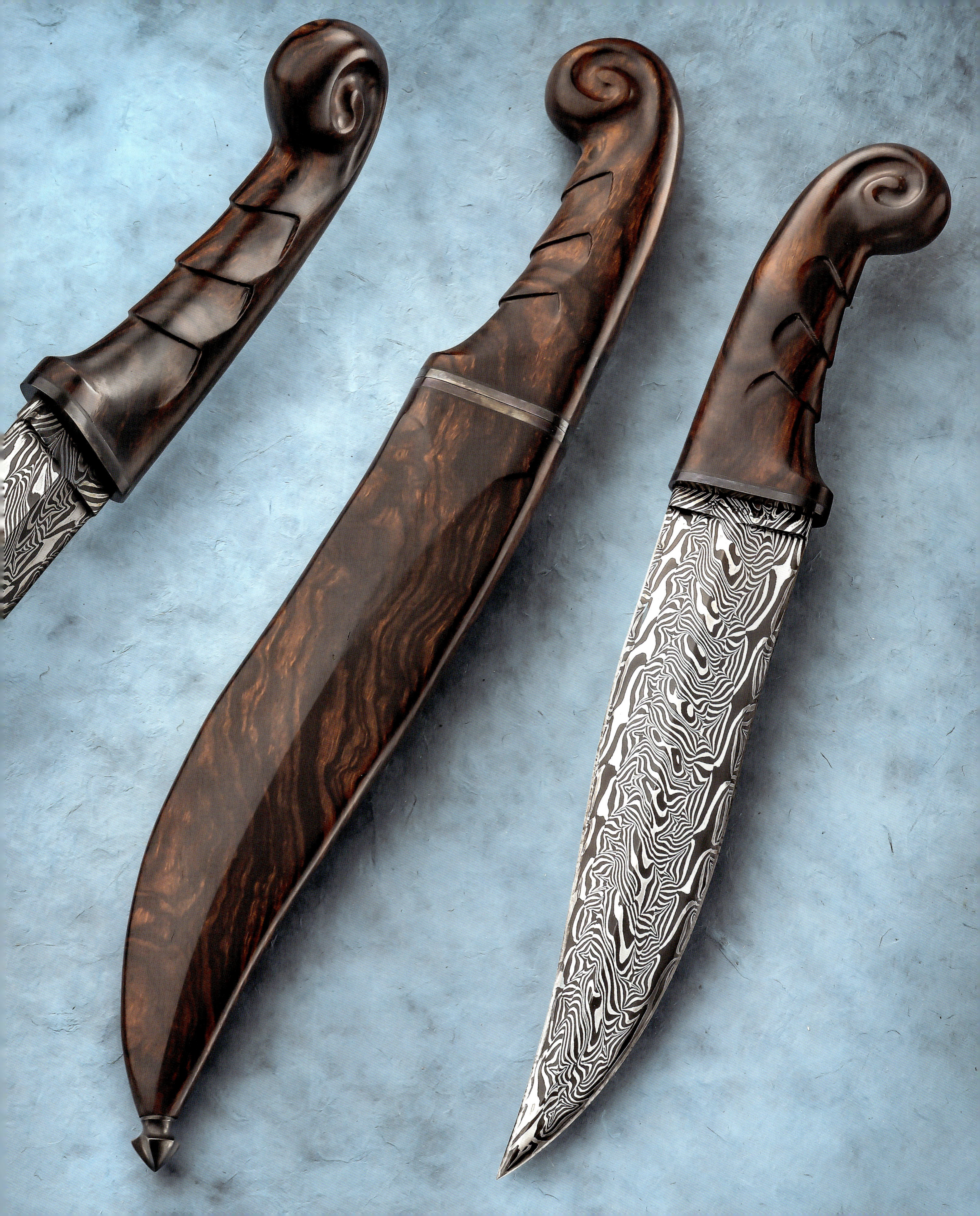

OWEN WOOD

Owen Wood aus Tuscola, Texas, ist sehr bekannt für seine exquisiten Gentleman-Taschenmesser im Art-Deco-Stil. Dieser Dolch wurde für die Art Knife Invitational 2021 gemacht. Owen verwendete für die Klinge seinen eigenen Explosionsdamast mit einem sich verjüngenden Streifen aus Damast mit Fischgrätenmuster in der Mitte. Noch mehr Damast gibt es als Einlage im Griff zu sehen. Er wird teilweise durch ein Goldschildchen verdeckt, in dessen Zentrum sich „Blacklip"-Perlmutt in Regenbogenfarben befindet.

Owen Wood from Tuscola, Texas, is very famous for his exquisite gent's folders in art deco style. This dagger was made for the Art Knife Invitational 2021. Owen used his own explosion pattern damascus for the blade with a tapered bar of herringbone damascus in the center. Even more damascus can be seen inlaid into the handle of stainless steel. It is partly covered by a shield of gold with a center of rainbow-colored blacklip mother-of-pearl.

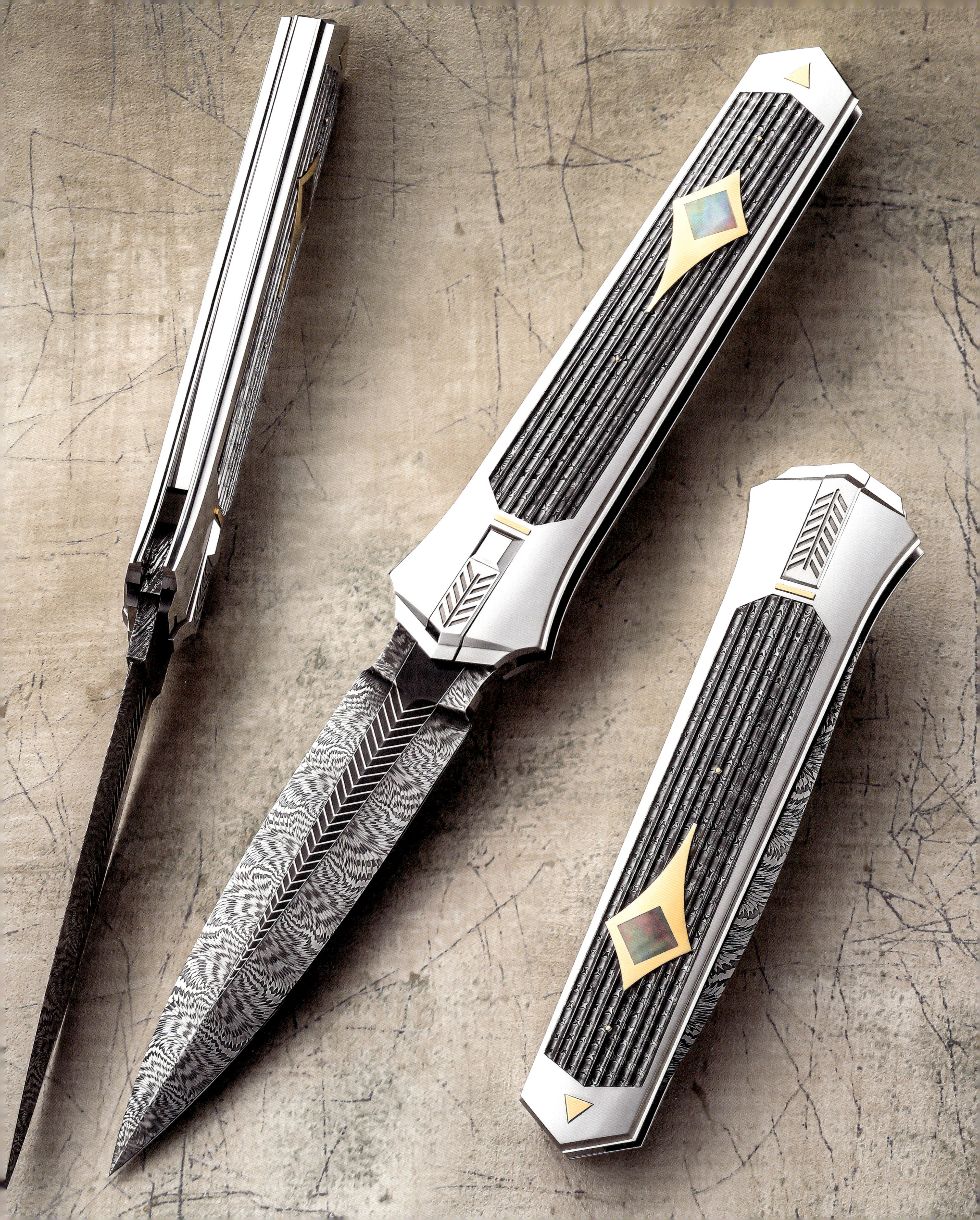

JOHN WORTHINGTON

Der Schöpfer dieses feinen Küchenmessers ist John Worthington aus Clyde, Neuseeland. Er liebt es alles selbst zu machen, auch die Wärmebehandlung seiner Messer. Für dieses *K-Tip* verwendete er „Ziegelstein"-Damast von Andrew Condick. Der Griff besteht aus tasmanischem Schwarzholz, das nur durch einen dünnen Bronzering von der faszinierenden Klinge getrennt ist.

The maker of this fine kitchen knife is John Worthington of Clyde, New Zealand. He loves to do everything himself, including the heat-treatment of his knives. For this *K-Tip* he used brick damascus forged by Andrew Condick. The handle is shaped of Tasmanian blackwood, which is only separated from the intriguing blade by a thin bronze ring.

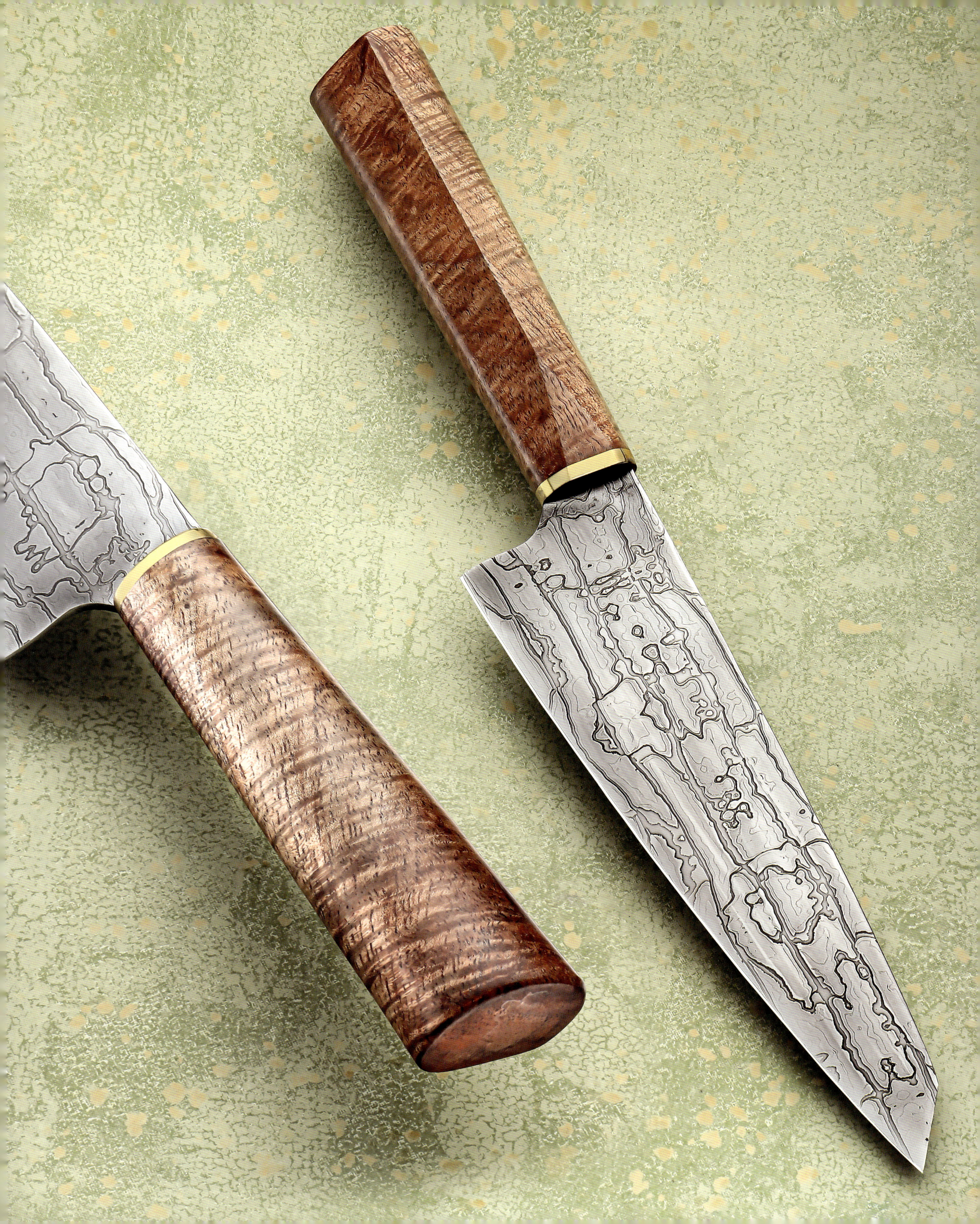

EBENFALLS IM WIELAND VERLAG ERSCHIENEN

Rudolf Dick

DIE KUNST DES SCHNEIDENS

Japanische Messer in der Küche
152 Seiten, über 200 Abbildungen,
Format 300 x 300 mm, Hardcover,
ISBN 978-3-948264-02-4
EUR 39,90

Rudolf Dick

DIE KUNST DES SCHNEIDENS
Japanische Messer in der Küche

Japanische Meisterköche haben für dieses Buch ihre Küchen geöffnet und enthüllen ihre Geheimnisse der kunstvollen Verarbeitung von Fisch und Gemüse, den Grundpfeilern der japanischen Küche. Sie geben dem Leser einen authentischen Einblick in die japanische Koch- und Esskultur und demonstrieren ihre Kunst auf höchstem Niveau. Für Profis und ambitionierte Hobbyköche ist dieses Buch eine faszinierende Anregung und Anleitung für die eigene Arbeit mit dem Kochmesser.
Darüber hinaus erfährt der Leser alles Wichtige und Wissenswerte zu japanischen Kochmessern, ihrer Technik, ihrer Herstellung und der richtigen Pflege – einschließlich dem fachgerechten Schärfen.

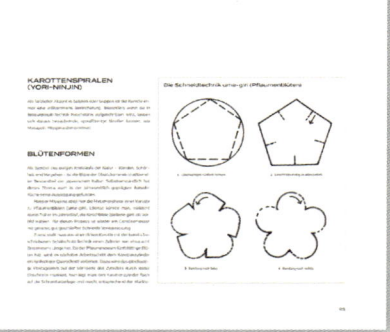